Revisting America

Inda Lou Lambert Schell
with
Janie Leona Lambert Gass

Writerspace Publishing

Editor: Judith Richards
Photo Editor: Lee Carpenter
Cover Design: Cissy Hartley

Writerspace Publishing
Mobile, Alabama

FIRST EDITION 2014

Hardcover Edition: ISBN 978-0-9889004-3-1
Softcover Edition: ISBN 978-0-9889004-4-8
E-book Edition: ISBN 978-0-9889004-5-5

Publisher's Cataloging-In-Publication Data
(Prepared by The Donohue Group, Inc.)

Schell, Inda Lou Lambert.

Revisiting America / Inda Lou Lambert Schell and Janie Leona Lambert Gass. -- First edition.

pages : illustrations ; cm

Summary: Author retraces the route taken by Charles Kuralt in Charles Kuralt's America.

Issued also as an ebook.

ISBN: 978-0-9889004-3-1 (hardcover edition)

ISBN: 978-0-9889004-4-8 (softcover edition)

1. Schell, Inda Lou Lambert--Travel--United States. 2. Gass, Janie Leona Lambert--Travel--United States. 3. Older women--Travel--United States. 4. United States--Description and travel. 5. United States--Social life and customs--1971- 6. United States--Civilization--21st century. I. Gass, Janie Leona Lambert. II. Based on (work) Kuralt, Charles, 1934- Charles Kuralt's America. III. Title.

E169.Z83 S34 2014 917.30493

10 9 8 7 6 5 4 3 2 1

To my four wonderful children,
Robby, Milton, Kay, and Ellene,
and their spouses, Lou Ann, Lyná, Scott,
and Richard (deceased).
Eight grandchildren, six with spouses,
and soon to be nine great-grandchildren complete
my beautiful, loving family.

Contents

Charles Kuralt

In 1957, Charles Kuralt accepted an offer from CBS and moved from the *Charlotte News* in North Carolina to New York City where he became a *CBS News* correspondent.

Ten years later he was producing his famous "On the Road" segment for *CBS Evening News.* Kuralt's road-trip adventures took him half a million miles on repeated visits to all fifty states, and provided material for his series of best-selling books, including *On the Road with Charles Kuralt* and *Dateline: America.*

Foreword

First of all, thank you for picking up this book. It doesn't matter if you bought it, received it as a gift, borrowed it from the library, or found it abandoned in a public place.

We just hope that you will read and enjoy it.

I am Lou Schell, and many years ago I gave my husband, Fletcher Schell, a copy of Charles Kuralt's travel book, *America*. We both read and loved the book, and talked about making a similar trip when Fletcher retired. But Fletcher's death in December 2004 changed my life completely and, I thought, also ended that dream.

Then in 2009, I reread Kuralt's book and began reconsidering the trip Fletcher and I had once imagined taking together. I mentioned it to my youngest sister, Janie Leona Lambert Gass, who had retired and was then living in Austin, Texas.

Janie and I grew up in the rural setting of a small town in southwestern Alabama. Chatom is the seat of Washington County where our maternal grandfather was tax assessor for nearly forty years and our roots there run deep. We had wonderful, loving, strict parents—necessary attributes to keep five daughters in line. We matured and went our separate ways, but always kept in touch and reconnected at family gatherings.

Janie and I never imagined that we would undertake such

an adventure as revisiting Charles Kuralt's America, but once the idea bloomed, our decision was made and we began to prepare. My first priority was to reassure my family that I would be okay even at my advanced age to make the trip. And my second priority was telling them I was using their inheritance to finance it. Their reply, "Mom, go for it."

The itinerary, based on Kuralt's journey, was rearranged because we would drive rather than fly and go directly from one place to the next in logical geographical order. We would carry four seasons of clothing, personal belongings (medicine, makeup, and accessories for all occasions), and some kitchen essentials.

The best part of all, we would stay a month in each place, which would give us an opportunity to get to know both the people and the places.

This book chronicles our ten-and-a-half month journey, using our blog, journal entries, expense reports, notes jotted on stray pieces of paper, business cards, newspaper articles about our trip, and our memories as sources for recollections.

We hope our book will serve three purposes: to encourage everyone, even those as old as Janie (seventy-two) and myself (seventy-nine), to actively pursue their interests in travel and discovery; to remind every reader of the kindness and goodness of people everywhere; and to take notice of, and maybe come to love, the awesome beauty of our country.

I wish to acknowledge that I am the recipient of God's wonderful love, watchcare, and blessings.

Lou Schell

Introduction

Saturday, January 1, 2011. I am up at the crack of dawn, packing last minute things, and putting the house in order. I'm realizing that this will possibly be the most unusual year of my life.

With the blessings of family, friends, neighbors, and lots of doubters and a driveway lined with well-wishers and a police escort, I am changing my life's course. I'm not sure if the police escort is a send-off or a way to ensure that I will leave (just kidding). I couldn't let myself think about all I was leaving behind, but only of what might lie ahead.

Janie's departure from Austin was quite different. She said she sneaked out at dawn without any send-off, except for early birds chirping. Driving alone gave her a lot of time for thinking. She had mixed emotions—euphoria and apprehension. Euphoria, because of leaving behind her everyday routine; apprehension, because of leaving behind her everyday routine.

One of Janie's concerns about our trip was how to transport enough books since she is an avid reader. There certainly wouldn't be room in our car or lodgings to pack books for a year. Her family had solved the problem with the gift of a Kindle for Christmas. Best Christmas present she ever received, she says.

We agreed to meet at Extended Stay of America in Kenner, Louisiana, a suburb of New Orleans—our first destination. The inn would be our home for the month of January. Even with Janie's long drive from Austin, we arrived within twenty minutes of each other.

Our first task was to unload Janie's stuff from the rental car and turn the car in. My Buick Enclave with OnStar was packed with every kind of clothing, staples from my kitchen, computer and printer, camera, and everything we imagined we might need for a year's journey on the road. The looming question: could we also fit all of Janie's belongings into the car when we left for Key West, our next stop?

We knew this first month would be the litmus test, both of us having lived alone for years, having been very independent and opinionated, used to having our own way, and just about as different as two people could be. One area of concern—temperature. I am hot natured and Janie is cold natured. One morning when the outside temperature hovered at 34 degrees F, Janie actually complained because I had the air conditioner on in our room. However, we are sisters, and committed to making this trip work.

Our New Orleans accommodations are adequate: one large room with two double beds, an open closet area, desk/eating/card-playing table with two chairs, kitchen with a full-size refrigerator, and a two-burner stovetop. There's no oven but sufficient cabinet space. Really, everything we need. And, as my late husband used to say, "There's a Walmart on every corner."

Moving in was quite a chore. We had to find a place for all our belongings, and still leave room to walk around. Shoes were lined up along the walls, and out-of-season clothes, purses, and the like were stored under our beds using collapsible plastic bags. The available corners of the room are stacked high and wide with other stuff.

We divvied up our trip responsibilities. I am the driver and

Janie is our "techie" and financial recorder, documenting expenses. We agreed to each keep our part of the room in order, taking care of our own clothes; I am cook, and Janie is dishwasher when there is no dishwashing appliance available.

One of my goals for the trip, a departure from Kuralt's travels, is to attend a different church every Sunday. Being the pianist at Chatom Baptist Church since I was nine years old, I haven't had the opportunity to visit many other churches.

Our first outing Monday morning was to the grocery store since we had a full kitchen and didn't want to eat every meal in a restaurant. It's always fun to see what a local grocery is like, and we even ate lunch from the grocer deli. We met a lady pastor while in the store who invited us to visit her church the following Sunday.

Janie hasn't been a churchgoer for years, but had promised she would attend Sunday morning services with me. We're grateful nothing catastrophic happened upon her entering the sanctuary.

We had made an effort to contact several people we hoped to see in New Orleans. One is Robert Guyton, a relative of a friend at home, a retired doctor who has been living in New Orleans for years. Robert agreed on a time to meet next week, and we are pleased, knowing we cannot expect all our contacts to materialize. People are busy. We must remember, not everyone is vacationing for a year.

Chapter 1

New Orleans, Louisiana

January 2011

WHEN MOST OF YOUR life has been scheduled, learning to enjoy complete freedom without guilt can be difficult. But Janie and I were working on it. It's Monday, January 3, 2011, and we're off on our adventure. After all Charles Kuralt didn't travel to all these wonderful places and then just sit in his room.

Our first stop: New Orleans, the largest city in Louisiana and one of the world's busiest ports. Its mix of exotic culture and food and history, along with authentically American music, has made New Orleans one of America's most unique cities. New Orleanians are famous for enjoying life every day regardless of their circumstances. Having lived in close proximity to New Orleans all our lives, Janie and I had given much thought to how we'd spend our month here in our first stop "on the road."

We had reserved accommodations just outside the city because lodging was cheaper, but we splurged on a taxi for our first trip into New Orleans. As the cab let us out in the French Quarter, the oldest neighborhood in the city, we heard live music—a perfect welcome. Apparently we were two blocks from the form-up for the Sugar Bowl parade. A couple of ladies connected with the parade gave us festive boas, which we proudly donned. At Jackson Square on the south end of the Quarter bordering a curve in the Mississippi River, a group of entertainers called the Dragon Masters performed: dancing, tumbling, rapping and joking. These four guys had competed and made the top twenty on *America's Got Talent*. Artists, musicians, tarot card readers, and mimes perform almost every day on the streets lining Jackson Square.

New Orleans was founded as *Nouvelle-Orleans* in 1718 by the French explorer Jean-Baptiste le Moyne de Bienville. Bienville chose this relatively high ground because of the Mississippi River's regular springtime flooding, as well as its proximity to portage between Lake Pontchartrain and the river via Bayou Saint John. The portage, established by Native Americans long before Bienville's arrival, constituted part of an important trade route.

The city was ceded to the Spanish Empire in 1763, returned to France in 1800, only to be sold by Napoleon in 1803 to the U.S. In 1812, the British were determined to take New Orleans and sent a large military force up the river. General Andrew Jackson successfully held them back with critical assistance from French pirate Jean LaFitte, which explains the monument in the middle of Jackson Square honoring the General and references throughout the old city to the daring pirate.

Jackson Square is a favorite among tourists. Working artists occupy space along all four sides of the fence that surrounds the statue of General Jackson poised astride his bronze horse. On the north end of the square is Saint Louis Cathedral, established as a parish in 1720. We stood in awe of its beauty. Triple steeples tower over neighboring buildings. In front of the cathedral is a large public space with open-air seating on scattered benches—plenty of room for those dancers, musicians, and other street performers. It's January and some of the Christmas decorations are still in place. Stationed at the other end on Saint Peter's Street, horse-drawn carriages decorated with flowers (carriage and horses alike) are available for rides. We couldn't resist that.

New Orleans is an appealing blend of old, due to the preservation of historic sites, and new. Urban renewal has replaced decaying structures with modern buildings. As in most cities, there are problems of crime, poverty, and slums. Janie and I heard a few tourists complain that New Orleans is dirty, hot, old, and crime-ridden. But we loved the city. It is old, but rich in history and interesting characters. It is hot, but we grew up in South Alabama, so we don't mind. It is dirty, but if you were three hundred years old and besieged by tourists, you would be dirty too. As for being crime-ridden, was it so much worse than other port cities its size? We never felt threatened or even uneasy in all of our roaming about the city. Of course, we didn't ask for trouble either.

A visit to New Orleans would not be complete without taking Hurricane Katrina into account. The hurricane, a Category 5 with sustained winds of up to one hundred and sixty miles per hour, stretched over four hundred miles of coastline on the Gulf of Mexico and made landfall the morning of August 29, 2005. New Orleans was buffeted by winds, but according to Ivor van Heerden, deputy director of Louisiana State University's Hurricane Center, the worst damage was from flooding due to "catastrophic structural failure" of the levees along the Seventeenth Street and Industrial canals and the London Avenue floodwall.

By the time Katrina hit, heavy rain had been falling for hours. The force of the storm surge (a wall of water that piles up during a hurricane) moving into the city via the Mississippi River-Gulf Outlet canal (called Mr. Go by locals) undermined the levees. Pumps meant to counteract heavy rains were overwhelmed. Nearly eighty percent of the city flooded. More than eighteen hundred people were killed. The day before Hurricane Katrina made landfall, Mayor Ray Nagin ordered the first-ever evacuation of New Orleans, but one-quarter of the city's residents hadn't the means to leave the city. In the few days after the storm, the Coast Guard rescued more than thirty-four-thousand people. Many citizens commandeered boats and helped their neighbors as best they could. The French Quarter remained remarkably unharmed.

Information regarding the aftermath of Hurricane Katrina, compiled by the Greater New Orleans Community Data Center, reported that about eighty percent of the pre-storm population returned to the city. Retail outlets reopened. New ones were established. Investment in a major medical corridor and an influx of technology-related companies offered diversification from the city's traditional dependence on tourism.

Yet tourism remains an important New Orleans industry. Attracted by Mardi Gras, jazz festivals, and sports events at the Superdome, tourists still revel in New Orleans' lifestyle and motto: *laissez les bons temps rouler*, let the good times roll. The Cajun French phrase strongly conveys the *joie de vivre* attitude of the old city.

For our first meal in New Orleans, we chose Café Pontalba. The Upper and Lower Pontalba apartments, on opposing sides of Jackson Square, are four-story brick buildings wrapped in wrought-iron lacework balconies. Constructed by the Baroness Pontalba in the 1840s, they are said to be the oldest apartment buildings in America. At ground level are shops and restaurants. We knew we were in a building laden with history . . . and the fried shrimp and oysters were wonderful!

We had discussed what to collect as a souvenir from each place we visited. Within the confines of cost, storage, and availability, we decided on refrigerator magnets. Our initial magnet purchase was at a card shop along Jackson Square. A taxi ride back to Kenner ended our first day on the road to visit Charles Kuralt's America.

One of the considerations that Janie and I had to work through was our sleeping arrangements. We've already mentioned that our space is one large room plus the bath. Janie reads incessantly and is in the habit of reading in bed until she falls asleep. That means a light must be on in the room. I tend to go to bed and hopefully to sleep before my Requip kicks in (we both have restless leg syndrome), and I like it totally dark and quiet. We found a solution, not to each of our liking, but something that worked. Janie would sit in the bathroom and read until I fell asleep. I'm an early riser, and I would reside in the bathroom each morning until Janie had slept to a reasonable time. One night when nothing seemed to work I pulled the linens off the bed and slept in the tub, if you can call that sleeping. It would be awhile before that problem arose again.

We had made a reservation to attend the cooking class of Chef "Big Kevin" Belton at New Orleans School of Cooking in the

Louisiana General Store on Saint Louis Street, three blocks from Jackson Square. It was such fun! "Big Kevin" is a former football player, six foot nine inches tall, nearly four hundred pounds, and a natural comedian. He's billed as the "human taxidermist" because he loves to stuff people. Over the course of his two-and-a-half-hour class, he made biscuits served with cane syrup and cooked jambalaya, gumbo, bread pudding with whiskey sauce, and pralines. The jambalaya and gumbo were the best we'd ever eaten. How Big Kevin kept his mind on his cooking is a mystery as he told stories the entire time. He kept us laughing, which made for excellent digestion. Big Kevin was such a delight. Janie asked him if he'd make the rest of the trip with us (I think she was hoping to improve on my cooking), but he had other obligations.

La Provence and August are the names of two famous restaurants owned by John Besh of New Orleans. From our hotel in Kenner, we crossed Lake Pontchartrain on the way to Lacombe, Louisiana, where La Provence is located. The restaurant wasn't open. Joyce Bates, the manager and a poet published under the name Just Joyce, invited us in. We asked if John Besh was there. Ms. Bates said no, but offered us a tour of the establishment. The décor was Country French, with beautiful hardwood floors, columns, mahogany paneling, and antique mirrors. Little seating areas set off a large dining room. Several other dining rooms and a huge banquet room were available as well. White linen cloths, place settings of old silverware, china, and crystal covered all of the tables. Fires burned in the big stone fireplaces. Fresh flowers scented the air and made an already elegant space all the more appealing. A grand piano in a waiting area caught my eye. I sat and played several pieces despite Ms. Bates having just told me that the best pianist she had ever heard usually played there. I'm not bashful. Ms. Bates continued our private tour by showing us the vegetable garden and a livestock pen. There's also an office building. We were invited back inside for refreshments: French-press coffee, paté, and thin baguette slices.

We suspected Chef Besh was back in his office, but he had generously extended his hospitality to us through his intermediary. Thanks, Chef Besh! Hopefully, we'll meet next time.

The drive west from Lacombe to Mandeville, Louisiana, is short, and we headed to a so-called dive, Louie and the Redhead Lady, which had been featured on the Food Network show, *Diners, Drive-ins, and Dives*, hosted by Guy Fieri. A trip to the colorful ladies' room is worthy of note: chartreuse being the main color with splashes of other bright hues and black. Vintage hats and lace and some of the Redhead's costume jewelry doubled as decoration. Very original. After a look about, Janie and I ordered, starting with artichoke and shrimp chowder, followed by fried shrimp, fried catfish, green beans, delicate onion rings, and a fresh green salad. We met Chef Louie Finnan and spoke briefly to him. He said he would be with Guy Fieri on the Food Network again next month. Finnan excused himself to leave early as he wasn't feeling well. We wished him good luck and agreed this was some of the best food we had ever eaten. Quote of the day on Louie and the Redhead Lady website: "One cannot think well, love well, sleep well, if one has not dined well."

Driving outside the city of New Orleans, we passed a large area of marshland: acres of slender, spiky, limbless tree trunks protruded from the water. Even without branches, Spanish moss hangs from the trees. The marsh water is dark, the trunks a lifeless shade of brownish-gray, and the moss is gray—bleak, but nature's perfect rendition of winter in the marshes.

Lakes, marshlands, and bayous extend from the city outward, reminding us that New Orleans is partly peninsula with miles of waterfront in three directions.

The heart of New Orleans spreads around a curve in the Mississippi River—thus the nickname Crescent City—while edging Lake Pontchartrain on the north and a lagoon that connects to the Gulf of Mexico. Many people visiting New Orleans do not realize that the Mississippi River flows south for one hundred and five miles before reaching the Gulf.

The varied habitats of Louisiana—marshes, woodlands, and prairies—offer a diversity of flora. Among the state's wildflowers are the ground orchid and several species of hyacinth. Spanish moss, which has become rare in the northern part of the state and much of the Southeast, grows profusely in the Southern regions of Louisiana and is evident on any tree-lined street of New Orleans.

We'd planned to get together with a relative of a friend from home, Robert and his partner, Bob. Not wanting to be late, we left Kenner early. Sometimes if I don't listen closely, OnStar takes us on a scenic detour. Robert and Bob's house is in the French Quarter, fronted by a gate with landscaping that led us to the entrance. Constructed in 1840 as a townhouse for plantation owners, the building is old New Orleans architecture at its best, including columns and a gallery with decorative wrought iron. Inside, every wall space is used to display valuable art. The beauty of Robert and Bob's home overwhelmed Janie and me. We tried to take it all in: the chandeliers, sculpture, elegant rugs, brick walls, eleven-foot ceilings, and custom-made draperies. Hollywood memorabilia filled the den, including a letter signed by Joan Crawford. In the dining room, a table for ten was set with a floor-length cloth, gold chargers, and elegant china, crystal, and silverware. French doors opened from the dining room to a large patio and seating around the swimming pool. You get the idea.

Meeting Robert and Bob was the best part though. Bob is from California and a great conversationalist. Robert, a retired doctor from Birmingham, has lived in New Orleans for years, is a man of many interests, and easy to talk to. After being offered some wine and having enjoyed some casual conversation, we walked around the corner to the Louisiana Pizza Kitchen. The menu was unusual. Janie ordered a grilled eggplant pizza, which she said was delicious. All in all, the evening was delightful, with good food and camaraderie that left us hoping we would see Robert and Bob again before leaving New Orleans.

On Sunday, having been invited by Pastor Erica Jenkins, we attended Thomas United Methodist Church in Kenner; it is an African-American congregation and one of the oldest in the state. Janie and I were asked to tell about our trip, which we did, and we joined everyone for fellowship after the sermon. Then, we were happy to have an afternoon to do nothing.

We'd been away from home for only a little while, but our location has become an attraction for visits from friends, and we benefited from that. Later today we're meeting several friends from Chatom, Alabama, at the LaQuinta Inn on Camp Street.

Leaving Kenner midmorning, we made our first stop: the Musee Conti Historical Wax Museum of New Orleans. Instead of solitary figures, tableaus depicted historical events. The educational tour wove together stories of French Creoles and three hundred years of history that included explorers, pirates, and Mardi Gras Zulu kings. Marie Laveau and her voodoo dancers and casket girls were there, too. *Filles à la cassette* is the term for virtuous young girls brought from France to the French colonies to marry. The girls were prized as brides and came to be called "casket girls" for the small chest of clothing they carried.

Lunch in the French Quarter at Oceana/Olde N'Awlins Cookery left us drunk on food. The atmosphere was so relaxed we succumbed to the best crab cakes, enhanced by crawfish cream sauce. That should have been enough but Janie and I foolishly also ordered the seafood platter with shrimp, oysters, catfish, slaw, and fries. After so much food what could one do but sit?

Starting with the Riverfront streetcar, we rode the line forward and backward. Next, we took the Canal Street line to Saint Charles Avenue, all the way down and back, which took us through a beautiful residential area called the Garden District, which is bordered by Magazine Street, Saint Charles, Toledano, and First, an area cut from four French long-lot plantations that belonged to Ursuline nuns and the Panis, Livaudais, and Delassize families. The district was later subdivided into streets and parcels. Luxury houses and gardens were built in this sector, which was considered the American district in the 1840s to 1870s by the rising mercantile elite.

The streetcar ride was a little long but worth it, though we were late meeting our friends from Chatom. Our walk from their hotel on Camp Street was preceded by a small Mardi Gras parade complete with bead throwing and bands and floats, but no Moon

Pies—a tradition in Mobile, Alabama. We continued a short distance down Poydras Street to Mother's for supper.

Beginning in 1938 Mother's owners Simon and Mary Landry cooked po-boys and homestyle meals for longshoremen, laborers, newspapermen, and lawyers until 1986 when they sold the "must eat" place to Chef Jerry Amato. During World War II, Mother's became a hangout for Marines. Five of the seven Landry children served in the Corps, including Francis Landry, the first woman in Louisiana to be accepted. The Landry family's special connection with Marines earned Mother's the title of Tun Tavern New Orleans. The original Tun Tavern in Philadelphia was the birthplace of the U.S. Marine Corps in 1775 during the Revolutionary War. A Mother's speciality is Roast Beef Debris Sandwich, made from the "debris" roast beef that falls into the gravy while baking in the oven. Having eaten a hefty lunch, Janie and I chose selections from the breakfast menu. Janie said if her order of eggs was only two, they must have been ostrich eggs. We shared bread pudding with rum sauce. Neither of us needed a whole dessert.

Hand and Foot, a variation of canasta, is our favorite card game. When a few friends or family are gathered, we play. Little space was available in our hotel rooms, but we asked permission to play in the hotel breakfast area. The game went on for hours, and it seemed we saw hundreds of people check in accompanied by their dogs. This dog-friendly motel we learned later had an entire floor designated for people with animals. How unique.

A visit to New Orleans would be incomplete without *café au lait* and beignets from Café du Monde in the French Quarter, and part of the fun is that before it is all over everyone would be covered with confectioners' sugar from the beignets. Café du Monde is naturally followed by a stroll through the nearby French Market—a long line of vendors in an open-market space with goods of all kinds that appeal to tourists.

Janie and I had discussed Hack Bartholomew, a trumpet player featured in Charles Kuralt's book, and wondered if we could find him. We noticed a statuesque man standing right at the entrance to Café du Monde playing trumpet. Without hesitation, Janie walked up to him and asked, "Are you Hack Bartholomew?"

"Yes," he said, and we launched into a delightful discussion about Charles Kuralt and his visits to New Orleans. According to Kuralt, Hack had once asked Kuralt if he was a Christian. Kuralt's reply was, "More or less."

"More is better," Hack said. Hack's grandfather had been the preacher at Mount Maria Baptist Church, the family church of New Orleans musical celebrities, including the Neville Brothers and Mahalia Jackson. Hack himself is minister of music at Trinity United Methodist.

Speaking of churches, we would visit two more during our time in New Orleans. A telephone call from friends in Chatom produced an invitation to attend the Norwegian Church or Sjomannkirken—Seaman's or Sailor's Church—on Prytania Street. The Norwegian Seaman's Mission founded in 1864 offered moral and religious education to Scandinavian seafarers.

The Norwegian church in New Orleans looked quite ordinary from the street, but the inside was impressive what with its spire ceiling in the worship center, the large fellowship room, and an area for vending machines filled with Norwegian foods. A ship's model hung suspended from the ceiling of the sanctuary. Displayed on the grounds at the church front was the anchor from the real ship. We learned that seamen and members of other Norwegian churches were offered housing when visiting in New Orleans. It is easy to imagine the comfort these services gave Scandinavians who found themselves far from home.

Pastor Erland Grotberg asked if we understood the sermon, which was entirely in Norwegian. Our answer: "Only the words *alpha* and *omega*." But we would have been disappointed if the service had been in English. A visiting choir of young people from Norway sang, too. Following the service a bountiful lunch of ham and roast beef sandwiches, shrimp, burgers, potato salad, stuffed eggs with strips of salmon on top, crusty breads, and cones filled with flavored whipped cream and cake were served. Each lady attending received a long stemmed red rose. Janie and I left even more impressed than we had been on arrival.

I know the whole world has heard of Auburn University in Auburn, Alabama, and is interested in the BCS Championship game in California. My son Milton Schell and neighbor Jack Thompson had attended the game and then they flew back via the New Orleans International Airport, which was only two miles from our motel. Janie and I met their flight, visited, and were informed that the game was great, quite intense, and well worth the time and effort to go all the way to California. We enjoyed a meal together, and I reassured Milton everything was okay, and the trip would continue as planned.

Returning to Kenner, I followed OnStar without a single wrong turn. I'm mostly on good terms with OnStar, but I have imagined that when my name pops up on its screen there's the question of who will have to route me. I don't always listen to or read the directions that are on the dash; I make unauthorized moves. OnStar doesn't allow for little scenic side trips. I am accustomed now to, "As soon as possible make a legal and safe U-turn." The streets of Kenner have been perfect for this maneuver. That may not be the case elsewhere, but I am getting the hang of it here.

Driving out of town to see areas surrounding New Orleans presents a different landscape. It's January and the bare trees offer a clear view of the swamps, Spanish moss on the trees, and endless bayous and bays. We crossed the Mississippi River via Huey P. Long Bridge to Gretna on the West Bank in Jefferson Parish. Boats and fishing tackle shops were plentiful but very few people were about. Algiers, a small community that is a part of the city of New Orleans and also on the West Bank, must have been off the map that day. We never did find it. Returning to Kenner for our first Mexican food on the trip soothed that disappointment. The meal at Casa Garcia was very good, and inexpensive, which amazed me because we were served such large portions.

After years of teaching school I am well aware of the fact that Thursday is the favored day for school field trips, yet Janie and I chose that day to visit the Audubon Aquarium. Thousands (it seemed) of shrieking four- and five-year-olds darted around us like schools of fish. Other groups of older children seemed intent on getting answers to questions for their assignment sheets. They were fun to watch.

Audubon is a world-class aquarium with state-of-the-art exhibits including major marine and submarine habitats of North and South America, the Caribbean, and Amazon rainforests. Thousands of fish, reptiles, and birds native to those habitats are in residence. The reconstructed Caribbean Reef tunnel is thirty feet long and allows an eye-to-eye view of Caribbean sea life. A rare white alligator found in a Louisiana swamp can be seen there too. In Cajun folklore, seeing the white gator is considered good luck.

The Audubon Zoo, park, and aquarium are named in honor of America's most famous naturalist and artist John James Audubon, who lived in New Orleans starting in 1921 as a part-time resident for nine years. The aquarium is in a beautiful building at One Canal Street on the bank of the Mississippi River near the French Quarter. It opened in 1990 and has become one of New Orleans' most popular attractions.

No doubt you know a meal is coming as we'd been away from home for several hours. But this one would be a meal above all meals. We were headed to August, another John Besh restaurant, at the corner of Tchoupitoulas and Gravier. (Tchoupitoulas is Janie's all-time favorite street name. The local pronunciation is *chop-a-tew-liss*).

John Besh is winner of many culinary awards: one of the Top Ten Chefs in America and recipient of the James Beard Award for Best Chef. One of his establishments has also been named one of the Top 50 Restaurants in the United States by *Gourmet* magazine. You get the idea. What a treat, what a bill, but we expected it and after the fact it didn't matter. We'd do it again just to see if Besh could make everything perfectly twice.

Arriving at August, we felt elevated to celebrity status. From the moment we stepped inside the door until we left we were treated like we were their only guests in an atmosphere of total elegance: white tablecloths; exquisite china, crystal, and silver; beautiful old oak floors; high ceilings and sparkling chandeliers.

Huge but tasteful bouquets of flowers were everywhere, and waiters in white coats hovered about our table.

Our mid-day feast began with what Janie called an *amuse bouche*, or small bite. Thank goodness Janie is so well read she knew what we were being served. Ours came in the form of a custard-like concoction in an eggshell with a tiny breadstick and caviar on top. The taste was subtle to cleanse the palate in preparation for the meal.

Rainbow trout, the entrée, was presented to us on a plate covered with mushrooms, crab meat, and a hollandaise sauce aerated we were told to make it light and fluffy. Nothing else was on the plate. My first thought, since I'm a big eater, was, "Will this be enough?"

The waiter took the time to describe each dish as it was brought to the table and answered questions we had about the food. Service was impeccable. The meal was perfect (I did have plenty), and dessert (Pere Roux's Banana Rum Cake with Creole Cream Cheese Icing—two tiers, three inches high, and covered in white icing decorated with leaves of white chocolate and shavings of the same on top) was almost too beautiful to eat. But we managed. Wow!

We had asked in advance to visit the kitchen and meet the chef, which we had heard was a customary accommodation if so desired. Again, we were told, John Besh was not on the premises, but we did receive a tour of the kitchen where several chefs including the pastry chef were available.

Janie hugged the pastry chef and thanked her for the rum cake. The staff all applauded as we entered, and again as we left. What a wonderful way to treat people. That must be another reason John Besh is so successful, and why he does own three other restaurants.

If you choose to go to August, save up, but you'll never mention the price again. It is that good.

The New Orleans Museum of Art sits on the southeast section of thirteen hundred acres of New Orleans City Park, a wide-open expanse of beautiful landscaping that includes the five-acre Sydney and Walda Bestoff Sculpture Garden and a large lake with swans on the front lawn.

More than forty thousand art objects are on display in NOMA, with an emphasis on French and American artists such as James Tissot, Camille Carot, Maurice Vlaminch, Edgar Degas, Claude Monet, Jackson Pollock, and many, many more. Early pre-Colombian and Native American pieces, art indigenous to the Pacific Islands and Australia, and African designs are all part of the huge NOMA collection.

And there's food! Brennan's restaurants are a New Orleans tradition. In the museum is a Brennan café. We ate turkey and bacon paninis with pickled artichokes and onions on the side. Delicious. I have never had so much time to spend on something as enjoyable as this: art and food.

Janie and I discussed what we had seen. She is a fan of Tissot's Victorian neoclassic oils, which she'd first been exposed to through a computer game. Her favorite painting today, though, was *Portrait of an Old Man*, by the seventeenth-century Dutch artist Jan Lievens. The old man was so very life-like that she was waiting for him to breathe, Janie said.

We were thrilled to have another opportunity to visit with our friends Robert and Bob on our last night in New Orleans. One of their favorite places is Palm Court Jazz Café, a café with fine dining and live classic New Orleans jazz.

The *New York Times* deemed the café "one of the most appealing in a rich bouillabaisse of New Orleans clubs offering Louisiana music."

Zagat, a national publication reviewing restaurants in New Orleans, said, "Absolutely fabulous traditional jazz, great ambiance; hepcats say it should be made a national treasure."

Nina Buck opened Palm Court in 1989 to provide a tasteful atmosphere for listening to live jazz while dining on excellent Creole cuisine. The café at 1204 Decatur Street in the French Quarter is in a restored early nineteenth-century building that reflects old New Orleans elegance. The bistro area is decorated with a wide selection of compact discs and LPs of music by famous and some not-so-famous jazz artists.

Nina's husband, George Buck, produced his first jazz disk in 1949 in New York City. Buck worked in radio, eventually acquired several stations, and bought up jazz labels all along the way. When he and Nina moved to New Orleans, Buck needed ten trucks to transport his jazz-label inventory. With that, he and Nina transformed an historic building into this famous music hall and dining room.

On our visit, the Crescent City Joy Makers—on piano, clarinet, trumpet, bass fiddle, and drums—performed for the café diners. Nina, dressed in a tight-fitting silver lame gown, floated about the dance floor. Everyone enjoyed just watching her, and Nina seemed to enjoy visiting with her guests as she danced around the room.

For Janie and me, the greatest pleasure was sharing the delightful food, music, and atmosphere with Robert and Bob. These men are well traveled, versed in New Orleans history, and made delightful companions. They made us feel very special and we know we have two friends for life.

Janie and I realized we won't be able to see every place Kuralt mentioned in his book, or contact every person, but we wanted to include as much as possible while still doing our own thing. Yet, I suspect, we'll probably be asking ourselves at the end of each month, "Did we make the most of our time and effort while here?" This had been our first month, our first city. We didn't know all the answers, but felt we'd done well in adjusting to our accommodations, to each other, and to keeping on task.

We were leaving a place we'd enjoyed tremendously for Key West. Once we started packing, thinking about where we were going and actually getting everything in the car (with maybe just enough space at the top for a sheet of paper), we got excited.

On some locations we would have a kitchenette or even a full kitchen, but I asked Janie to stop me from shopping for anymore cooking utensils. In addition to all the gadgets we'd brought—crockpot, toaster oven, handheld mixer, and two coffee pots—we'd acquired mixing bowls with lids for storage, sets of different size plastic bowls and lids, and foil baking pans, etc. We had stretched the limits of a Buick Enclave's capacity for stuff to be packed therein.

Reservations were firmed up for our next three stops, and then for Ketchikan, Alaska, in October at the Black Bear Inn. Move over Charles Kuralt. Here we come!

Chapter Two

Key West, Florida

February 2011

OUR JOURNEY TO Key West from New Orleans lay ahead of us: 1,045.9 miles. We made a quick stop in Creola, near Mobile, Alabama, to meet several family members at a McDonald's restaurant. They shared our excitement that this trip was actually happening. Driving ever closer to Key West, the scenery became more tropical and beautiful as we entered the lower regions of Florida. From Miami we picked up the extension of Highway One sometimes called the "highway that goes to sea."

The 113-mile, two-lane road with forty-two bridges from key to key first opened in 1938. This was after Henry Flagler's railroad, once the only route to Key West, was mostly destroyed by a hurricane in 1935.

The State of Florida bought the old railroad bed from Flagler and built the Overseas Highway. Due to heavy traffic, limitations of the two-lane road, and a forty-five-mile-per-hour speed limit, it took four hours to reach Key West. The magnificent view made up for any inconvenience.

Have you ever seen a mangrove tree? You have if you've driven to the Florida Keys. The mangrove lives in saltwater and lines the Overseas Highway from Key Largo to Key West. They also make up those islands alongside the highway. Some of the islands are only one tree. Mangroves were once thought to be of no value, but it is now recognized that the mangrove is important to the ecosystem. Clams, snails, and crabs depend on decomposing mangrove leaves and branches for their entire diet. The root system provides a protective nursery for reef fish and many water birds. All sorts of birds were flying as we drove Highway One. We were looking at the bluest water we'd ever seen, and the air was cool and crisp. It was, after all, February.

Our rental on Sugar Loaf Key, about seventeen miles from Key West, was similar to the setup we had in New Orleans: one large room with a spacious living and dining area, nice bath, and a big walk-in closet. After several phone calls from home though, we realized this space would not accommodate all our guests.

Key West is the last in the string of islands making up the Straits of Florida. The entire island is only four miles long and two miles wide. It is 3,370 acres, the size of a modest cattle ranch in Texas or Central Park in New York City. The highest elevation on the island is eighteen feet.

We drove into Key West and ate at Southernmost Café and

Bar, the southernmost point of the contiguous United States of America. Pigeons swarmed around us. The temperature was in the seventies. Everyone in the restaurant wore beachwear. We were definitely in Key West—the place where it is said one minute everyone is napping, and the next they are partying. Chickens run loose in the streets, and the island is famous for its liberal attitudes. A man wearing only a tiny Speedo bathing suit provided a visual of a different sort. He seemed quite proud of his appearance and well aware of his audience as he paraded across the sand.

On our way back to Sugar Loaf Key we saw a sign for Mia Howe Realty. Janie suggested we stop and see if they had anything available that would accommodate our future guests and us. On Ms. Howe's desk was a photo of a two-story house she hadn't had time to list. We asked to see it and signed a lease on the spot. Two bedrooms were a plus. The spacious bath and living/dining/kitchen area with sliding glass doors that enlarged the space were definitely enhancements. On the upper level an eight-foot-wide balcony with screens allowed light and air and kept out the bugs. The house felt wonderfully open and bright. And it was seated on a canal overlooking Sugar Loaf Bay. Not too shabby.

We hated to move again, but the chore was quickly forgotten as we settled into the new house, and Janie, our techie, hooked us up for Internet. We were ready to go, set for the next twenty-two days to search for people, places, and great food.

There are many ways to obtain information about a city: computer searches, phone books, brochures, and what is beginning to be my favorite, just asking. People are usually eager to talk about their hometown. That's how I found the Sugar Loaf Key Baptist Church a few miles from our house, a small friendly congregation, a mix of young and old, no choir but a pianist about my age (please forgive me if I'm wrong), and a wonderful message just for me: The scripture John 10:10 reminds us of the "true abundance of God," and that Jesus is the only door to God's presence and abundance, the amazing greatness and goodness of God. I needed that message.

We drove into Key West needing haircuts and camera advice. Supercuts took care of our hair, but we found no camera shop in Key West. Since every tourist is carrying a camera, that seemed odd. Luckily we found the help we required at Radio Shack.

Charles Kuralt visited Blue Heaven Restaurant in Key West and declared breakfast the place's best meal. We went for lunch. Blue Heaven at 729 Thomas Street in Bahama Village is a place with history. The property has hosted cock fighting, gambling, and Friday night boxing matches refereed by none other than Ernest Hemingway. It's an old two-story building with a courtyard paved in slate pool table tops from long ago. It has a water tower and a rooster cemetery. At one time or another the upstairs has housed a dance hall, a bordello, and a playhouse. Currently that upstairs space is the Bordello Gallery.

We dined outside on the patio. Roosters were running about or perched in trees, but not once did we see one attempt to flutter near patrons or disturb a table. Two of the birds crowed back and forth, and while I don't know the language, it did prove that roosters crow at times other than daybreak.

Our lunch was excellent: shrimp sautéed in butter, with squash, zucchini, and onions; refried beans; brown rice; asparagus spears; diced tomatoes; and a huge slice of fresh-baked cornbread. The presentation was beautiful, but nothing compared to the taste. We shared a slice of Key Lime Pie with a four-inch meringue. An incredible, edible meal. Should anyone leave Blue Heaven hungry, it's no fault of the restaurant. The ambience was completely laid back, but the owners obviously take food preparation seriously.

Key West offers several modes of transportation for seeing the sights. Walking or cycling is popular, and there is the pedicab—a two-wheeled cart accommodating a pair of passengers, powered by a man peddling an attached bicycle. We chose the World Famous Conch Train, which looks like a big toy, its engine pulling a string of bright yellow canopy-topped open cars that snake along behind. *Florida Monthly Magazine* voted the Conch Train the "Best Guided Tour in Florida." Our guide/engineer (who can make or break a tour) shared political, cultural, and geographical facts of the island—four hundred years of history. The main focus was Olde Town, that part of the island formed by nature, essentially the western side, and New Town, the man-made section.

Key West was first settled in the 1820s and was America's richest city, per capita, in 1886. It is a tropical paradise that has become a magnet for artists, hippies, and cruise ships. Populated by gingerbread cottages and white picket fences, and Victorian mansions with widow's walks, it's also crowded with sidewalk cafes, T-shirt shops, and famous local characters. One of those characters was Mayor Dennis Wardlow.

In the 1980s President Ronald Reagan declared a War on Drugs. To curb the flow of illegal drugs into the U.S. through the Florida Keys, Reagan commanded the U.S. Border Patrol to set up a blockade on U.S. Highway 1 at Florida City just north of the Keys. All vehicles headed north from the Keys were stopped and searched. Identification was required, proving U.S. citizenship in order to proceed. The blockade quickly curtailed Keys tourism and severely inconvenienced local workers and businesses. Mayor Wardlow of Key West sought an injunction to stop the federal blockade but to no avail. Upon leaving the Monroe County Courthouse one April day, the mayor stood on the steps and announced to the world by way of assembled TV crews and reporters, "Tomorrow at noon the Florida Keys will secede from the Union." At noon, April 23, 1982, Mayor Wardlow stood in Mallory Square in Key West, where he read the proclamation of secession and declared the Conch Republic an independent nation. "We've raised our flag, given our notice, and named our new government," he said.

The Conch Rebellion began with the symbolic breaking of a loaf of stale Cuban bread over the head of a man dressed in a U.S. Navy uniform. The now Prime Minister Wardlow announced that the Conch Republic was officially at war with the U.S., and demanded $1,000,000,000 in economic aid to rebuild his nation after the federal siege. Then he turned to the admiral in charge of the Navy base at Key West and surrendered to the Union forces.

President Reagan immediately removed the blockade to the Keys. The Conch Republic continues to celebrate its independence each year with week-long festivities in April.

I routinely took my morning walk alongside the Sabal palms that line the streets of our neighborhood. The Keys are a paradise of exotic trees, flowers, and animal life. The Sabal, state tree of Florida as well as South Carolina, is also known as cabbage palm, or palmetto. Its edible core is used in heart-of-palm salad. Extracting the heart kills the plant, as the terminal bud is the only point from which the palm can grow.

The Sabal is well suited to the local environment. It is hardy, tolerant of cold, drought, salt winds, and standing and brackish water. But it suffers in salt water flooding. The tree grows to a height of sixty-five feet, with a trunk that can reach two feet in diameter. Its yellowish-white flowers, produced in large compound panicles up to eight feet long, extend out beyond the trunk. The palm's elegant height and graceful limbs add exotic beauty to an already magnificent tropical landscape.

On my morning strolls, the faces of school kids and dog-walkers had become familiar. We'd met several neighbors who had welcomed us to the community. Wayne and Chuck lived next door with their two Vizslas, Tootie and Zuzu. Vizslas, a breed of sporting dog originating in Hungary, are known to be gentle, well-mannered, and affectionate, but Tootie and Zuzu are rescue dogs and very skittish. Janie's effort to make friends with the dogs required intervention from Wayne and Chuck. She never overcame their defenses but was finally able to pet them.

Janie has been unable to walk distances due to arthritis (first disabling bout at age eighteen), and she misses the dog show encounters each morning on my walk. She is a dog lover and is known to stop to pet any dog in range.

We agreed no pets would be allowed on the trip, but we've adopted an iguana at our rental. Iguanas are odd-looking creatures and one of them had become competition for our yard space.

He is an herbivore and can grow to five feet in length, weighing twenty pounds. Although not on an endangered species list, iguana trade is controlled to protect the species for the future. They are popular pets and a food source in Latin America. We'd named our iguana Iggy. Iguanas are often found near water, are agile climbers, and can fall fifty feet yet land unhurt (their secret is they use their hind legs to grasp leaves or branches to break the fall). Iguanas prefer to remain on the ground for warmth during cold weather.

Iggy is green, although some iguanas are blue, black, or even pink. He (or she) seemed to have a calm disposition. He did possess a row of spines along his back and tail which act as protection from predators. We were aware that Iggy could deliver a painful strike. His sharp teeth are capable of shredding leaves or human skin. If cornered or threatened, he extends and displays the dewlap, stiffening and pumping up his body, hissing and bobbing his head at the aggressor. Social interactions such as courting a mate are evidenced by head bobs and puffed dewlaps. The frequency and number of head bobs are said to have particular meaning to other iguanas.

All this iguana information to explain what we faced while sitting in the backyard overlooking the beautiful lagoon. There was plenty of space, but it was shared with Iggy. I walked fast when headed to our entrance, believing I could get to the steps before Iggy. But just in case, I always kept some edibles such as leaves, flowers, or fruit nearby to toss and distract him.

February is Key West's top tourist month of the year. In Olde Town the narrow, tree-lined streets are difficult to traverse, with barely enough space for two vehicles to meet and pass. Sidewalks and shops and restaurants are crowded, yet the atmosphere is relaxed, non-hurried. Service people are friendly and helpful. And always, there is the ever-present breeze from the Atlantic Ocean on one side of the island, or the Gulf of Mexico on the other.

Our visitors would be coming soon and we were planning things to do and places to see. The weather was perfect: cool, sixtyish, and not a cloud in the brightest blue sky. It was the beginning of a new fishing season, a very important part of the Key West lifestyle and the focus of many of Charles Kuralt's visits.

We aren't fishermen, boaters, or water babies, but our neighbor across the street happened to be office manager for the new *FishMonster* magazine, in only its second month of publication.

FishMonster is the creation of publisher Diane Scott and her husband, Captain Marlin Scott, editor. (How ironic his name is Marlin like the fish.) The magazine is filled with fishing, diving, and boating information that is pertinent to the sportsmen's interests and livelihood. One of the most important and helpful features in the magazine is the reprinting of rules and regulations—of which there are many—for fishing the Florida Keys, taken directly from a publication provided by State of Florida Fish and Wildlife Conservation Commission, Gulf of Mexico Fishery Management Council, and the South Atlantic Fishery Management Council.

Even though I'm not a fisherman or boater, I enjoyed reading the issue. My favorite section included stories by legendary captains of the fishing and boating world. I just know this magazine will be successful.

Captain Scott also hosts an afternoon talk show, and he had invited Janie and me to be guests on it one day. Of course, we accepted. It was such fun watching Marlin, who is a hoot, maneuver microphones and phone-in guests, all the while talking to Janie and me. He asked about our trip and our upcoming book about our trip. And, like his magazine, the show was loaded with tips, information, and suggestions for his listeners.

We left feeling grateful and happy to have met these incredibly talented people.

Our guests have arrived, and we're headed to the Key West Butterfly and Nature Conservatory, voted the No. 1 attraction in Key West by the People's Choice Awards. The environment of the conservatory is a tropical paradise within a tropical paradise. It is magical, inviting, relaxing, and breathtaking as we view hundreds of the most fragile and beautiful creatures in nature. I speak of an impressive collection of flowering plants, colorful birds, cascading waterfalls, and trees. It is the setting for viewing a variety of fifty to sixty species of butterflies from around the world, all under a domed, climate-controlled, glass-enclosed habitat. Janie said she felt like an interloper, but the butterflies were gracious hosts and would sometimes land on us for a short visit.

The Learning Center of the Conservatory explores the anatomy, physiology, life cycle, feeding, and migratory world of the Monarch. It offers a close-up look at a variety of live caterpillars that are feeding and developing on the plants. In the Conservatory gift shop we found original art work and nature items. It all was amazing and the No. 1 vote is deserved.

I never thought Ernest Hemingway, a Key West icon and legendary writer, handsome. Most photos show him unshaven and wearing unkempt clothing, but while touring his home we saw earlier photographs of a very handsome younger man. Hemingway's home from 1931 to 1939 was at 907 Whitehead in Key West, a Spanish colonial two-story house built in 1851 by Asa Tift, a marine architect. Hemingway wrote some of his best work there including *The Green Hills of Africa*, *A Farewell to Arms*, and *Death in the Afternoon*.

The house is now a Registered National Historic Landmark. Our guide gave an excellent tour of the house with its very Key West-style of open porches, floor to ceiling windows, louvered shutters, and high ceilings. The house is light and airy, spacious enough for gatherings and furnished for comfort. It sits right on a busy street with the property covering almost a city block.

Hemingway's writing studio/study is on the second floor of a separate, small building; it is connected by a suspended walkway to what was his bedroom in the main house. While not exactly a "man cave" the studio felt masculine and held an extensive library. The writer's routine was to write each morning from six until noon. After work, he went fishing or to Sloppy Joe's (his favorite bar in Key West) until whenever. He was back at work by six the next morning. Janie has always been a fan of Hemingway, particularly of his stories of Africa. Hemingway worked as a reporter for the *Kansas City Star* after he'd graduated from high school in Oak Park, Illinois. A defective eye kept him from military service, but he served as an ambulance driver for the American Red Cross during World War I.

His first solid success as a writer came in 1926 with the publication of his novel, *The Sun Also Rises*. Much of the writer's macho reputation seems to have been earned during his time as a war correspondent in World War II and the Spanish Civil War. In that time, Hemingway lived in Paris, Cuba, and Key West.

He was a fancier of bullfighting and big game hunting and many of his stories were of men of action, outdoorsmen, soldiers and expatriates. In 1953 Hemingway was awarded a Pulitzer Prize for his short novel, *The Old Man and the Sea.* The Nobel Prize for literature was given to him in 1954.

Why would we sit for more than an hour on a concrete pier waiting for the sun to set? Because it's a Key West tradition . . . what you do in Mallory Square. Early arrival was required to find a good viewing spot, so one could enjoy all the entertainment by jugglers, tightrope walkers, fire-eaters, magicians, and musicians. Once the sun had set there was a collective sigh of satisfaction.

We'd had a physically exhausting afternoon and were ready to find a good place to eat, which we did: The Conch Republic Seafood Company. At 631 Greene Street, the Conch Republic Seafood Company overlooks Key West Marina and Historic Seaport. In the early 1900s, Key West was called the Sponge Capital of the country. The location of Conch Republic was where "mother ships" of sponge fleets docked to unload their cargo.

Vast beds of pink shrimp were located just off the Dry Tortugas in 1949. Soon hundreds of shrimp trawlers were operating out of the Bight. The Singleton Fish House and Ice Plant was the point of unloading and packing shrimp in ice, and it became the largest such operation in the world. All this at what is now the location of the Conch Republic restaurant.

During construction of the restaurant in the 1990s, materials salvaged from the docks and ice plant were integrated into the new building. Today the Conch Republic Seafood Company is a popular open-air restaurant with a Caribbean-influenced menu. Fresh seafood is still delivered to its dock daily. We enjoyed a wonderful meal. My entrée, Snapper Wellington—fish and crab baked into a crust, like Beef Wellington—was delicious. And of course there was Key Lime Pie for dessert. After such a busy day, the only thing to do was to go home, play cards for a while, and then try to sleep. Which we did.

On July 20, 1985, Mel Fisher finally found his dream—the priceless treasure cargo of a lost Spanish galleon, *Nuestra Señora de Atocha*, which sank in 1622 during a hurricane off the Florida Keys. The ship held forty-seven tons of gold and silver. Fisher's dream of finding lost treasure began when he was a boy after reading *Treasure Island* by Robert Louis Stevenson. He continued throughout his life to read of sunken ships and treasure hunting.

In the 1950s, Mel Fisher opened the first dive shop in the world in Redondo Beach, California. Mel's Aqua Shop was a success. He and his wife loved scuba diving, and visited Key West for vacation. It was there that Mel decided to search for treasure at the bottom of the ocean. Mel, his wife, Deo, and their children spent sixteen years in pursuit of the *Atocha*'s buried riches. After "the day" that the Fishers achieved their goal of raising the Spanish treasure, they spent years fighting courts for the ruling that finally gave them "rights of admiralty." The treasure was valued at more than 450 million dollars. Fisher had spent several million raising the treasure from the ocean and battling to keep it.

We visited the Mel Fisher Museum at 200 Greene Street in Key West. The Mel Fisher Maritime Heritage Society is a non-profit organization charged with accumulating and disseminating information and providing educational services on maritime and colonial activity in the New World. Portions of the treasure from *Atocha* and other ships are showcased at the museum. Jewelry made from those treasures can also be purchased. We spent several hours in the museum. It was not nearly long enough to absorb all of the information, but we did get a feel of the importance of Fisher's ambition and discoveries.

Our wonderful friends were leaving us in Key West. We saw them off and went for lunch at Blue Heaven and, of course, a serving of the island's best Key Lime Pie and a photo with the owner, Susanne. Though she was not owner when Kuralt visited Susanne does remember him eating in the restaurant. We later learned our friends, supposedly on their way home, also couldn't resist returning to Blue Heaven for one last slice of Key Lime Pie. Now it's just Janie and me again. We'd had a break from being alone, and we'd had a fun, busy, good time with our friends.

A subsequent morning found us visiting the Little White House, President Harry Truman's getaway in Key West. Preserved just as it was when Truman last visited, the sunporch has a poker table still laid out with cards as they were dealt when Truman played his last game there. The site is peaceful, well cared for, with a beautifully manicured lawn. Tourists took advantage of the opportunity to just sit in the white lawn chairs, and chat and rest.

It was time for me to make a few appointments, as our time in Key West was growing short. Cade and Braden, a neighbor's children, attend Big Pine Academy, an A-rated charter school on

Big Pine Key. Big Pine serves pre-school through seventh grade. I have never had the chance to talk with anyone about a charter school and as a retired educator I was curious. This was an opportunity to learn. Cathy Hoffman, director, allowed me to visit three classrooms: Braden's kindergarten, a second-grade computer class, and a fourth-grade writing group. I was impressed: the classes were small, the teachers interesting and from different parts of the country, and choices for electives were many with scheduling that allowed time for the "extras."

I thoroughly enjoyed talking with Ms. Hoffman. A charter school is a public school, she said, operated independently of the local school board, often with a curriculum and educational philosophy different from other schools in the system. The charter school can receive public money and private donations, but is not subject to some of the rules, regulations, and statutes that apply to other public schools. In exchange some type of accountability for producing certain results is required and set forth in the school's charter. Charter schools are attended by choice. They are part of the public education system, are not allowed to charge tuition, and provide an alternative to other public schools.

Sloppy Joe's Bar in Key West became famous because it was Ernest Hemingway's frequent haunt, as mentioned earlier. It's open to the street, so we strolled through just to be able to say we'd been there. The bar was on our path to an ice cream shop we'd ignored all month, but it was worth the wait.

I had been trying to connect with a good friend Adam Carages, who lived in Chatom, Alabama, when he was a teenager and was a member of my Sunday School class. Adam is deputy of the Monroe County Courthouse and a bailiff during court sessions.

Thanks to Adam, Janie and I received a private tour of the beautiful new courthouse, even getting to view the holding cells and basement. We met Adam's judge and several other local public officials still in their offices working at four-thirty on a beautiful Friday afternoon. I wish we could have had more time with Adam, but he was working and we were loafing. Thank you, Adam, for taking the time to show us about.

Our last Sunday in Key West, February 27, we visited Big Coppitt First Baptist Church. I was curious to meet Pastor Darrell Robinson, thinking he was the former pastor for a large Baptist church in Mobile, Alabama, and had moved to Florida. Wrong!

This Pastor Robinson spells his first name differently, is quite young and energetic, and African-American. He leads a very lively church with many activities for youth and children. The church provides meals four days a week. The children were studying *Pilgrim's Progress*; the adults, the Book of Acts. Experiencing God was offered as a new spiritual-growth opportunity.

I know that I have already said this about other churches we have attended on this trip, but isn't this the sort of service that churches should be about? A small church doesn't necessarily mean a *small* church.

It was our last evening in Key West. We had invited our neighbors, Wayne and Chuck, over for supper. Our verbal invitation went something like this, "We're sorry we haven't done this sooner, but we're cleaning out the refrigerator before leaving and would you come help us eat up our leftovers?" They said, Yes, with a chuckle, and we had an enjoyable evening.

Such nice people, good neighbors, and again I couldn't help but think, what interesting and talented people we have had the privilege of meeting.

We absolutely couldn't leave the Keys without eating once more at Blue Heaven, our favorite restaurant. It didn't disappoint. Breakfast was, "Oh, so good."

Then it was home to finish packing. It had been so easy to call our house here home. It had been quite accommodating for our visitors and us. Indeed, it was our home on Sugar Loaf Key.

Chapter Three
Charleston, South Carolina
March 2011

WE ARE RESIDENTS on a barrier island called Kiawah Island, fifteen miles south of Charleston. South Carolina has hundreds of islands fronting the deeply indented southeastern Atlantic Ocean coastline. This broad, swampy plain extends nearly seventy miles inland, crisscrossed by dozens of rivers.

Kiawah Island was named for the Kiawah Indians who inhabited the territory before the 1670 arrival of English explorers. Today it is operated largely as a beach and resort with villas, condos, cottages, and acclaimed golf courses. The resort includes shopping areas, pools, tennis courts, the beach, golf courses, and trails for walking and biking. Workers are everywhere, all the time. Every time a leaf falls, there is someone there to blow it away. Loud, but effective.

Our approach to the island was a narrow two-lane country road bounded on each side by towering trees strewn with long strands of Spanish moss. The trees line the road and their trunks bear reflectors that reflect headlight beams, an effort to prevent drivers from veering off the road. In open areas, marshland and low growing vegetation appeared periodically, exposing a lot of blue sky, though none as vivid as in Key West. This habitat was quite different from where we had just been, more like the marshes and swamps around New Orleans. We had loved New Orleans with all its exotic history, food, street scenes, art, and music. We had also loved Key West with its laid-back atmosphere, conchs, Iggy, miles and miles of water, awesome sunsets, and delicious food. Now Charleston's Lowcountry charm awaited us.

Janie and I, both in our summer whites, looking all Key Westy, checked in at the resort office where others sported long trousers, sweaters, and jackets. The morning temperature had been in the fifties, winds of fifteen miles per hour, and a wind chill factor of thirty-eight degrees F. But we have packed well and have exactly what we need for the change.

Charles Kuralt didn't do an awful lot while in Charleston—an assumption we made based on what is in his book—but we had a schedule that didn't sound unbusy. We would start with a carriage ride around Charleston, a harbor tour, and a visit to the Charleston Museum, Magnolia Plantation and Gardens, and the Hunley submarine. We looked forward to a concert featuring jazz, gospel, spirituals, Gershwin, and Civil War songs, and then an evening at Charleston Fashion Week with a runway show, award-winning designers, and fashion from local boutiques. Visiting the Calhoun Mansion was on our list, and other things that struck our fancy.

Our Kiawah Island cottage was on a lagoon near the ocean. We were quite comfortable with two bedrooms and two baths; a fireplace in our nicely furnished sitting room; and a full kitchen with dishwasher, JennAir stove, and a full complement of dishes, silverware, and glassware. We were also blessed with a washer and dryer, two back porches, and a small front porch. From our porch we had already watched a pelican and a duck, fish jumping, and birds landing on the lagoon. No Iggy, though.

Since there was an electric dishwasher, Janie worried about her usefulness. To combat that she'd begun cataloging all the receipts, memorabilia, and business cards we had collected. This should help us in planning ahead, as well as providing details when we begin writing our book. Janie was comforted knowing she was not only the techie but also the trip's accountant and archivist.

On our way up the coast we stopped in Savannah, Georgia, and asked OnStar to take us to Paula Deen's restaurant, The Lady & Sons. Back in 1989, Paula started The Bag Lady food service out of her home. That humble beginning grew into a famous restaurant and full-service catering business. In 1999, *USA Today* chose The Lady & Sons as home of its "International Meal of the Year." The restaurant at 102 Congress Street requires reservations and we had none, but we're never too shy to ask. We mentioned our revisiting Kuralt's America trip, and with that the kind hostess found us a table.

We were a little rushed for time due to a parking meter and the need to be on Kiawah Island by five o'clock, so we chose the lunch buffet. It began with a cheese biscuit and hoecake, and ended with dessert. I had banana pudding and Janie tried Paula's original and famous Ooey Gooey Butter Cake. We had hoped Paula or her sons, Jamie and Bobby, who have become famous in their own right, might be on the premises. They were not.

Leaving the restaurant, we had a near catastrophe. I had not noticed that the back lift was open on the car. I must have accidentally pushed the button and now people were waving at us, hollering, and pointing at the back of the car. I slammed on brakes, and we both hopped out to see what was lost. Only our computer and printer! We found them undamaged, but what a scare. We couldn't thank the people (who flagged us down) enough for making us aware of our predicament.

Charleston, South Carolina isn't called the "Holy City" for nothing. According to our guidebook, one hundred and eighty-four church spires are visible on the skyline, not to mention the many churches in the surrounding countryside and on the nearby islands. We'd be visiting the French Protestant Huguenot Church and taking in its history a little later. Our Charleston adventure would begin with a carriage tour, provided by the Old South Carriage Company at 14 Anson Street and operated by the same family since 1983. Its ads beckon tourists to stop by the stables to meet the staff. Tour guides are well trained and much care and attention is given to the carriages, horses, and historic detail.

Our guide, Steve, wore the Old South Carriage uniform of Confederate gray pants, white shirt, a red sash around his waist, and the Rebel soldier's cap. His horse, George, is a huge Percheron, a French breed of draft horse, and a mottled light gray. Both he and Steve handled their jobs quite well. We saw the Battery, Rainbow Row, Broad Street, historic churches, and many beautiful old Southern homes. One home that we passed while on the tour belongs to the Piggly Wiggly magnate. Pigs (the symbol of Piggly Wiggly) made of iron, graced the front porch.

We asked the staff at the carriage office what to do around

town. They recommended three things: their tour; Hyman's Seafood Restaurant, voted most popular restaurant in the southeast, they said; and the Magnolia Plantation and Gardens. We started with lunch at Hyman's. I had a shrimp po-boy with at least twenty shrimp in a foot-long bun accompanied by slaw and hush puppies. Janie and I disagreed on the quality of the lunch. The high note to it was meeting a couple of delightful women who walked into the restaurant, looked at the menu, and had turned to go when one of them observed the place had no Sweet and Low. I piped up and said, "I have some in my purse," and offered to share it with them. They thanked me profusely. So much so, I thought I might get a thank you note from them. Just kidding.

SpiritLine Cruises Harbor Tour offers a different perspective of the city. On the waterfront is Pineapple Fountain, a magnificent creation in the shape of a pineapple, lit like a Christmas tree, and a symbol of welcome and hospitality. We saw Fort Sumter, Fort Moultrie, the Battery, and the aircraft carrier Yorktown. Charleston Harbor was once the playground of Blackbeard the Pirate, a man who deliberately made himself look horrifyingly frightening—like the Devil incarnate—to the crews of ships that became his prey. Most were more than willing to jump ship and leave Blackbeard to it. Little is known about the man. Rumor indicates he was an educated person, and that his name may have been Edward Teach.

Many questions listed on the harbor tour brochure were answered by our guide. Did you know that South Carolina is called the Palmetto State because of the Civil War action at Fort Moultrie? The fort was constructed of palmetto logs, which are quite spongy. Most of the cannon balls shot by the Union Army either lodged in the logs, or bounced off. Rebels would then harvest the cannon balls and shoot them back. What other tree can claim such a history?

Did you know that the Boston Tea Party had an impact here on James Island? The tea party was part of a wave of resistance that originated when Parliament tried to rescue the financially weakened East India Company. The British wished to continue their benefit from the company's valuable position in India. The Tea Act, passed by British parliament, adjusted import duties in a way that allowed East India Company to undersell even smugglers in the colonies. Consignees in Boston, Philadelphia, New York, and Charleston were selected by the Brits to receive a large shipment of tea, more than 500,000 pounds. Under pressure from the Patriots, a group for revolution, consignees refused to accept shipment, but some merchants would not concede. Tension mounted. In Charleston, the tea was rejected, then stored. But Sam Adams in Boston led a small group of the Sons of Liberty, disguised as Mohawk Indians, to board the ships there and jettison the tea.

England took the act to be confirmation of Massachusetts' role as a core of resistance to legitimate British rule and responded harshly. The episode escalated into the American Revolution.

Did you know that the Civil War began with a cannon shot fired on Fort Sumter? In December of 1860, six days after South Carolina announced secession, U.S. Army Major Robert Anderson abandoned the North's Fort Moultrie post and relocated his companies E and H to Fort Sumter. South Carolina's Governor Pickens called for the fort to be evacuated, an order Robert Anderson ignored. Confederates fired on Fort Sumter April 12, 1861, and the North returned fire, but the North surrendered after thirty-four hours of the siege. In an effort to retake the fort, the North fired more than 46,000 shells during a two-year period, but the South held onto the fort until February 1865 when it was finally evacuated. Fort Sumter remains a significant monument.

These questions came from a brochure about Charleston harbor, and were all answered on the ninety-minute narrated tour as we cruised past the sights, enjoyed in ideal weather conditions: cool and sunny, breezy. Perfect.

Our third "must do," the Magnolia Plantation and Gardens, sits only ten miles from Charleston and is listed on the National Register of Historic Places. It is home today to the eleventh generation of Draytons, having been established by Thomas Drayton and his wife, Anna, who arrived from Barbados to the new English colony of Charles Towne in 1679.

The Draytons cultivated rice during the Colonial era. Later the estate was occupied by British and American troops of the Revolutionary War. The Draytons were both statesmen and soldiers, and fought British rule.

To keep the estate in the Drayton name, Thomas Drayton, great-grandson of the first, willed his estate to his daughter's sons on condition they assume their mother's maiden name. Young John Grimké Drayton, a second son, became heir when his older brother was accidentally killed by a deer hunter's bullet. Despite his inherited wealth, John pursued a ministerial career and entered the seminary in New York. There he fell in love with and married Julia Ewing, daughter of a prominent Philadelphia attorney. John returned to Charleston with his bride.

Drayton fell seriously ill under the burden of estate management and his practice as a minister. He devised his own cure by working in the estate gardens. He wanted to create a romantic garden for his wife to make her feel more comfortable in South Carolina. A few years later, his health returned, and his gardens had been much expanded.

Magnolia is the oldest plantation on the Ashley River and a centerpiece of Charleston history. The current house, the third one on the property (two previous houses were destroyed by fire), was originally a hunting lodge, a rather large one, that was disassembled and floated down the Ashley River to be reassembled at the current site. Our guided tour showcased the Drayton's collection of early-American antiques, porcelain, quilts, and other heirlooms. We were told the Draytons have been host to many notable guests, including Eleanor Roosevelt, George Gershwin, Henry Ford, and the actor Orson Welles.

Magnolia Plantation has nearly five hundred acres of gardens and grounds to explore, with miles of biking and walking trails winding through different habitats.

To think we actually paid to ride in a boat and shoot pictures of alligators—huge ones, the largest I'd ever seen—when any day of my life I can go to the river at McIntosh Bluff in Alabama and see alligators aplenty, but that's what you do as a tourist. The nature boat tour followed canals through a one-hundred-and-fifty-acre former rice field.

The diversity of living things in the swamp garden is said to be unequaled anywhere else in the U.S. Thousands of plant and animal species coexist in the sixty acres of blackwater cypress and tupelo swamp on the plantation. Much of nature can be viewed from the boardwalks, dikes, and bridges that allow access: nesting herons, egrets, otters, turtles, alligators, moorhens or gallinules, anhingas (snakebirds), and hundreds of species of plants. The grounds are not manicured, but natural, a feature I liked very much.

Janie and I found our visit to the plantation and gardens quite worthwhile, and were thrilled to have our picture taken next to a plaque that read, "Remembering Charles Kuralt, America's Favorite Travel Writer and Friend of Magnolia Plantation." Kuralt described it as, "My greatest pleasure."

Speaking of gardens and trees, we passed a sign on our way to and from Charleston that said, "Angel Oak" and finally one day we took the time to see the tree. The statistics were amazing: it's a live oak, more than 1,500 years old, (it would have sprouted before Columbus's voyage), height of more than 65 feet, diameter of spread reaching 160 feet, trunk circumference of nearly 25 feet, and it covers 17,100 square feet of ground. Do you remember the last line of Joyce Kilmer's poem, "But only God can make a tree"? Well, he did, and Angel Oak is a magnificent one. One happy thought, it made Janie and I look so small.

Our worship experiences in Charleston were varied. The first Sunday, I went alone to Stono Baptist Church. We had passed it one day and I liked the looks of it. Once again, I was pleased with the many opportunities offered to every age at the church.

At Stono, there were multiple jobs: church cleaner, lawn team, money counters, prayer chain leader, recovery and crisis leader, budget and finance team, and the music ministry. Not to mention many fellowship activities for all ages. It seemed there was a place for everyone to plug in, to serve in whatever way one might be led, and to feel a part of a fellowship.

Stono is a place where you, and I, would like to have our names on the prayer list, knowing we would be prayed for daily.

The message that day, "Lessons for Forgiveness," brought by Rev. Tim Squire, pastoral care minister, will be remembered.

The historic Charleston City Market is open three hundred and sixty-five days a year. Market Hall faces Meeting Street, the main entrance to four blocks of open-air buildings. The market sits on land ceded by Charles Cotesworth Pinckney to the city in 1788 with the stipulation it was to be a public market in perpetuity. The original buildings were constructed between 1804 and the 1830s, with stalls for meat, vegetables, and fish stretching to the waterfront. After a fire, the current building, designed by Edward Brickwell White, became the replacement. Today stalls for everything from jewelry, art, carvings, photography, old signs, linens and purses to food and leather goods can be found on location. We strolled unhurriedly, to look and sample bites of food offered, including the benne seed wafer, considered a Charleston favorite. Crisp and delicious.

Most notable in the market were the famous sweetgrass baskets woven by local artisans (sometimes while you watched) in various sizes, shapes, and prices. The sweetgrass craft is one of the oldest forms of African artwork in the U.S., a tradition passed down from former slaves, one generation to another. A basket can take from twelve hours to three months to complete and each is a unique design and shape. Once in great demand on rice plantations of the old South, the baskets were used to collect and store fruits, vegetables, and other staples. Some slave owners sold the baskets for added income. No secrets of this local craft of the Gullah community are shared and many from the community have abandoned the land for other pursuits, making the baskets increasingly rare. Large-scale land development has also overtaken much of the wild marshes and swamps where sweetgrass grows. Baskets now command prices from one hundred to twenty-thousand dollars. Examples of this fine art can be seen at the Smithsonian Institution in Washington, D.C.

We liked Charleston. The weather was beautiful, the scenery ever-changing, the beach almost private, and there was so much to see and do. March is an ideal time of year to visit. Some would say a little cool, but we'd say just right. Light jacket weather.

Someone had told us about a good restaurant on John's Island called The Fat Hen, which was on our way home to Kiawah Island. Ensconced in what looks like two old houses joined together, The Fat Hen has a glass-enclosed porch with tables, outside seating, twinkly lights in the shrubbery and trees, white tablecloths, and candles that add to the folksy ambiance. The Lowcountry cuisine gives a nod to its Southern and Huguenot origins and is prepared by nationally acclaimed Chef Fred Neuville.

Our waiter, Hy, spent time with us explaining the menu, tending to our drinks, and checking in every few minutes. Hy never seemed hurried. We began with an appetizer of fried green tomatoes. My entrée was a salmon steak with *béarnaise* sauce; Janie ordered mahi mahi. Each entrée was served with locally grown, roasted vegetables. Our dessert, shared, was a wonderful coconut cream cake. A delightful experience.

Now to a different experience—our first ever. We attended the runway show of this year's Charleston Fashion Week, its fifth annual event. Charleston Fashion Week is a five-night celebration with more than thirty-five runway shows and competitions for Emerging Designers and the Rock the Runway model competitions, both have launched many a career. Charitable partners are organizations such as Center for Women, Lowcountry AIDS Services, and the Medical University of South Carolina Children's Hospital.

Huge white tents had been erected downtown on the lawn of Marion Square, under which were now gathered hundreds of people, dressed every which way—some quite tastefully and others, just awfully. Basically, anything could have been worn and it would have been okay. Not knowing what to expect, Janie and I had dressed up a bit—pretty traditional. General admission tickets got us in the door. Then we worked our way up to be seated on the third row. We found ourselves near the end of the runway, a good position to view the models as they made their turns and posed for photographers, of whom there were many.

Our special treat was seeing the design of a children's line of clothing and models ranging in age from about three to nine. The clothes and the children were both adorable. One show-stealer was a boy of about three years with a mop of dark hair who walked ever so slowly. When the first of the line passed him on their way back, he immediately turned and followed them off the runway instead of completing his walk. That brought cheers and laughter from the audience.

Following was a very long forty-five-minute intermission.

After intermission we saw clothing from three boutiques and five new designers. Most of the clothes were beautiful, practical, and something ordinary people might wear. The beautiful and practical was interspersed with outlandish styles that left one wondering who would buy, much less wear them. Each designer presented eight looks, complete with jewelry, appropriate hairstyle, makeup, accessories, and shoes. We especially noted the shoes, some of which seemed to have no relationship to the dress with which they were paired. Undoubtedly our ideas of fashion are dated, but an outfit patterned in red, black, blue, white, and beige was worn with shoes of a pale green. Clunky shoes were paired with delicate, feminine dresses.

A featured designer, not one of the competitors, presented twenty outfits inspired by cathedrals and graveyards, an idea that taxed the imagination. But we heard it from the designer himself. The models throughout the show were beautiful, pale, gaunt, and expressionless—not one weighed a hundred pounds, even those six feet tall—but the clothes did look so elegant on their slender frames, and that was what we were meant to focus on.

A winner was to be chosen from the sixteen semi-finalists in the Emerging Designer Competition, East. We were given the opportunity to vote for our favorite. Neither Janie nor I picked the winner. But it was a fun night, and we felt quite sure it was something Charles Kuralt would not have done. At least, he hadn't written about it in his book.

On Sunday, March 20, we attended the French Protestant Huguenot Church at 136 Church Street. Built in 1844, it was designed by architect Edward Brickell White. Mr. White, you may recall, also designed the Charleston City Market.

The oldest Gothic Revival Church in South Carolina, it is designated a National Historic Landmark. Its congregation traces its origins to the 1680s. It's the only independent Huguenot church in the U.S. Services still follow eighteenth-century French liturgy, but are conducted in English.

Huguenots were French Calvinists facing suppression in France when they began to settle in other areas such as South Africa and Britain. In 1598, King Henry IV of France issued the Edict of Nantes, granting certain rights and protections to the Huguenots. Louis XIV revoked the edict in 1685, prompting an exodus of Huguenots from France.

We entered the old sanctuary on the left side. Pews were enclosed with solid wood dividers between sections. Four rows of the boxes—two on either side of the center aisle—were available. On the exit end of the pew by the aisle was a little latch just inside the entry door. The seating would have been comfortable for three, but four people made it crowded unless all four were small, which was not the case. The *prie dieu* (for kneeling during prayer) were available but not used. A hymnal, Bible, and liturgy had been placed in each of the holders on the pews. The beautiful old church with its stained glass windows, wooden floors, and sparkling chandeliers created a worshipful atmosphere. We learned to just sit when unsure whether to stand, sing or speak, read or pray, but the message was there when we listened. After hymns, readings, and responses, only a short time was left for the sermon. It was good, and brief.

After the service, a member gave us a short history. On April 30, 1680, a ship from London, the *Richmond*, dropped anchor off Oyster Point in the new province of Carolina, a settlement that had been moved from Albemarle Point. On orders from King Charles it was renamed Charles Towne. Forty-five French Protestant Huguenot refugees arrived on the *Richmond*, seeking asylum from religious persecution in France. They had fled to England and waited months for transportation to a land where they could work and worship in freedom and peace.

King Charles subsidized these skilled people in their effort to establish in a British territory crops and industries that had been French monopolies.

The church founded by the refugees has quite a history of closings and different ministries. Firemen blew it up once to make gaps in the flames of a fire in 1796 that started in a nearby stable and spread, ultimately leaving many citizens homeless. Today's church stands on the original site of Queen and Church streets.

One of our favorite places to visit is a museum. Charleston has America's first: Charleston Museum, founded in 1773. It is unique. Its purpose is not to preserve or showcase paintings but to preserve and interpret the cultural, architectural, and natural heritage of South Carolina Lowcountry and the City of Charleston. At the museum, Janie and I saw ancient fossils, an enormous whale skeleton, and, at the other end of interests, elegant costumes and Civil War artifacts. A hands-on section for children offered opportunities for them to see and learn on another level.

Outside the museum in front of the entrance lay a full scale model of the *Hunley*, the world's first successful combat submarine. The *Hunley* was built in Mobile, Alabama, in 1863 and shipped to Charleston. The forty-foot vessel was used to battle Union ships during the Civil War. It sank twice in 1863, killing five of the crew the first time and all eight the second, including Horace Hunley, inventor of the sub. After each tragedy the submarine was raised and returned to service.

February 17, 1864, *Hunley* attacked and sank the sloop USS *Housatonic*, which was on Union blockade duty in Charleston's outer harbor. Lt. George E. Dixon, commander of the *Hunley*, and his crew of seven volunteers embedded a torpedo into the hull of the *Housatonic*. As the torpedo detonated, they backed the sub away, sending the *Housatonic* and five of its crew to the bottom of the harbor. The same detonation killed all eight on board the *Hunley*. Research conducted long after the sub was raised indicated it was only twenty feet from the *Housatonic* when it suffered the same fate.

In 2002, a researcher examining the area, found close to the commander Lt. Dixon's skeleton a misshapen twenty-dollar gold piece, minted in 1860. The coin had been sanded on one side and engraved with this inscription: Shiloh April 6, 1862 My Life Preserver G.E.D. (Lt. Dixon's initials). A forensic anthropologist examined Lt. Dixon's skeleton and discovered a healed injury to his hipbone. Dixon had been wounded in the thigh by a bullet at the battle of Shiloh. The bullet struck a gold coin in his pocket, saving his leg and possibly his life. Family legend said Dixon's sweetheart, Queenie Bennett, had given him the coin for protection. He carried it thereafter as a lucky charm.

We had an appointment with Gedney M. Howe III, a prominent Charleston attorney who spent twenty-five years and five million dollars restoring the Calhoun Mansion, one of the most talked about sights in the city. We wanted to meet the person responsible for such an amazing transformation—if only because he is mentioned in Charles Kuralt's book. We called Mr. Howe's office, spoke to his secretary, and told her of our adventure. She passed our request to Mr. Howe and arranged an interview. He said his time was limited but he would love to meet us. Janie and I were overwhelmed with the grandeur of his law office and could hardly imagine what the house would be like. We were leaving the office to go to lunch and mentioned having to move our car to find another parking space. Mr. Howe gave us a slip to use his private parking spot across the street for as long as we needed. A true Southern gentleman.

Lunch time found us wandering the streets, looking for something a little different. After reading menus posted in the window of several restaurants, we chose Magnolias at 185 East Bay Street. Naturally it was decorated with paintings of magnolias, many of them, but in a tasteful way. Magnolias is much written about and described as serving "upscale Southern cuisine." We had an adorable waiter named Giles and probably the best food we had eaten in Charleston. I think I said that about The Fat Hen, but this time Janie agreed with me.

After lunch we walked along the waterfront looking up close at things we had seen from the tour boat, and took a ride in a pedicab along the Battery. We found the Harris-Teeter supermarket mentioned by Kuralt in his book. The store is huge, with many specialty sections and a Starbucks. It's also open twenty-four hours a day. We hoped to taste one of the hot apple fritters that Kuralt also mentioned, but talked to the manager and found the store no longer has them. Janie and I each bought a box of cereal instead so we could say we had shopped at the same Harris Teeter as Kuralt.

And now—to the Calhoun Mansion, the largest residence in Charleston at some twenty-four thousand square feet, with thirty-five rooms and thirty-five fireplaces, a grand ballroom, private elevator, a seventy-five-foot-high domed stair hall ceiling, a ninety-foot cupola, and five levels of piazzas.

Calhoun Mansion was designed by architect William P. Russel and built for George W. Williams in 1876. Italianate in style, the architecture was adapted to Charleston with rope moldings adorning every door and window. Iron fencing signified the wealth of the owner. The woodwork is described as exotic, complex, and dazzling, with woods in each room varying one from the other. Elaborate plaster moldings grace the ceilings. The flooring is inlaid wood.

George Williams' daughter married Patrick Calhoun, a railroad financier and grandson of Vice President John C. Calhoun. At the turn of the century, the Calhouns hired Louis Tiffany to design and install lighting in the mansion.

Calhoun was forced to sell the home after the great stock market crash of 1929. The mansion then passed through various owners and fell into a dilapidated condition. It was condemned in 1972.

Mr. Howe bought the house for approximately $250,000, not much more than its original cost, but now the roof was caving in and walls were falling down. The place was in almost total ruin, but he could not see letting such a treasure be demolished. Howe had worked as a bricklayer while in law school.

Just out of law school, he purchased the mansion and began personally the work of restoration. He lived in one room of the house and cooked on a hot plate, finishing work a room at a time while maintaining an increasingly successful law practice. Howe restored the home, furnished it with period pieces, and improved the grounds with manicured shrubbery, trees, and statuary.

Mr. Howe told Janie and me that during renovation his mother came at one point to help by cooking and doing some cleaning. One day she announced that her sister, his Aunt Rose, wanted to visit, and asked that he finish a bedroom and a half bath for her.

"Why only a half bath?" he asked. His mother replied, "If you give her a full bath with a shower, she won't ever leave."

After marrying and having children, Mr. Howe decided he didn't want his children to grow up in such a rarefied atmosphere. He sold the mansion in 2004.

Philip Simmons was the "poet of ironwork," according to John Paul Huguley, founder of American College of Building Arts in Charleston. We wanted to find the home of Simmons or someone related to him, and hopefully, see some of his work. His ability to endow raw iron with pure lyricism is known and admired throughout not only South Carolina, but is also evidenced by his many honors and awards. Simmons apprenticed with a former slave in the 1920s, Peter Simmons—no relation. Philip Simmons began to do specialized ornamental ironwork in 1938 and fashioned more than five hundred decorative pieces: gates, fences, balconies, and window grills. He was the most celebrated ironworker of the twentieth century. The city of Charleston is literally decorated from end to end by his hand.

Our clue to finding his home on Blake Street was a wrought iron fence, the only one on the block. The modest house is on Charleston's East Side where Mr. Simmons lived all his life. We talked to his nephew, Carlton Simmons, who was raised by Philip, taught by Philip, and had worked with his uncle since his youth. Carlton continues the work today. The shed behind the house contains his tools of the trade: pieces of iron, an anvil, and an eighty-year-old forge still in use. We asked Carlton how much he worked. Was it according to job requirements, or number of orders? "No," he said, "it's what mood I'm in." Carlton gave each of us a small, pretty scroll-like piece of iron he had worked.

Simmons' small home is being transformed into a museum. His most famous work, the *Star and Fish Gate*, purchased by the Smithsonian Institution's National Museum of American History, was designed by Simmons while on a flight to Washington, D.C. He said he had no idea what the design would be when he boarded the plane. By the time of his arrival, he had completed the design.

Simmons was known as a kind and gentle man who willingly shared his experience and wisdom with anyone he met. His favorite quote was, "If you want your prayers answered, get up off your knees and hustle." He was thoroughly professional, his work his only advertisement, and his legacy is one of excellence and pride in his work—an inspiration to youth and other professionals around the country. Janie and I drove about the city looking for examples of Simmons' work.

When I look at the letters f-i-g, they spell fig, the fruit. But at the restaurant we chose for supper one night (because Janie had read about it) FIG is an acronym for Food Is Good. Chef Mike Lata's local neighborhood restaurant focuses on using fresh products from local growers. There's no giant walk-in refrigerator at 232 Meeting Street, just a few small ones. Lata is a James Beard Award-winning chef, and FIG has been featured in *Bon Appetit, Food and Wine*, the *New York Times*, and on the Food Network.

We were able to chat with Chef Lata for a few minutes about the restaurant, his food philosophy, and his hopes for the future. On the FIG restaurant website, Chef Lata says: When you eat at FIG, you taste produce grown in Lowcountry's distinctive sandy soil, fish caught in our briny waters, and livestock raised on our pastures, all of which is grown and harvested by people I have grown to know and love. FIG provided one of our best meals so far. Sounding familiar, isn't it? We hurried our dinner a little, though, as we had a concert starting soon.

Janie and I were excited to be able to attend *The Sound of Charleston*, produced by Charleston Musical Heritage Productions. It's a weekly presentation during the first six months of the year held in the Circular Church. Musicians from the Saint Cecelia Society, a string quartet, started the program playing Fuchs, Pachelbel, and Haydn. Using guitar, banjo, and concertina, a duo performed Civil War songs like "The Yellow Rose of Texas," "Wait for the Wagon," "Goober Peas," and "Oh, Come, Angel Band." Soprano D'Jaris Whipper-Lewis sang selections from *Porgy and Bess*—"Summertime" and "I Loves You, Porgy."

Our favorite, which was absolutely wonderful and amazing, was a piano duet of *Rhapsody in Blue* played by sixteen-year-old virtuoso Micah McLaurin and college junior Irwin Jiang.

When we all sang "Amazing Grace" at the end of the concert, it could not have felt more appropriate. John Newton, an officer on a slave ship, visited Charleston for several weeks in 1749 and attended the Circular Church. A sermon there led to his conversion. He later became a cleric and wrote "Amazing Grace," one of the most popular hymns in the English language.

Dissenters—English Congregationalists, Scots Presbyterians, and French Huguenots of the original Charles Towne settlement —founded the Circular Church in 1681 at 150 Meeting Street. In a spirit of diversity and free thought, they erected the meetinghouse in the northwest corner of the walled city. In the late 1700s, prominent members of the church often spoke for political and religious freedom. From 1820 to 1860 both black and white citizens were part of the congregation, which was called by many names over the years, but finally became known as Circular Church.

Robert Mills, Charleston's most prominent architect in 1804, designed the vast circular hall, the third structure to house the Circular Church congregation. A fire in 1861 destroyed the church. Bricks from "Old Circular" were used in building the present sanctuary, completed in 1892. It is beautiful and a perfect setting to showcase "The Sound of Charleston."

The Holy City has more than one church of historical note. The First Baptist Church of Charleston is referred to as the "Mother Church of Southern Baptists." It is the earliest Baptist church in the South, organized September 25, 1682 in Kittery, Maine. Due to persecution there, pastor William Screven and twenty-eight members of his church relocated to Charleston. Near that time, two groups of settlers arrived in Charleston, one from southern England and one from Scotland. The Baptists among them were soon drawn into Screven's church, and by 1708 the membership numbered ninety-eight souls. During the Revolutionary War, the church was seized and used by the British for storage of salt beef and other provisions.

Today's church was just what we had wanted it to be: old, beautiful, wooden floors, and stained glass windows but recently renovated and refurbished. Designed by Charleston architect Robert Mills, the church building was dedicated in 1822. Mills, a man of generous civic spirit, is known for having championed sustainability in his buildings and the use of fireproof materials. He considered the Greek style and grand proportions of the Charleston Baptist Church to be the "best specimen of correct taste in architecture in the city." After 1860, the history of the building was marked by three disastrous events: the Civil War, the hurricane of 1885, and in 1886 the largest recorded earthquake in the Southeast. Each time the brave congregation restored the edifice for the worship of God.

A hundred and twenty-five years later, the organ music, the sermon, and the visiting African-American choir continued to uphold the church's heritage and its position of leadership and service, providing ministries for all ages, international missions, and a school. The church members were very friendly to Janie and me. Isn't it amazing how the Lord uses such a variety of ways to reach people?

Janie and I have so many pictures of the Charleston area, in our heads and in our camera. Huge trees making a canopy that drips with Spanish moss, and creates a shadowy path, line the mostly two-lane roads approaching Charleston. Suddenly we'd drive into the sunlight and see miles of Lowcountry marsh. Looking across the bay waters, every color the sun could make was reflected, and there was Charleston Yacht Club with hundreds of moored boats of every description. Along the waterfront, huge old homes are well kept—a perfect picture postcard. Each day, as we made our drive from Kiawah Island into Charleston this view was repeated, and we never tired of it.

Janie and I have tried to give you a true picture of Charleston. We were so impressed with its downtown: its cleanliness, beautiful historic buildings and monuments, and, of course, the people of Charleston and the surrounding Lowcountry area. On Kiawah Island we hadn't really had neighbors and so did not meet people there as we had in Key West, but everywhere we went the citizens of Lowcountry exhibited true Southern hospitality.

Can't believe Janie and I will be doing this for a whole year: moving into a place, becoming part of the community, enjoying all that is offered, then packing up and leaving. I suspect it will get harder to leave each time. But it was exciting, too, to know there would be something totally new and different each month. These were our last days in Charleston. We would pack on Wednesday to leave Thursday, and would be in Blowing Rock, North Carolina, on Friday, April 1.

Chapter Four
Blowing Rock, North Carolina
April 2011

LOOKING AT THE MAP, the road from Charleston, South Carolina, to Blowing Rock, North Carolina, looks as if it's much longer than the actual 294.1 miles. We expected scenery quite different from the Lowcountry of Charleston but had not anticipated a lush, green mountainous landscape.

Janie and I hadn't researched each destination before arrival, preferring instead to enjoy the excitement of surprise as we traveled to each new place. Such was our drive to Blowing Rock.

Our arrival on April 1 was greeted by lightly falling snowflakes. At first miniature flakes fell, but soon those became larger flakes—lots of them—covering the ground. We couldn't believe what we were seeing. This was no April Fool's joke, but a real snow and getting harder and harder. We found our condo and instead of going in made a beeline to a grocery store and stocked up in case we were snowed in. Janie and I were the only people shopping who smiled about the snow. Most folks we encountered said they were tired of it.

We asked the store manager if he knew someone who might help us move into our condo. Our place was on the second floor; we had a car full of stuff, and it was still snowing. Warren Davis was recommended and Janie called him immediately. He agreed to help and met us at the condo. We liked him. Warren lingered to visit a while after getting everything upstairs. He didn't leave until he'd invited us to visit his church, Laurel Fork Baptist, off the Blue Ridge Parkway just a few miles out of town. We assured him we would be there on Sunday. Several more days of snow with intermittent sunshine made the scenery gorgeous to us Alabamians, and gave us an opportunity to settle in, plan our itinerary, and stay snug and warm while doing nothing, without guilt.

Blowing Rock is a cliff, four thousand feet above sea level, high above the Johns River Gorge three thousand feet below. The rock walls of the gorge form a chute through which the northwest wind sweeps with such force, it returns any light object tossed into the void. *Ripley's Believe It or Not* says of the phenomenon, "The only place in the world where snow falls upside down." From the rock, Hawksbill Mountain and Table Rock can be seen to the southwest; Grandfather Mountain—highest peak in the Blue Ridge—is visible to the west, as is Mount Mitchell, the highest mountain east of the Mississippi River.

A bishop of the Moravian Brethren, August Gottlieb Spangenberg and his party of settlers were the first known visitors to Blowing Rock. In 1752, the 2nd Earl of Granville offered a hundred thousand acres of land to Spangenberg if he'd settled there. Spangenberg and his followers arrived and were greeted by severe wintry weather, heavy winds, and snowfall. Little is known of their time in Blowing Rock, save that it was short, and white settlers did not inhabit the Granville District again for many years.

Before Spangenberg, these windy cliffs of North Carolina were home to Cherokee and either Catawba or Chickasaw tribes. Accounts of which warring tribes occupied the area differ, as do details of the famous legend of star-crossed Indian lovers. A popular version of the legend of the "blowing rock" says a Chickasaw chieftain traveled with his beautiful daughter far from his home in the plains because he was fearful of a white man's admiration for her. One day while sitting on the rock gazing into the valley below, the young maiden spied a Cherokee brave wandering in the wilderness. She playfully shot an arrow in his direction. Soon the handsome young man appeared at her wigwam and courted her with songs of his land. They became lovers. One day a strange reddening of the sky brought the brave and the maiden to the blowing rock. To him it was a sign of trouble, commanding his return to his tribe, but the maiden urged him to stay with her. He was torn, having to choose between duty and love. He leapt from the rock into the wilderness below. The grief-stricken maiden prayed daily to the Great Spirit for his return, until one evening a reddening sky appeared and a gust of wind blew the young brave back onto the rock and into his lover's arms. From that day on a perpetual wind has blown onto the rock from the valley below, and the Blowing Rock legend lives today.

The Blue Ridge Parkway, maintained by the National Park Service of U.S. Department of Interior, is four-hundred and sixty-nine miles long, extending along the crest of the southern Appalachians and linking two national parks, Shenandoah and the Great Smoky Mountains. Because of the varying elevations along the parkway, flowers and trees bloom at different times. Tulip and serviceberry trees bloom in spring. In the fall all of the leaves burst into color; tulips and birches turn yellow; the sassafras, orange; and the maples, red. It culminates in a brilliant show of color. The oaks present hints of russet and maroon, and evergreens such as Virginia pine, white pine, and hemlock; spruce and fir add green to round out the color wheel. This display in itself would make the drive worthwhile.

The village of Blowing Rock, with its fifteen hundred permanent residents and nearly eight-thousand summer residents, offers the best of small-town living: a safe environment, year-round outdoor activities, beautiful churches, an award-winning school, and the finest accommodations with superb restaurants and shopping. A major preservation effort has been in place for many years to protect the proud historic heritage of the village, and to maintain the community character that makes this small town unique. In addition, attractions such as Tweetsie Railroad, Grandfather Mountain, Linville Caverns, and galleries, museums, festivals, and performing arts of professional quality draw vacationers as well as locals.

Our first impression of Laurel Fork Baptist Church and its locale had us shooting pictures the moment we stepped out of the car. The church is small, the front faces the mountains, and the building is surrounded by incredible views of hills, valleys, trees, and homes—just like a painted picture. Pastor Daniel Featherstone saw us wandering around with our camera and came to meet us. Then we saw Warren, who had unloaded our vehicle upon arrival to Blowing Rock, and he extended an invitation to church. We were introduced to many nice people in the congregation. Dr. Featherstone preached a beautiful sermon on "The Humanity of Christ," about the Man and the words of agony He spoke, from Hebrews 4:15. I wish I could have taped the message. It was a reminder that in Jesus's humanity, He faced every temptation we face, and He provided a way for our repentance, forgiveness, and restoration of a right relationship with Him.

Dinner inside the fellowship hall was a spread of every food imaginable, and so much of it. I believe I'd never seen so many desserts at one meal. It was difficult, but I think Janie and I sampled almost all of them. A young man who sat with us for lunch shared some of the church's history. One interesting event in recent years was the filming of scenes around the church for the movie, *The Green Mile*. Another local site used during filming of the movie is Moses Cone Manor, or Flat Top Manor (a reference to nearby Flat Top Mountain), a mansion built in 1901. In the film it was called the Georgia Pines Nursing Home. After lunch, we were entertained with a concert by the Backroom Bluegrass Band, a group of four: F-style mandolin (with fancy curlicues at top and on the head stock), stand-up bass, guitar, and banjo. The bass player and banjo picker were husband and wife and exceptionally good singers and musicians. The banjo itself was custom-made by a man of regional renown, Homer Ledford. His widow was present for the concert. Our visit to the church was a most enjoyable time. Thanks, Warren.

I usually access OnStar the minute I get in the car, but when we left Laurel Fork Baptist I did not do it. I took a wrong turn and we ended up in Boone, North Carolina, about six miles north of Blowing Rock. It was a gorgeous day, and the town was teeming with students from Appalachian State University—walking, running, biking, and skate boarding. We had planned to visit Boone at some point, and it looked quite interesting. We'll definitely make another trip here soon.

Referring to his time in Blowing Rock, Charles Kuralt titled a chapter "Grandfather Mountain." Staying in a cabin on the mountain as Kuralt did isn't feasible for Janie and me, but we will check the spectacular views on this, our first tourist outing. Driving up the mountain, we enter one hairpin curve after another—you know the kind, where you meet yourself coming back.

Our brochure describes the drive as 5,946 feet up a summit in which one enters a different world. It also warns, this is the most rugged mountain in eastern America. Summertime rarely reaches the mountaintop. The warmest temperature ever recorded (in 2012 after our visit) was eighty-two degrees F. Mountain temperatures are generally ten to twenty degrees cooler than on the flatlands below.

At the gate to Grandfather Mountain, a fee is paid for entry. Once inside the park, visitors can hike or picnic, spot black bears and cougars in their natural habitat, or dare someone to walk across the "Mile High Swinging Bridge." There was no question that Janie and I would walk across the 228-foot suspension bridge. After all, we're on an adventure!

The bridge was the vision of Hugh Morton who was put in charge of Grandfather Mountain and sought a way to get visitors from the gift shop parking lot to the rocky overlook. Charles Hartman of Greensboro, South Carolina, designed the famous suspension bridge. The 360 degree view extends for miles and miles, with a vista of mountains, valleys, and gorges. We were told to take a jacket as it could be quite cool and windy, but on that day we were gifted with warm sunshine and little wind.

Because of the vast gain in elevation, there are sixteen distinct ecological habitats on Grandfather Mountain. Profile Trail, 2.7 miles up, offers a rocky stream enveloped by rhododendron and a canopy of trees. Rich Cove, a lower section, is open and airy with ground cover of ferns. Acid Cove is covered with dense shrub. The Coves give way to hardwood forest: red spruce and Canadian hemlock. The mountain is said to have greater plant diversity than all of Europe. The pink-shell azalea, native only to northwest North Carolina, is found here.

Interesting facts: The Mile High Swinging Bridge "sings" when the wind blows, sounding much like a harmonica; some of the highest wind speeds recorded are in excess of two hundred miles per hour. Only Mount Washington in New Hampshire has had stronger winds. It's called Grandfather Mountain because from a certain vantage point, the ridgeline resembles the profile of a bearded man looking toward the sky. Some of the film *Forrest Gump* (from the book by Winston Groom of Mobile, Alabama) was filmed on the mountain. Daniel Boone walked these same forests in the 1760s and provided the town name for Boone, North Carolina.

As much as we have ridden around town, and as much as I have walked, Janie and I kept dodging the ice cream/chocolate shop. The aroma took my breath away. At last we decided to indulge, buying our ice cream cones and walking across the street to sit on one of many benches that line the sidewalk around the town square park. It's a scene typical of many small towns, and it was a pleasure for us to sit and observe the world as it slowly went by.

First Baptist Church of Blowing Rock is only a mile from our condo. We visited there and were introduced to Doris and Marshall Edwards. The Edwards soon became our Blowing Rock "angels." My definition of an "angel" in this situation is a person (or persons) who helped us integrate into a community. The Edwards invited us to lunch at Canyon's Restaurant after church, where the food was good and the view even better.

The congregation of First Baptist refers to Marshall Edwards as "The Reverend Holy Rascal." When anyone new arrives, Marshall takes him or her on a tour of the village, not stopping or allowing them out of the car for two hours. We got his delightful narrated tour, which didn't seem two hours long. It thrilled us because we saw and heard about people and places we would not have know about otherwise.

Doris and Marshall met at Baylor University in Waco, Texas, where he was a divinity student and she was a music major. Marshall began his ministry in Batesville, Texas, moving back to Waco and then to Austin. Now retired, he still serves as pastor emeritus of First Baptist in Blowing Rock. Doris leads seminars, groups of missionaries in English classes, and otherwise devotes her time and expertise wherever and whenever she is needed. She is pianist at First Baptist.

In a phone conversation, my sisters Shirley and Janie decided that Janie should call Doris and tell her that I had been a church pianist in Chatom for more than fifty years, and ask her if I could play at one of the services, as the organist was to be away Sunday.

Doris offered to play organ, thereby giving me an opportunity to take the piano. How nervous might one be after not having played for months, and in front of totally new folks? The answer, very nervous. I spent some time alone at the church, practicing music for the Thursday night Maundy service, the 6:30 sunrise, and the 11 a.m. worship service. I thought I did well, didn't embarrass Doris or my family, and it felt good to play again.

Janie and I liked Pastor Randy Guenther and his very good and well prepared messages. Janie said she felt as if he were speaking to her personally, the mark of a great speaker. Guenther is leader of a very busy, wonderful, and caring church family.

Doris Edwards invited Janie and me to every church activity, beginning with a ladies' Bible study class. We met Linda Chastain from Birmingham, Alabama, when we attended a Women's Missionary Union meeting in her home.

Linda and her husband, Robert, own a mountain that has been in his family for years. On it the couple built a large beautiful home, and we enjoyed a seated luncheon with good food and companionship there. Linda entertained us with the story of a visit from a fully-grown brown bear one afternoon while she and Robert were sitting on their front porch. They were alerted by a noise from the side of the house where a bird feeder hung from a tree limb. The bear was standing on his hind legs, swatting at the feeder. Robert, always a gentleman, spoke nicely to the bear requesting that he leave the premises. The bear ignored his polite appeal, so Robert went inside and returned with a gun. He fired into the air. The bear skedaddled.

Kathy Williamson, owner of the local ice cream/chocolate shop, was also in the Bible study class. She recommended that Janie and I meet Jeff Eason, editor of *The Blowing Rocket*, a local newspaper, to be interviewed.

Jeff Eason conducted a good interview with us that resulted in an article on the front page of the newspaper. He teased us saying no murders had been committed that week, leaving him with space to fill on two pages of the paper. Janie and I bought quite a few copies. We hope enough remained for the locals of Blowing Rock.

Prior to our interview, another newfound friend from church, Dee Lutz, told us not to leave Blowing Rock without seeing the *fresco* paintings by Roger Allen Nelson, a local artist. Jeff Eason at the newspaper kindly gave us Mr. Nelson's telephone number, and a meeting was arranged for the next day. We had no idea it would be a day we would never forget.

Roger Allen Nelson arrived at our condo with his eight-year-old daughter, Rachel, who joined us for the day. Rachel is quite a little lady. Our adventure turned into an entire day of riding in Roger's Toyota van, which he said has three hundred thousand miles on it. We wound up and down mountain roads at what felt like sixty miles an hour.

Roger looks like a hippie of the 1960s: tall and slim, bearded face, and a head full of long, unruly dark hair. He's a very handsome man and sooooo nice. An accomplished artist, Roger trained in classical realism; he holds degrees in Fine Arts/Art History from the University of Minnesota. He later studied the French academic tradition of painting under Richard F. Lack, who established the Atelier Lack School of Arts after a long apprenticeship with Ives Gammel in Boston. Both Lack and Gammel were accomplished in the style of the Old Masters of Europe. Roger developed a taste for larger works and public art. He was commissioned by the City of Minneapolis to design and paint murals.

Roger bought land and a home in North Carolina and turned to carpentry and renovation; then plans, renderings, and elevations for local architects; and set designs and drawings for movies. When he met the world-renowned *fresco* master Ben Long and signed on as a volunteer assistant, it was a turning point in his life. Ben Long had begun a *fresco* at Saint Peter's church in Winston Salem. Roger became chief associate artist to Long, working with him on *frescoes* in North Carolina and France. He also became instructor at the Fine Arts League of Asheville, teaching artistic anatomy and life/figure drawing. It wasn't until the year 2000 that Roger began accepting solo commissions.

Fresco painting is said to be the most ancient of art forms and perhaps the most arduous. During the Renaissance, *fresco* came to be known as the mother of all arts. Learning to master pure pigments and natural elements of *fresco* painting gives an artist insight into every aspect of art. *Fresco* means fresh in Italian, and refers to an art form using a canvas of wet plaster. Pure pigments, suspended in distilled water, are absorbed into the surface as the plaster dries. Though refined, methods used today are similar to those practiced for many millennia, predating recorded history.

Before any work proceeds, the artist spends months planning and committing a design to paper. Figure studies, cartoons (detailed drawings to scale), figure types, and poses all are meticulously executed, along with overall logistics and preparations.

Lime is quarried, kiln-fired, slaked, and added to the *fresco*. Soon a chemical reaction takes place between the calcium hydroxide in the plaster and carbon dioxide in the air. Colors must be applied during this time, since they will adhere to the new limestone crystals that are forming. The lime then dries, sealing pigment in as it reverts to its original rock-solid state.

Depending on size, *frescoes* are painted in sections with each portion completed in a single day. Being an unforgiving medium, if a mistake is made, the plaster must be removed and the entire section begun again. Many *frescoes* are created by a team of collaborators because of the multiple steps in the process, the magnitude of the work involved, and the importance of timeliness. The entire project could include the artist, an assistant, an associate artist, the mason, and the architect. When completed, the *fresco* is married to the building that houses it, creating a permanent masterpiece for the ages.

The nearly twenty-year restoration of the Sistine Chapel in the time of Pope John Paul II has sparked renewed interest in *fresco* painting. The magnificent works of artists like Botticelli and Michelangelo, using natural materials, has appealed to new generations of artists and art lovers.

Roger Allen Nelson believes *fresco* is the best medium for painting on a grand scale because vast surface areas can be covered. Further, because of the fundamental plasticity of the lime plaster, it conforms to many platforms: curved or domed surfaces, flat walls, or odd shapes. Modern building methods and materials have greatly improved the stability of the *fresco* wall, preventing cracking and moisture problems. New pigments have greatly enhanced the colors of the *fresco* artist's palette. Today's heating, air-conditioning, and air-filtering systems provide an ideal environment for *fresco*, something unknown by masters of the past.

Roger went to great effort to find someone with a key to show us a *fresco* at Crossnore School, an orphanage. In the E.H. Sloop Chapel is a wonderful work—Benjamin Long IV's *fresco* depicting the Bible verse, "Suffer the little children to come unto me." The size of the work, the shades and colors so beautifully melded together, and the expressions on the children's faces in the *fresco* brought tears to our eyes. I know we would have been disappointed if we had not seen this extraordinary work of art.

Janie and I had no idea we'd be viewing *frescoes* in private homes, but Roger's friend, Brett Schwebke, owner of Tynecastle Builders, facilitated this very thing.

Roger and Brett are friends and artists together. Brett builds homes on a five hundred-acre mountain that has been owned by his family for three generations. Having spent the better part of the last three decades there, Brett still sees his mountain through the eyes of a child as he shares the enchantment of the land with us. Brett drove us up to the peak of his mountain, something he does for very few people. We felt especially honored to see the magnificent view.

Tynecastle, tucked into the Blue Ridge Mountains between Banner Elk and Linville, gives Brett Schwebke challenges in building unlike any other location. Brett considers timing the key to successful construction—a shorter building season demands careful planning of the months required to put foundations to grade after choosing a proper site and orienting the house to it. Most of all, Brett interprets the owner's lifestyle and desires and integrates those into the building of a Tynecastle home.

The presence of many fine craftsmen and artisans in the area give Brett and his team what is needed to offer his clients a home limited only by their imaginations. Each home is uniquely designed and built with centuries-old timbers, native materials, Old World-style *frescoes*, hand-forged iron, custom-made light fixtures and cabinetry. Brett, when unable to buy the desired furniture or fixtures, designs those himself to create just the right look. He builds only one home at a time and devotes all his effort and concentration to that project. Janie and I were taken into three privately owned homes built by Brett and shown *frescoes* painted by Roger.

In the first home, the first *fresco* was in the dining room, a scene set in the mountains with a couple of men seated at a table on a deck and a woman standing nearby. The *fresco* had a border done in *trompe l'oeil*—an art technique using realistic imagery to create the optical illusion of three dimensions or other materials. The illusion continued the painting onto the tile of a beautiful sideboard. While working on the *fresco*, Roger asked Brett what he liked to eat for breakfast. Brett said, "Eggs Benedict." Roger painted the egg concoction onto the plate in front of one man seated at the table. His figures looked as if they would step from the painting and speak. The depth of Roger's talent amazed us.

In the second home, the *fresco* was painted over a mantel in the living area. Roger's subject was the American Indian. For several months, Roger spent time with a local Native American named Two Bills, learning stories about his life and the life of his tribe. Two Bills posed for several figures in the *fresco*. Again, Roger's incredible work brought to life the history, religion, and art of the American Indian.

The last house was unfurnished and the largest of the three. Two *frescoes* graced opposite walls of the living area: one depicted a life-size Daniel Boone, in the other, his wife, Rebecca. Their figures were incorporated into authentic living conditions of their time, complete with cabins, gardens, and livestock. In the dining room of the same home, a third *fresco* of landscape orientation portrayed frontiersmen, horses, and mountains. A spirit-like figure had been painted into the mountains, one hand raised, making a fist. We asked Roger what the figure represented. With an enigmatic expression, he replied, "You have to answer that for yourself."

It would be difficult to accurately describe the beauty of the homes we visited or the *frescoes* within, or the views. Imagine standing on top of a mountain, on the highest peak, where you can see for miles and miles—the wind is blowing, but no sound other than your own voice can be heard.

Janie and I agreed that our favorite house toured was the first, the smallest of the three, though not small by any standard. It was designed, built, and furnished by Brett, including the beautiful and large light fixture in the living area created especially for that space.

Brett suggested his grandfather's barbecue restaurant for lunch. It was near the bottom of the mountain, he said. Brett didn't go with us, and we had just ordered when he appeared at our table asking if we had everything we needed. Then he went to the kitchen and made sure we were served their locally famous homemade banana pudding for dessert. The barbecue and the sauce were outstanding and we had all the trimmings. Brett insisted on paying for everything. We thanked him profusely, although inadequately we felt, for his time and effort on our behalf.

After all this, Roger took us to his home and studio where he showed us paintings in different stages of completion, as well as how he ground the pigments for the *frescoes* himself. Roger's house and studio are two separate buildings in the middle of nowhere, on a dirt road in a glorious stand of timber on the side of a mountain. Magnificent.

Janie and I returned home at 4:00 p.m., exhausted, still full from lunch, and giddy with amazement at what we had seen and heard. We were the only two people who had been given such an awe-inspiring gift. Roger Allen Nelson had made it possible for us, and we were deeply grateful. We would cherish the time Roger and Brett spent with us.

Our condo was so nice, as were our landlords, Susan and Blake. We had a little plumbing problem shortly after moving in, and Blake came and quickly fixed it. Although we never met Susan, we did e-mail back and forth and felt as if we knew her.

We're in a building with four condos, one of four buildings in a complex. Our entry hall opened into the dining area and living space that look upon a small balcony with a view of Grandfather Mountain. A bedroom and bath sat off to the left of the dining room; a large master bedroom and bath were by the living area. Furniture, wall hangings, lamps, other lighting, and a beautiful stone fireplace perfectly suited to the space and atmosphere finished the picture.

We could not have asked for more.

Janie and I were fortunate to be adopted by Betty Pitts, who writes for a newspaper in Blowing Rock, and her daughter, Lynn Lawrence. Betty is the "go to" person here, we had been told by everyone, when you want to get things done.

Betty and her late husband, Hayden, grew up in Blowing Rock and owned several businesses there. Hayden served as mayor for many years. Betty knew everyone and shared many a witty anecdote with us. We were invited to visit her home to eat "leftovers"—a feast to us—from Easter. Betty's house is next door to the former home of Jan Karon, the author of the Mitford series of books.

Lynn Laurence, wife of the current mayor and Betty's daughter, is a special friend of Jan Karon, who has admitted to using people from the community of Blowing Rock as characters in her books. Of course, she changed the names.

Lynn speaks to Jan quite often and had told her of our special reason for being in the community. Jan had relayed a special hello to us, wishing us well on our adventure. Jan is in town many times during the year for fund-raising events, and would return the first week of June this year for several lectures and gatherings.

You wouldn't think things could get any more exciting for us, but they did. We had received a call from friends in Chatom, Alabama, saying they would be in Blowing Rock for Easter.

The week of Easter we attended Holy Week communion services at Saint Mary of the Hills Episcopal Church. Each day, Monday through Wednesday at noon, there was a devotion with a different speaker and a different church furnishing the meal. I had walked by this church every morning and was pleased to see inside. It is beautiful. We met many nice people at the gathering, including Meg and Frank Fary, Margaret Joffrian and her husband, and Luella Rundel, who were members of the Rumple Presbyterian Church.

On Easter morning after a sunrise service at the Baptist Church, the men of Rumple Presbyterian hosted a community breakfast, which we attended. Janie and I sat with an adorable couple, Jack and Lori Sharp, who were expecting their first child. Jack is a civil engineer. The two hope to reopen a camp for handicapped children on property they own here. As I write I wonder if the project has become a reality because Jack and Lori were so excited about its potential.

Our Chatom friends, John and Paula Beech, attended the late church service with us. We lunched together at an expensive restaurant in an exclusive resort, Chetola. We had chosen the restaurant as our treat for them, and never intended that John would pay for the meal, but he did.

It was a special day and we enjoyed talking with John and Paula about family and everyone in Chatom.

Kent Tarbutton, who has a marvelous rags-to-riches life story, owns Chetola Resort. Having heard about Kent, we called asking for an appointment to meet and interview him at the resort. The few minutes we requested turned into two hours, thanks to Kent, a fascinating person, a Bible teacher, entrepreneur, quite handsome man, and possessor of a great personality. He is all of the above, and yet I still feel I have not described him adequately.

Kent was born in Norfolk, Virginia, ran away from home at age fourteen, later obtained a GED, then a college degree in psychology. He went on to work with autistic children and later with addicts and prostitutes. He was fortunate to have an uncle who believed in him and helped him find himself. He moved to Blowing Rock as a single dad with a twelve-year-old daughter. Kent considers Blowing Rock a village and works hard on projects with different organizations to retain that village atmosphere.

There is no doubt Kent's daughter, Morgan, is dear to his heart. A few weeks after moving to Blowing Rock, Kent's security people asked why he felt the need to pick up his daughter every day after school.

"So she can go to the park, play with her friends, eat greasy hamburgers, and if ever there is a problem someone will call me," he replied.

That described the kind of place he wanted for his daughter to grow up. Morgan is now twenty-seven years old, a graduate of Appalachian State College, has taught English in Japan for seven years, loves photography, and has traveled extensively. Kent is a proud father.

Kent Tarbutton's vision for Chetola Resort is to "make memories." The resort boasts forty-eight time-share owners and 226 wholly owned condos with one to five bedrooms. Many of the condos are for rent.

Every kind of native tree, shrub, and flower grace the beautifully landscaped grounds. A gazebo is available for social affairs. There are old stone buildings and cobblestone walkways, and all are meticulously cared for by his staff.

Kent teaches a Bible study class for male employees and holds staff prayer meetings. He encourages female employees and gives them time for their own Bible studies. Much of the staff has been with him since the early days of his ownership of Chetola.

One of Kent's interests is Cone Mansion, which sits on a high hill overlooking Blowing Rock. Moses H. Cone and his brother, Caesar, made their money in textiles in the late 1800s. The Cone Export and Commission Company of 1891 was built on efficiency—the company used an assembly line.

In 1894 the business was moved to Greensboro, North Carolina. Roads were beginning to be improved, prompting Moses Cone to purchase thirty-five hundred acres near Blowing Rock. The acreage included Flat Top and Rich Mountains. Cone built a thirteen-thousand square foot mansion on Flat Top.

The Cones had no children but fed and clothed many children of the community when their families were down on their luck. A local story about the Cones is that when they came home to Flat Top, whether for a short visit or the entire summer, people would run ahead of the carriage clearing the trail of rocks and debris to assure that the carriage and Mrs. Cone, who was in poor health, would not be jolted.

The Cone Mansion is now home to a Southern Highlands Craft Guild shop. Southern Highlands is one of the nation's strongest craft organizations, second only to Boston Society of Arts and Crafts. Southern Highlands operates Blue Ridge Parkway's Folk Art Center and represents some nine hundred craftspeople in nine southeastern states.

Our Wi-Fi connection left much to be desired. After consulting with AT&T, we bought an air card. Janie, our techie, hooked it up per instructions, but we still didn't have the strength needed to blog. Looking for a better connection, we went to Kojay's in town. Kojay's is a wonderful little café-type restaurant with all kinds of gourmet sandwiches, soups, many flavors of coffee, and most important to us, Wi-Fi. The café is closer to a cell tower than our condo is. And the bonus, Kojay's has its own bakery, turning out delicious confections. Very tempting.

Tables are available inside Kojay's and also on an enclosed patio with a waist-high fence on the front of the building. Owners Phyllis and John allowed us to come sit on the porch even when the café was closed. We did this quite a few times. No doubt passersby wondered why two old women were climbing over the rail, dragging a computer and printer. We made ourselves at home.

One day while inside the café with all our equipment spread over a pair of tables, a couple came in and sat at the next table. We always put Kuralt's book, *America*, our inspiration, out in plain view so that people might notice and give us an opportunity to tell them about our trip.

This time was no exception. (In our defense, we also use the book as a reference.) The couple, Kitty and Harley Gaston from Charlotte, North Carolina, own a home in Blowing Rock. Kitty began to tell us that she knew Kuralt in high school in Charlotte, even though he was several years older than she. He was in a class with one of her brothers. Kitty recalled that Kuralt had performed in a play, *Antigone*. In the ancient Greek play the chorus was instrumental to the story, and "Charlie," as Kitty called him, was in the chorus. He didn't play sports, but was a good scholar and born with "that wonderful voice." Interested in journalism early on, Kuralt worked with the local newspaper while in high school. We were pleased to hear first-hand information about Kuralt. It was just one of our little serendipities. Our admiration for Charles Kuralt continues to grow because everyone speaks so highly of him.

Remember when we took a wrong turn and ended up in Boone? Now we were going back. Boone is the county seat of Watauga County, with a population of about 17,000. It is home to Appalachian State University and more than 20,000 students, the sixth largest institution of the University of North Carolina system. (A side note: Janie's daughter-in-law completed her degree in history at UNC, Wilmington.) We made several trips to Boone for shopping, haircuts, restaurants, and a visit to the oldest store in the area, Mast General Store.

The original Mast store was built in 1882 by Henry Taylor and opened in 1883. By 1897, Taylor sold half interest to W.W. Mast, a member of a pioneer family who had settled in the valley. Taylor and Mast lasted until 1913. Mast bought out Taylor, and the general store remained in the Mast family for sixty years. The Masts endeavored to carry every item a family might need, from plows to cloth, cradles to caskets. This policy led to a popular saying about the store, "If you can't buy it here, you don't need it."

Mast's functioned as a store, a community gathering place,

a doctor's office, the place for wildcrafters to bring their roots and herbs in exchange for store credit, and after the 1940 flood it provided a site for mourners to gather in honor of their lost loved ones.

There were other branches of the Mast General Store, but this flagship store in Boone offered something quite unique—five hundred old-fashioned, hard-to-find candies that overflow from barrels. We had a great time wandering the store and staring at the awesome amount of merchandise under one roof.

I haven't mentioned lately the relationship between Janie and me, our getting along, mainly because it isn't an issue. Did I say everything is hunky-dory? Well, no. But here we are on this adventure and neither of us intend to go home before we've finished.

We fuss, even had a shouting match or two, but neither of us will give in to the other. We each want the last word. We sort of say all we can think of to one another, turn and walk away, maybe for a few hours, and then get back on an even keel. I tell Janie she brings out the worst in me. She says I drive her absolutely over the edge. We're both stubborn, used to having our own way, and want what we want, when we want it. We're just two sisters spending 24/7 together and loving what we're doing. We haven't had to call 911. So far.

There is no way to name every interesting person we'd met, or recount all the happenings as there had been so many. It had been fun to stroll through town, in and out of shops, chatting with owners. Everyone had been friendly, ready to offer helpful information, and we felt we instantly made new friends for forever. I know that Janie and I would both love the opportunity to return to this special place. The only way to realize the beauty of Blowing Rock and the surrounding area is just go and see for yourself.

At this point each month we would begin to think about how to say good-bye. We always felt a reluctance to leave. It had been true in other places, and we found it to be true here, too.

Our moving angel, Warren, asked for us to please call him when it came time came to pack up and load the car. We did just that, taking advantage of his kindness and strength to go up and down the stairs many, many times.

It's April 29, 2011, and we were leaving Blowing Rock, planning to drive 426.3 miles to Washington, D.C. for a quick visit, then on to New York City. We took a last ride through town, capturing a final picture of all of it in our minds. Seeing Kojay's open, we stopped by long enough to thank Phyllis and John for their hospitality. They were representative of the kindness of everyone we had met, so it felt like saying good-bye to all.

Chapter Five

New York, New York

May 2011

HOW MANY TIMES had we heard the lines from the famous Broadway musical of 1944 that starred Frank Sinatra and Gene Kelly?

> *It's a wonderful town.*
> *The Bronx is up but the Battery's down,*
> *The people ride in a hole in the groun'*
> *New York New York*
> *It's a wonderful town!*

Now to know that Janie and I were going to spend a month in that "magical place" was just too exciting. I had been there at least five times before. Janie's first trip was a stopover at the airport to change planes for a flight to Reykjavik, Iceland.

First things first: New York City is the proper reference to the City of New York, as opposed to the State of New York. Five boroughs: Brooklyn, the Bronx, Manhattan, Queens, and Staten Island make up the City of New York. The boroughs were consolidated into a single city in 1898.

New York City lies at the mouth of the Hudson River in the southernmost part of the state, and is the most densely populated major city in the U.S.; its 8,244,910 people are distributed over a land area of 305 square miles. On the streets of New York City as many as 800 languages may be heard. In some areas even street signs, business names, and signs in the subway change languages, giving New York City the distinction of being the most linguistically diverse city in the U.S., and perhaps the world.

Directional designations in the borough of Manhattan define the 33.7 square miles as Uptown, Downtown, Midtown (between Thirty-Fourth and Fifty-Ninth), West Side (west of Fifth Avenue), and East Side (east of Fifth Avenue).

Approximately fifty million people annually visit the many districts and landmarks of New York City. Times Square, referred to as "Crossroads of the World," is a brightly lit hub of the theater district, one of the world's busiest pedestrian intersections and a major center of the world's entertainment industry. New York's financial district, anchored by Wall Street in Lower Manhattan, is home to the New York Stock Exchange. Chinatown incorporates the highest concentration of Chinese people in the Western Hemisphere.

You can see that New York City is a metropolis of mosts. Add to all the others, New York's subway system is the most extensive rapid transit system in the world, with 24/7 service taking you within minutes of every kind of opportunity, be it colleges and universities, theaters, restaurants, parks, bridges, museums, libraries, the Statue of Liberty, or the United Nations headquarters.

New York City is an important center for international diplomacy, and has been called the cultural capital of the world.

We rode and rode and finally found our brownstone apartment in Brooklyn, in the middle of Bedford-Stuyvesant, at #395 Madison Street (not Madison Avenue). Bed-Stuy is in the north central part of Brooklyn, formed in 1930, and the cultural center for Brooklyn's black population—many of whom moved over from Harlem. Bed-Stuy's name derives from Bedford, the first major settlement (in pre-Revolutionary days) east of the Village of Brooklyn on the ferry road to eastern Long Island, and Peter Stuyvesant, the last governor of the colony, New Netherland.

Arriving at our address, we were met by Roy Colvin, landlord and caretaker of #395, who has lived here since 1955. Roy asked a neighbor, David, to help us move in. David also offered advice on where to shop, things to do, and safety tips. He hauled our belongings up to the second floor and put them wherever we asked. Janie and I jokingly wondered if he would be around when we were ready to leave.

Our loft apartment is about a thousand square feet without partitions or doors. There's a bedroom at either end, with Janie's in an alcove facing the street out front. My bedroom on the opposite end was advertised as having a garden/patio view but in reality doesn't come up to the photo. The apartment-size kitchen (tiny) has a two-burner stovetop, microwave, and under-the-counter refrigerator, which will mean more frequent shopping. On the positive side, we do have a television in each bedroom-and Wi-Fi, which is great.

Although a little uncertain about the safety of our location, due to Bed-Stuy's reputation, we decided to give it a try while making other inquiries. In the end, other places were much more expensive, we were settled in, and Roy and David were such friendly help, we decided to stay put.

It's May 5, 2011, and our biggest problem is finding a space to park the car for a day without getting a ticket. We decided to bite the bullet and take the subway into Manhattan. New York City's transit system is 656 miles of track and 468 stations, the busiest system in the United States and seventh busiest in the world. It operates in four of the five boroughs. Staten Island has a separate line. In 1869, a demonstration of the first subway ever built was held in New York City. The Great Blizzard of 1888 had shown the need for underground transit in the city, and by 1904, the first line opened.

We were only ten blocks from a subway entrance and thank goodness Janie is good at figuring out diagrams, routes, and schedules. We took the A train (remember the song?), an express to Times Square. There we would exit for theater outings, but to visit the Metropolitan Museum of Art required us to take the A train, transfer to a local, then a bus, and walk several blocks. Janie had worked this out, and the reverse order. Today, the trial run.

President Obama was in town, having lunch at one of the fire stations near Times Square, and we couldn't get closer than a couple of blocks.

We walked about, sat on bleachers, and watched people. Junior's restaurant at 1515 Broadway was our choice for lunch. Originating in Brooklyn on Flatbush Avenue in 1950, the Manhattan restaurant is known for good food, fast service, and, of course, the cheesecake. The funny thing about Junior's is that nothing is junior. A bowl of grits, or a cup of coffee, seriously looked the size of a Kiddie Saucer Ride at the amusement park.

Here's my take on what we were doing in New York City. Charles Kuralt had been here in December, which would be very different from the month of May. Janie and I would do our own thing, although I imagined some of what we would do, Kuralt would also have gotten to at some point.

It's Saturday, May 7, and we're headed into Manhattan to see the musical, *Billy Elliot*. Our concern about what to wear was not warranted. We soon realized that anything goes. A quick lunch, good luck in finding a parking space near the subway entrance, and we were on the easy ride to Midtown. Walking the streets was more difficult; the mass of people crowded us between sidewalk and buildings. We could hardly move without bumping someone.

Arriving at the packed Olympia Theater, we settled in our seats, congratulating ourselves on their excellent location. Expensive, but worth it. The play was the best I'd ever seen. An eleven-year-old boy carried the show, smiling, singing, and dancing for two hours and forty-five minutes. Even the bows at the end were another number. We met two interesting couples during the short intermission, a doctor and his wife from Pennsylvania and a couple from Berlin, Germany.

Sticking to the advice we had been given, we were home by six, before dark. Being a Saturday night, it was noisy in our Bed-Stuy neighborhood. Lots of traffic, both foot and vehicular, with boom boxes blaring. When I think of the sights and sounds of New York City compared to the peacefulness of Blowing Rock, North Carolina, the difference is infinite. In New York, I heard whistles, screeches, the roar of airplanes overhead, car horns, and sirens from fire trucks, ambulance, and police cars, all with different tunes—a cacophony of noise.

While out walking my first morning I had noticed airplanes about to land at John F. Kennedy Airport, and when I was out again later in the afternoon I observed twenty-six planes land at three-minute intervals. I was fascinated to watch them from my bedroom window, too, but the noise factor was less appealing.

Janie and I began looking for a church to attend for Mother's Day, passed two in our neighborhood, but finally found one via OnStar that was listed as "Southern Baptist." We drove for miles and miles and in heavy traffic before reaching our destination. At the church we weren't allowed to choose our seats, but were ushered to a spot.

We sat through a good hour-and-a-half of preliminaries: singing a chorus some fourteen times; visiting—which was fine; the passing of the collection plate (once for tithes and again for the offering); the reading of several pledges concerning money; introduction of all the mothers, collectively, and then all visitors, collectively; and at last at 12:30 p.m., the pastor opened his Bible. It would have been a good message, we think, but Janie's legs had begun to twitch due to restless leg syndrome, and she had to stand and move to the back. The usher informed Janie that no one was allowed to sit in the back during the sermon, even after Janie explained her condition. Janie motioned for me to come to her and we quietly left the church. By now, it was 1:30. Isn't it said in Baptist circles that the Holy Spirit leaves at twelve noon? We felt a bit guilty, but the service had started at 11:00 a.m.; it was not what we had had in mind; it wasn't the Southern Baptist service we'd grown up with.

Happy Mother's Day calls from children and grandchildren made our day. I had gone out walking early in the morning and every older gentleman and even some young men called out, "Happy Mother's Day," leaving me with a blessed warm feeling of welcome.

We arrived at the Metropolitan Museum of Art just in time for lunch in the Met cafeteria. That gave us a moment to plan how we might see some of the two million objects in the permanent collections and special exhibits. The Met has an interesting beginning. Its concept was nurtured in Paris, France, in 1866 by a group of Americans who wanted to create a "national institution and gallery of art," to take art and art education to the American people. In April 1870, the Met opened at 681 Fifth Avenue in the Dodworth Building, and in a couple of years acquired a Roman sarcophagus and 174 European paintings. Works by Anthony van Dyck, Nicolas Poussin, and Giovanni Battista Tiepolo were among the Met's first acquisitions. In 1880, the museum was moved to its current location at 1000 Fifth Avenue.

Peopled with family greeters, family programs, lecturers, and volunteers at information desks speaking Chinese, French, German, Italian, Japanese, Korean, Russian, Portuguese, and Spanish, the Met is a world all its own. Janie wanted to see the Old Masters and Impressionists, and that is where we spent most of our time. Seeing it all would have taken weeks. We compromised by viewing the works of Rembrandt, Vermeer (one of Janie's favorites), Manet, Monet, Van Gogh, Toulouse-Lautrec, Hals, Bonnard, and Tissot. Janie spotted a portrait of Tissot painted by his friend, Degas. To ease her way, Janie used a wheelchair to tour the museum. Despite our weariness upon returning home, we agreed it had been a fun day.

We love Broadway! We were going to see *Jersey Boys*, the story of Frankie Valli and the Four Seasons. Yes, tickets for musicals are expensive, and we spent forty minutes finding a parking spot near the subway entrance. Once the subway deposited us near our destination's station, I ran to the theater to pick up our tickets. We were barely seated at 1:57 for the 2:00 p.m. performance.

This was our kind of music: "My Eyes Adored You" and "Can't Take My Eyes Off of You." We remembered dancing to these tunes and singing along, too, when we were young. These Jersey Boys were so very talented, had we closed our eyes we would have sworn they were the original group. It was all worthwhile—even the cost and the hassle to get there. We enjoyed every moment.

At some point every day our landlord, Roy, and neighbor, David, could be found sitting out on their steps or patio, and we always stopped and visited with them. David gave us a tour of his brownstone, all three floors. He has done a lovely restoration with custom drapes and a completely renovated kitchen. We'd also become acquainted with the lady at the laundromat, the barbershop, and a couple from Trinidad who live in the basement apartment. Our neighborhood is different from any place we have lived before, very multicultural. On our way to the laundromat, we passed Pee Wee's, a barbershop frequented by hip-hop stars. Limousines and expensive cars are commonly seen parked at the curb. Pee Wee's is known to give good haircuts; cheap ones, too. Karen from the laundromat walked us to the shop and introduced us to Felicia while we made appointments for the next week.

In Bed-Stuy there are hundreds, maybe thousands, of brownstones. Most are the traditional brown color, but occasionally you'd see a bright blue, or even chartreuse, one. Many have also been painted off-white.

The original brownstone in Brooklyn or the New York City area was a multi-floor row house with a façade of brown sandstone. This construction material was quarried in New Jersey and Connecticut during the nineteenth century and became quite popular. Stonemasons of the time were artisans who found the sandstone easy to work with, allowing creations of varied and ornate design. A garden floor, or English basement, at ground level with the front entrance under an exterior formal staircase would lead to a garden at the back of the house. The kitchen was also on the garden floor. Another feature of ninetheenth-century brownstones is a parlor floor with ornate molding, arched doorways and discreet pocket doors, tall windows, and a large fireplace, all designed for elegant entertaining. Most of the original brownstones have been converted to multiple-family dwellings, but still maintain some of the finest architecture in Brooklyn.

As I walked past one building I saw it was a music studio offering lessons in theory, voice, piano, violin, and guitar, brass, as well as drums, reeds, acting, and modeling. I never saw anyone around but wish I could have met the instructors.

I'm impressed by the politeness of everyone we have met, and the care given their small plots of flowers and vegetable gardens. These old buildings each have a history, and it would be interesting to know something about the lives and circumstances of the people who had lived in them and who call them home now.

Sunday, May 15, dawned a rainy day, but a little sprinkle never hurt anyone and we had plans to visit Saint Patrick's Cathedral in Manhattan for the noon service. Unfurl umbrellas, everyone.

The first Saint Patrick's was built on Mulberry Street in Lower Manhattan in 1815. According to a news article in the *New York Gazette*, four thousand people from the "best families of New York attended the dedication." The cathedral was built to the design of Joseph Mangin and destroyed by fire in 1866. At the time of the fire, plans were already underway for a new cathedral to be built between Fifth and Madison avenues.

Viewing Saint Patrick's in its present form is moving, but it doesn't convey the woes that went into completion of the building. The cathedral was the dream of John Hughes, first Archbishop of New York, who with noted mid-nineteenth-century architect, James Renwick, realized their mutual dream on blueprints of a Gothic-style structure.

The horror and tragedy of the Civil War stalled the building of what should have been a testimony of man's love for his fellow man. Three years after the foundation had been laid, weeds were growing over structural groundwork. The Civil War ended and fourteen more years passed before the cathedral opened under direction of Archbishop Hughes and Cardinal McCloskey. Even then it was not in its completed form. The spires were lifted into place some ten years later.

Lady Chapel was added at the turn of the century, in the traditional Gothic-style common to European churches built from the thirteenth to fifteenth centuries. Saint Patrick's has always been an original. Its distinction is noted in the height of the spires—330 feet from the street. Seating capacity is approximately 2,400. The organ has 7,855 pipes, and there are nineteen bells (chimes) weighing a total 29,000 pounds. The rose window measures twenty-six feet in diameter.

The Mass we attended celebrated the Fourth Sunday of Easter with The Most Reverend Timothy Dolan, current Archbishop of New York, serving as the celebrant and homilist. It was beautiful; the organ music, sermon, rituals, and celebration were almost more than we could take in. More than any other church we'd visited, the beauty and awe inspired by the cathedral kept our eyes from wandering and our minds on the message.

Despite the soft rainfall, we went to Rockefeller Center's Rock Café and sat outdoors under umbrellas just for fun and the atmosphere. Tourists from round the world passed our table or sat nearby. I enjoyed an open-face shrimp omelet with cherry tomatoes and fava beans on top (delicious!), and Janie tried Eggs Benedict on a biscuit with ham and aioli mustard.

We finished with Mississippi Mud Cake, topped off by whipped cream, caramel sauce, and nuts. Thank goodness our trip home was uneventful. After that meal, we couldn't possibly have "run for our lives." What a good day.

While online checking "things to do" in the area, Janie asked if I'd like to attend a Yankee's baseball game. We were excited to get tickets, but not to the extent that we wanted to make the trip twice. Or so we thought. Saturday, May 21, we had a relaxed uneventful ride to Yankee Stadium in the Bronx. Yet obviously something was amiss. We had expected hordes of people gathering or rushing to their seats. In fact hardly anyone at all was about. We checked our tickets and realized we'd arrived several days early for a game scheduled for Wednesday. What a bummer. We made the most of our unnecessary jaunt by eating at McDonald's, and reassured ourselves that now that we knew the way to the stadium, Wednesday's trip would be easier.

Janie and I had been doing okay healthwise except for Janie's difficulty walking. She was in pain, but not complaining much. She did see a doctor for an ear problem, and received medication for pain and infection, just in case.

That Championship Season, a 1972 play written by Jason Miller and starring one of our favorite actors, Chris Noth, was on our list of plays we had to see. The play received a Pulitzer for Drama, a Tony for Best Play, the New York Drama Critics Circle Award, the Outer Critics Circle Award, and a National Summer Stock Award. Four former high school basketball champions and their coach meet annually to celebrate the year they won Pennsylvania's State Basketball Championship. But this year instead of indulging in the usual nostalgia, the friends unload all their secrets on one another, causing the foundations of friendship and their lives to crumble. Everything they have ever believed comes into question.

Brian Cox, Jim Gaffigan, Jason Patric (the playwright's son), and Kiefer Sutherland star in the production at the Bernard Jacobs

Theater. Jason Patric played the role of the drunkard, going from tipsy to falling-down believably drunk over the course of the play. Noth's character was a successful but sleazy guy who had an affair with his friend's wife. We were seated one row in front of Chris Noth's agent and hoped to get an okay for a backstage meeting with the cast, but it didn't happen. We tried though.

On another rainy Friday afternoon, we ventured into town and stopped by CBS studios with the desire to speak to someone about our trip. Because of Kuralt's affiliation with CBS, we had fingers crossed that someone might talk to us. A greeter took all of our information, gave us a number to call, and likely dismissed us as more hopefuls trying to get through the door in whatever capacity. All we knew to do was to give it a try.

Looking for a spot to get out of the rain, we stopped in a Starbucks. It was crowded and had not one available seat. Bobby Flay's restaurant, Bar Americain, was in our path, and Janie is a big Flay fan. The restaurant is large, with modern décor and excellent service, even though we only ordered coffee. We wished it had been the dinner hour, but we were only killing time and so had to settle for lingering over our cups.

Our next stop was Tom and Toons, a piano bar restaurant. We'd met the parents of Jordan Addison, pianist and vocalist at Tom and Toons, while in Blowing Rock. Jordan's father had asked us to stop in and see his personable and talented son. Jordan is credited with performances on cruise ships and in many clubs.

He has written music for other performers and even has some Broadway experience. Janie and I chatted with Jordan before his show, posed with him for a photo, and enjoyed a delicious dinner.

Since listening to a recording of the Brooklyn Tabernacle Choir many years ago, I had wanted to hear them in person. On May 21, we attended the Brooklyn Tabernacle Church. First established in 1847 as the Central Presbyterian Church on the corner of Willoughby and Pearl streets, the tabernacle is a multicultural, nondenominational church. Begun in a rundown building with a handful of members, the congregation now numbers ten thousand and weekly services are held at 17 Smith Street in the heart of downtown Brooklyn.

The tabernacle's first building was destroyed by fire, the second by a thunderstorm, and the third by another fire. By 1971, a congregation of only thirty met in a dilapidated building on Atlantic Avenue. When the former Carlton Theater at Flatbush and Seventh avenues was purchased and renovated, the congregation found new vitality through its Tabernacle choir. Pastor Jim Cymbala and his wife, Carol, put together nine untrained voices from the church membership.

Carol's innate musical sense for harmonies made the choir a great success. In her search for appropriate music to lift up the congregation in the greatness of God, Carol wrote music specifically for the choir. Her efforts brought money to make recordings and to distribute their music to friends and loved ones. The choir's recorded videos and numerous albums eventually won five Dove Awards and six Grammys. In New York City, concert venues included Carnegie Hall, Radio City Music Hall, and Madison Square Garden Theater. That kind of acceptance and recognition provided the Brooklyn Tabernacle Church a wide open door for ministry, presenting a gospel message through music to people all over the world. Another renovated theater, Loew's Metropolitan, became home in 2002. The choir is a unique cross section of humanity drawn together and lifted up by the power of Jesus Christ. Each rehearsal begins with prayer to ask the Lord to bless their music and anoint their songs for service. Janie and I sat in the theater, which seats 3,200 people, and I did not see an empty chair. The choir members drifted in and took their places in the most casual way, but with reverence. I would not soon forget the experience.

The parking situation on our street had become almost more than we could handle. Janie and I had gotten two tickets for parking violations, one for $115.00 and another for $45.00, and we'd begun to wonder if it spoke to our intelligence. Certain days, you must park on the designated side of the street, but by 11:00 a.m. your car must be moved to the other side. Some days are free and no move is required. All this scheduling is so the streets can be swept, and that's wonderful, but for the price we were paying I'd have gladly swept under my own car. Our good friend, Roy, had taken to blowing his car horn to signal that it was time to move our vehicle. Finding a spot in front of the brownstone wasn't easy. But lesson learned. We didn't like thinking we were the clichéd dumb blondes (with a little gray sprinkled in) or that we were being targeted because of our Alabama tag.

Janie and I are not even baseball fans, yet it was a thrill to be in the new Yankee Stadium, which is huge and befits the Yankees. Their opposition on this day, May 25, was the Toronto Blue Jays.

We'd made our trial run and so had an easy ride to the stadium. It was a bright sunshiny day, with a light breeze blowing, just like we'd seen so often on television, but this time we were there! After finding our seats we ate ballpark hot dogs, fries, and milk shakes (Coke not having enough calories). Janie even drank a beer.

We had good seats in left field with nice young people around us, including two young guys from South Carolina living in New Jersey and working in New York. They bought Janie the beer when they got theirs, and Janie said the ice-cold brew hit the spot.

It turned into a hot afternoon, and a couple of guys stripped off their shirts. We enjoyed the game and the ambience; don't remember the score, but do remember the Yankees won. We saw A-Rod and Derek Jeter play. Andre Jones hit two homers. (I may be showing my baseball ignorance, but wasn't Jones with the Atlanta Braves at one time?) Between innings, men with rakes or brooms dragged the field while "YMCA" played on the sound system. The guys stepped in time to the music and when the chorus began they dropped their tools and went through the hand motions for the crowd, just like the Village People. Lots of fun!

We couldn't be more excited. Our sister, Shirley, and her partner, Marge, are coming from Birmingham to meet us in Manhattan for a few days. Marge can't manage stairs easily so we decided it'd be mutually beneficial if we all met at their hotel. It would be a welcome change of pace for Janie and me. We possibly overpacked, taking suitcase, dopp kit, and one of the computers.

Janie and I always become angry when people say New Yorkers are rude, impolite, and not very nice. We have met with nothing but kindness and courtesy in the city. On our trek to and from the hotel, each time we encountered a flight of stairs a gentleman would offer to carry our bags. We were truly grateful to them.

Arriving at the Flatotel Hotel within ten minutes of Shirley and Marge, we settled in our rooms and set up a table large enough to play cards in Shirley's room. This was standard procedure for us when we're together.

Yes, Flatotel is an odd name for our hotel. It's derived from the word for European apartments, which are called flats, and hotel. Flatotel is known for the generous size of its rooms. Rooms and suites are available for short visits, as well as studio and one-, two-, and three-bedroom apartments for stays from one month to a year. We were right in the middle of the theater district on Fifty-Second Street between Sixth and Seventh avenues.

We crossed a concourse to find lunch at Duke's Café, where we would end up eating a couple of times during our stay in Manhattan. Duke's has at least thirty food stations with everything from sushi to barbecue; soup, salads, fresh fruits and vegetables, and pasta and seafood; multiple kinds of sandwiches and desserts. It boggled the mind to imagine how they kept it all ready for the busy flow of hungry customers.

Janie and I were returning to Saint Patrick's Cathedral, this time for a choral and orchestra concert, An Evening of Sacred Romantic Music. Marge and Shirley would attend with us. Tickets in hand, we all climbed into a taxi to the cathedral.

Saint Patrick's choir consists largely of volunteer singers and a small professional group. Music is prepared from different periods for liturgies and other special events. The late music director and organist John Grady, who also served with the Metropolitan Opera, established the choir in its present form. Today, Dr. Jennifer Pascual is the heart of the music program considered North America's most prominent Roman Catholic cathedral. Dr. Pascual is the first woman to hold her position. A former organist and choir director for the Archdioceses of Newark, New Jersey and New York City, she was on Artistic Staff of the Boys Choir of Harlem from 1994 to 2003.

Saint Patrick's Choir has performed for many heads of state (including the Secretary General of the United Nations); with soloists such as Renée Fleming and Placido Domingo; for Mass for visiting popes; and even in Yankee Stadium. The performance atmosphere was formal, but not stuffy. Ladies wore black and men were attired in tuxedos. The fifty members of the orchestra, thirty-five in the choir, and soloists were outstanding.

We topped off our evening with "to die for" burgers at Bill's Bar and Burger near Rockefeller Plaza, the largest stand-alone burger joint in the United States. The amazing thing about New York City is that on any street, any neighborhood, any building you see—there's something significant about it. You've heard or seen or read about every place, and it gets your attention. We couldn't see and do everything, but we paced ourselves, picking and choosing, and, of course, set limitations based on budget.

The cost of theater tickets, as noted before, added up, but one show we couldn't miss was the musical, *Priscilla, Queen of the Desert*. What a show—a tale of two drag queens and a transsexual crossing the Australian outback in a bus. The play is adapted from Stephan Elliott's film, *Adventures of Priscilla, Queen of the Desert.* Alan Scott, screenwriter and playwright, partnered with Elliott on the play. *Priscilla* won a Tony Award (2011) for Best Costumes—a dazzling array of more than five hundred creations. Acting and set design (especially the bus) and music—twenty dance floor favorites including "It's Raining Men," "Finally," and "I Will Survive"—were incredible.

Shirley, Marge and Janie and I loved every second of it. I would see it again, only on Broadway. It was Janie's favorite of all the plays we'd seen so far. If you have a chance, do yourself a favor and go.

All my life I'd heard of Sardi's, across the street from the Palace Theater at 234 West Forty-Fourth Street. The restaurant is known for the hundreds of caricatures of show business celebrities that are displayed on its walls. In 1921 Vincent Sardi Sr. and his wife, Eugenia, both born in Italy, opened their first eatery a short distance from the current Sardi's. They accepted an offer from theater magnates, the Shubert brothers, to relocate in a new building the Shuberts were constructing.

To increase business in the 1920s, Mr. Sardi borrowed an idea he'd seen in a Parisian jazz club called Zelli's: hiring an artist to do drawings of celebrities and then decorating the walls with them. Sardi's first caricaturist was a Russian refugee named Alex Gard, who he hired to make the images in exchange for one meal a day at the restaurant.

Gard's first caricature was of Ted Healy, one of the Three Stooges. Frequent mentions of Sardi's restaurant and his celebrities in newspaper columns by Walter Winchell added to the popularity of the establishment. Sardi's soon became known as a pre- and post-theater hangout, a place to see and be seen.

Shirley and Marge treated Janie and me with a souvenir from the *Priscilla* show. We proudly wore our neon pink boas to the restaurant and quickly became a topic of conversation. Soon we were friends with everyone within talking range, and enjoying the meal and visiting. By the time we departed Sardi's, almost everyone was aware of the trip Janie and I were making and we were sent on our way by many well-wishers with promises to buy our book.

A double-decker bus tour is a great way to see the Big Apple. While Marge went off with her son and grandson for the day, Shirley, Janie, and I took the triple-loop tour. We saw just about every neighborhood and building, statue, bridge, museum and theater and restaurant, river, boat, church, park, and most anything else you can imagine when you think of New York City, or the Big Apple, as it is known.

The appellation Big Apple was first applied as a reference to the city in the early 1920s. New York's many racecourses were sometimes called apples, and soon apple became a popular term for the substantial prizes awarded to winners of horse races. A *New York Morning Telegraph* sportswriter, John Fitzgerald, wrote in his column about horse races "around the Big Apple." Research suggests Fitzgerald had heard the term from racetrack jockeys.

In the late 1920s and 1930s, New York jazz musicians spoke of New York City as "the Big Apple," meaning it was the premier place to perform.

During a 1971 campaign to boost tourism, the moniker Big Apple was officially adopted to suggest a wholesome All-American city, an effort to dispel the reputation of the metropolis as a dark and dangerous place to visit.

The cheerful name stuck.

My sisters and I hurried back to Flatotel to get ready for the Broadway musical, *Memphis*. The play is loosely based on Memphis disc jockey, Dewey Phillips, the first white DJ to play race music, as it was called back in the 1950s.

In 2010, Memphis won four Tony awards. Despite the great choreography, recognizable music, and leading lady, Jasmin Richardson, we took a little catnap during the play. Janie said that, other than the leading lady's voice, it was hard to find anything to love. That's unusual for her, because she's usually an easy grader. Perhaps we were tired after such a busy day and not appreciating the beauty of it.

By the time we all went to Sardi's for dinner, we had perked up and enjoyed another fine meal and the friendly environment.

At the end of our evening, there's always a round of cards to help put us to sleep, and that night's lasted until the wee hours of the morning. Nevertheless, we were up again at 6:00 a.m., preparing for the 9 o'clock service at Metropolitan Community Church where the pastor is Marge's friend.

There weren't many people in attendance, but it was quite a nice church, a great message and communion, and the opportunity for Marge to visit her friend.

A churchgoer had brought his dog, a small breed that the

owner held in his lap during the service. Janie had to pet the dog before we left.

We only had time for a quick breakfast before Marge and Shirley departed for the airport. Janie and I called a cab to return us to our brownstone. We couldn't bring ourselves to lug our belongings back on the subway. The fare of $27.50 seemed a bargain, all things considered.

We presented Roy with a little "happy" for keeping our car moved to the right side of the street at the right time while we were gone.

On Monday, a block party to celebrate Memorial Day was in full swing in our neighborhood—lots of loud music, kids running and playing in the street, and wonderful smells of barbecue—typical of holiday weekends everywhere.

I welcomed a phone call from my nephew, Stanton Schell, a computer whiz who designs websites for high-powered companies in New York. He has been here for some time and lives in Greenwich Village. Stanton came by the following day and we had a pleasant, although short, visit. Amazing how many relatives I was getting to see on this trip.

Janie and I had been in Brooklyn, New York, for a month, and we had always meant to buy ice cream one day from the truck that passes through the neighborhood, tinkly music emanating from the vehicle. But despite our good intentions, we had only managed to enjoy watching neighbor children and adults sitting out on their steps, licking ice cream cones. Seemed the truck always arrived just after we had eaten a big meal. But we should have made the effort, because that's what one does in a typical New York neighborhood.

Our month in New York had ended. We were leaving two very special friends, Roy and David. I felt we had became a part of the neighborhood, and once again I thought: I would come back and do it all over again.

Chapter Six
Woodstock, Vermont
June 2011

MY MILEAGE CALCULATOR said it was 267.2 miles from New York City to Woodstock, Vermont. Janie and I regretted our month in the Big Apple had ended. Time was passing too quickly. This was our sixth month on the road, and it seemed we'd just left home. As happens at the beginning of each new month, we were anxious and excited to start our next adventure.

Conifers and northern hardwoods cover much of the state of Vermont. As we approached the hills and mountains and villages on two-lane roads, everything was green, all shades, and almost blinding at times. What a contrast to the iconic image of Vermont in the fall with its bright yellow, red, and orange leaves. The Green Mountain State, as it is known, looks fresh and beautiful this day, and quite different from the urban surroundings we had just left behind. The sky was bluer, the white clouds puffier, the air more crisp, and right now we were liking this place. The noise of horns, sirens, airplanes, and the incessant roar of traffic and humanity had dissolved into peaceful quiet, even though we're on the main highway to White River Junction, Vermont.

Our accommodations in Woodstock were not available to us until June 6. The Super 8 Motel in White River Junction, fourteen miles from our destination, would be home for a few days. It was an opportunity to see the surrounding area before we settled into exploring Woodstock. Several local restaurants caught our notice: Lui Lui's, mostly Italian; Crossroads Café, good old country cooking; and China Moon, a quite good buffet. One evening we enjoyed excellent food and service at the Tip Top Café—a surprise—because the name didn't fit the upscale atmosphere of the restaurant. A little pricey, but well worth it.

Bradford, Vermont, a nearby town, stages a "Farmway" promotion every year featuring music, lunch, and an open house at its famous Farmway Inc. Vermont Gear store. Farmway is located in an old Purina mill that had been vacant and neglected for years. With sixteen acres to explore, the company offers footwear, cold weather gear, sporting goods, and household items. People travel many miles for Farmway's saddles, boots, Cabot cheddar cheese, and even cream for a cow's udder.

Saturday, June 4, we rode a train from White River Junction, serenaded by live music during the ride. We departed the train onto a red carpet and became part of the huge crowd milling about. Everyone we met welcomed us. It was a sale day. People were shopping and there was much to see: swings, tables, hammocks, and Adirondack chairs; every sort of gear needed for camping, hiking, fishing or canoeing, hunting or riding horses, and for all weather conditions. A free lunch of hot dogs with beans and slaw and a drink was offered, followed by an ice cream sandwich for dessert.

The success of Farmway's family-owned business is attributed to what it makes its number one priority: customer service—listening to customers and stocking the items they need and want. The staff is made up of four husband/wife teams, thirty-six full- and part-time employees, and a whole bunch of great friends.

We spent hours and still did not see everything, but we did our best until time to take the train back to White River Junction. I hadn't ridden a train since the doodlebug train from Chatom to Millry when I was quite young. Janie recalled a trip on the Hummingbird, an express train, from Mobile to Montgomery, Alabama, when she was a teenager.

Zipping along now at twelve miles an hour seemed great fun. Two musicians played guitar and fiddle, and soft drinks and snacks were served. All in all, a fun day.

On Sunday, I attended Valley Baptist Church, a nondenominational church with a great sermon and music. Many of the churches we'd visited so far had been less formal in their services. A praise group often led the music; instruments included guitars, fiddles, and sometimes drums, with no choir. Often what I would call "special music" was offered. This church was well attended, but minus my sister, Janie, who hadn't felt up to it today.

June 6, we would at last be moving into our rented farmhouse just three miles west of Woodstock on Route 4. It had ended up being so "Vermont-looking," painted dark red and built in 1840. We had stopped en route for grocery shopping. I was looking forward to a good kitchen after the small idea of one we'd had in Brooklyn. Scott Chisholm, an architect in Boston and owner of the house, arrived before we did. He had engaged a neighbor to help with cleaning and preparing the house for us. We were thrilled with the farmhouse and happy to meet its owner.

The yard was big. We're on the main highway just across the road from Ottaquechee River, which at this location is wide and shallow—an ambling river making a beautiful rippling sound as it flowed over the rock bed, through the village of Woodstock, and on to Long Island Sound. I was excited because this is where I would walk every morning.

Our farmhouse, with its living room furnished in leather chairs, a huge fireplace, beautiful old tables and lamps, looked so very comfortable. The kitchen had everything, including a pantry and dishwasher. Sliding glass doors opened from the kitchen to a covered deck and patio. A fourteen-foot-long country table with benches graced the eating area next to the kitchen, the perfect space, light and airy, for Janie and me to play cards and to set up the computer. Stairs at the front entrance led to a master bedroom suite and bath and two more bedrooms and another bath. Slanted ceilings in the upstairs rooms gave the space a quaint look.

The whole house was furnished in the style of the 1800s when it was also built. Janie and I would have room to enjoy being together, but space for some private alone time as well.

The next morning at breakfast I heard a knock and opened the door to a policeman. I know my face went expressionless because my first thought was, "What happened to the check I mailed in New York for those parking tickets?" which would now be overdue. Or, had the policeman seen our Alabama car tag and found out about all the illegal U-turns?

James Cushing, corporal of the Woodstock Police Department, informed me he was simply making a routine check. The house had been empty for some time (we were the first renters ever), and it was on his beat and only several houses down the road from where he lives. What a relief to know we would be watched over. While talking, Corporal Cushing said the safest place to walk would be across the road, the very place I had already chosen. My walking had been curtailed by rain, but the cloudy days also kept the temperatures in the low seventies. I couldn't complain. On this particular morning it was sixty-five degrees F, perfect for shorts and a light jacket.

Question: what should one do when meeting a car while on one of the many one-lane covered bridges in Vermont?

Answer: You back up, quickly, which I had now done several times and without even running off the boards. Vermont has one hundred covered bridges, the highest number per square mile in the U.S. Authenticity of a covered bridge is based on construction, not age. An authentic bridge must be constructed using trusses rather than other methods such as stringers.

The trestle bridge near our farmhouse is one I'd yet to walk across. A sign said it has a three-ton limit, and with all my references to food and restaurants—well, you understand my concern. But I would attempt it before we left this place.

I haven't seen anyone while out walking: no dogs and few sounds other than the babble of the river. Loved the names on signs: Biscuit Hollow Road and, I smiled at this, Fletcher Hill Road. There was surely a message here. My late husband's name was Fletcher.

Something would have to be wrong for someone not to appreciate what a beautiful space we were in, and we should have been enjoying it to the fullest. But Janie was having such a hard time as she was in constant pain. We did get out a bit, rode to town, and looked in several shops. With our usual luck—our serendipities—Janie and I met a wonderful lady in the first shop we entered. Akankha Perkins instantly became our Woodstock angel. Akankha invited us to a Thursday night supper sponsored by Hand in Hand at the Unitarian church. She called the newspaper to say they needed to schedule us for an interview. And she contacted the Thompson Center suggesting we be asked to speak to Center's visitors about our journey.

Since Janie was walking with a cane, a conversation opened about getting some medical attention for her. Through staff at the Thompson Center for Seniors and Community, Janie secured an appointment at the Ottaquechee Health Center in town. X-rays were made, determining that arthritis, not back problems, was the culprit. Medication was prescribed, and cortisone injections ordered for when we arrive in Maine. Janie's physician in Austin arranged for blood work along with the X-rays.

Rest was what Janie needed most. Walking and driving contributed to her discomfort. It was painfully ironic that we were on a yearlong road trip.

The mission of the Thompson Center for Seniors and Community is to be the gathering place for multi-generations, with programs and activities that promote physical, intellectual, and social well-being of the adult community, enhancing dignity, self-worth, and independence of each individual.

Janie and I saw that mission being carried out each time we visited, which was often. The place soon became a haven for us. We were pleased to have been asked to speak to a Tuesday morning gathering, and nervous as we were, we accepted because we had a lot to share.

Our initial church outing was to First Congregational Church of Woodstock at 36 Elm Street. The "gathered church," founded around 1773, was based on a concept of believers who came together wherever they could, in homes or a barn, for worship and fellowship, without ties to any formal religious group. The church of colonial Woodstock organized with only nineteen members and voted to accept the Congregational plan as "the most agreeable to the Word of God."

Today, Pastor Norman Koop, son of the former surgeon general of the United States, Dr. C. Everett Koop, now led the "gathered church."

During our initial visit, Pastor Koop encouraged his congregation to stand and quote Bible verses learned in Sunday school and to share the meaning of each verse. Koop gave special recognition to first-graders and high school seniors as they were presented Bibles; he acknowledged Sunday school teachers; and the minister of youth who was leaving to attend seminary in Florida. Best of all was the message from Koop, whom we met later during fellowship.

Woodstock's history is fascinating. In October 1768, a hardy soul named James Sanderson built a cabin on Blake Hill near today's Woodstock. He moved his wife and baby into the dwelling in December of the same year. Known to be a great reader, Sanderson apparently was prepared to withstand a long winter's isolation. In the spring another young man arrived and soon three more healthy young men with families had settled into the area. Major Joab Hoisington built a gristmill in 1776, and later added a sawmill on the Ottaquechee River, south branch. Settlement of the area was slowed by the Revolutionary War, but resumed once the war ended. Waterfalls on the river provided waterpower for mills and factories, and manufacturing became a force in growth. A railroad between Woodstock and White River Junction brought tourists and hauled freight.

The spiritual and intellectual soul of Woodstock was influenced early on by two men: George Perkins Marsh and his father, Charles, who was Woodstock's first attorney and a leading citizen. Charles Marsh donated land in Woodstock on which a meetinghouse was built. He had contacted every citizen of the village, telling them he would not live in a town without a place of public worship. The frame of that first church was raised on Independence Day 1806 (it remains today).

The younger Marsh, George Perkins, became known as America's first conservationist. As an adult, George Perkins Marsh wrote that he first took notice of the Vermont landscape when just a boy, sitting on a little stool between his father's legs, as

Charles Marsh drove his two-wheeled chaise. Mr. Marsh pointed out trees to his son, and told him how to recognize each one. The lesson that stuck with little George occurred when his father reined in his horse at the top of a steep hill and pointed out how the water below flowed in three directions. That is a "watershed," his father said. George never forgot the word.

Graduated from Phillips Exeter Academy and Dartmouth College, George was elected to the House of Representatives in 1839. He moved to Washington, D.C., but on trips home became disturbed by changes in the Vermont landscape. He knew that the clearing of forests caused those changes. Marsh warned farmers, in an 1847 speech, of their peril and described forest management already in use in Europe. Soon after, he published *Man and Nature.* The book marked the onset of serious study of how people live, and how their lives affect the landscape they inhabit. Marsh urged farmers and citizens alike to recognize that human actions can have consequences both negative and unintended against the environment on which they depend.

The book George Marsh wrote influenced another Woodstock native, Frederick Billings. In 1883, Mr. Billings was out west building the end of his Northern Pacific Railroad when he read *Man and Nature.*

Billings returned to Woodstock and purchased the old Charles Marsh homestead. He also bought up failing farms and re-forested surrounding hillsides near Woodstock with Norway spruce, Scots pine, European larch, and species native to Vermont.

Billings was a highly principled man of deep Christian convictions. He erected Billings Chapel in Woodstock as a memorial to his parents. His wife, Julia, a strong supporter of one of America's best-known evangelists of the day, Dwight L. Moody, invited Moody to preach revival services at the new chapel.

Moody's history is intriguing, too. He was born into such poor circumstances, his mother sent him away to work for his room and board. Described as a poor reader even as an adult, and of a dark spirit, Moody nevertheless persevered to establish in Boston a Sunday school. Within one year, he had six hundred and fifty students and sixty volunteer teachers. Moody's school received so much attention it was visited by President Lincoln in 1860. In his teachings, Moody promoted use of *The Wordless Book*, an aid to instructing the illiterate. The book is still in use around the globe. Moody preached revival services in Woodstock in 1886 and again in 1887.

In 1934, Laurence Spelman Rockefeller married Mary Billings French, the granddaughter of Julia and Frederick Billings, at the Woodstock church. It was the beginning of the Rockefellers long and affectionate commitment to the town.

The legacy of the Marsh, Billings, and Rockefeller families blessed the fellowship of the First Congregational Church for many years. In 1991 at a town meeting, Mary French Rockefeller said a simple prayer, "Thank you, Lord, for the land and our heritage. We pray for guidance on how best to preserve it for future generations, knowing that trust in Thee and Thy love will be our strength."

The true work of the gathered church is told in the lives and testimonies of the more than two thousand persons who have been members since its founding in 1781.

I know I am giving this church a lot of attention, but the history was so exciting to me, I must share two more things.

E. Howard & Company of Boston originally manufactured luxury watches, but its finely made tower clocks, ubiquitous in New England, soon gave it a worldwide reputation. The tower clock was a matter of civic pride in colonial towns of the 1870s, and Woodstock was no exception. The tower clock of the First Congregational Church was installed in 1889 and is still rung on the hour and half hour each day. Estimates indicate that thousands of Howards remain in operation and have yet to be converted to electricity.

Understanding how the clock works is difficult for my unmechanical mind, but I was compelled to try. The tower clock is built in four sections. The driving mechanism is a weight or spring that provides power to run the clock. The transmitting mechanism (a series of cogged wheels) distributes power to the indicating mechanism—the actual hands of the clock face—at a pace set by the controlling mechanism, where the pendulum keeps time. Each section has a job to do.

The power of the driving mechanism comes from use of a windlass, weight on a pulley rope that wraps around a drum or axle and connects a ratchet and click. The weight is wound with a key. That power is transmitted by the series of cogged wheels working on one another—the time train—to the hands of the clock face, allowing the clock to run just so fast and no faster. It distributes the once-an-hour rotation to four other axles, one for each clock dial, and carries the minute hand for that dial.

Winding the windlass is the clock custodian's twice weekly duty, and one unaccustomed would consider it an aerobic workout. A website describing the Howard clock says the pendulum swings forty times a minute, not the sixty you would expect. Still, that is 57,600 swings in a twenty-four-hour period. A windlass also operates the bell mechanism of the clock. A hammer strikes the bell once for the number of every hour, plus one strike on the half hour. A calculation by a researcher once tallied the total at one hundred and eighty strikes in a twenty-four-hour period. Multiply that times the days of a year and be prepared to be impressed by the endurance and quality of these beautiful clocks.

The second thing I wanted to bring to your attention is the Paul Revere bell. Woodstock holds the distinction of being the only town with five bells manufactured in the foundry established by Paul Revere, the Revolutionary War patriot. The oldest of the five bells, and the only one cast in Revere's lifetime, is displayed on the south porch of the First Congregational Church. A committee of three journeyed from Woodstock to Boston in 1818 to purchase this bell at a price of forty-five cents per pound from Paul Revere and Sons. The bell weighed 711 pounds, making the purchase price $319.95. I don't know how long the trip home by horse and wagon would have been, or how a 711-pound bell was lifted up into the bell tower.

Paul Revere is noted in history books for his famous midnight ride to warn the Lexington Minute Men of imminent British invasion. But Revere was also an accomplished artisan and businessman. He'd apprenticed under his father, a goldsmith, and by the 1760s the young Revere was a master goldsmith. Upon his father's death, Paul took over the Revere foundry in the north end of Boston to support his mother and siblings. After the Revolution he went to work making iron and brass items such as stoves, hearths, anvils, and cannons. In 1792, he agreed to recast the cracked bell from what is now known as the Old North Church in Boston. Revere and Sons foundry cast a total of 298 bells between 1792 and 1828.

A crack was discovered in the Revere bell at First Congregational Church in 1974, after 156 years of use. Experts confirmed that it could not be repaired. A new bell was purchased from the Verdin Company and installed in 1976. It was tuned to the key of C as was the original, and cast bearing the words "Praise Ye the Lord ..." from Psalm 150. The faithful old Revere bell was then retired and can be viewed on the south entry to the church.

Three of Woodstock's five Revere bells still ring, one from the Masonic Temple (formerly the Christian church), one from Saint James Episcopal Church, and one from North Universalist Chapel. The fifth Revere bell rests on a pedestal behind Woodstock Inn near the inn's putting green.

The Marsh-Billings-Rockefeller Mansion—known locally as simply "the mansion"—was built in 1805 as a farmhouse. It was the boyhood home of George Perkins Marsh (previously mentioned as one of America's first conservationists and author of *Man and Nature*).

Frederick Billings purchased the house and the surrounding five hundred and fifty acres to begin his program of forest restoration. He developed a breed of prize-winning Jersey cattle on his two-hundred-acre dairy farm. Billings hired well-known architect Robert Morris Copeland to design formal gardens to surround the mansion.

The house was updated in 1885 with Queen Anne features, rounded arches centered with keystones, dentil moldings, oak woodwork, and oak flooring. It is tastefully furnished with nineteenth-century Victorian pieces, mixed with the Rockefeller's furnishings of the 1960s. The Billings were avid collectors of art, and their particular interest in American artists and American landscape paintings resulted in one of the largest private collections of Hudson River School paintings in the United States.

Mary French Rockefeller inherited the mansion in 1954. After forty years she and her husband, Laurence, turned it over to the National Park Service. Since 1983, the Woodstock Foundation has run the property as an operating farm and living museum of Vermont's rural past.

I'd never had a tour or lecture by a park ranger that wasn't top-notch and the tour of the mansion was no exception. Janie and I missed the garden and farm tour because she was unable to walk that distance, but we nonetheless took away a good idea of what life was like in the time of the home's heyday.

In Janie's defense, she always carried a book and suggested I go on any side venture I wanted to while she sat and read and waited for my return.

In 1892, the Rockefellers opened the Woodstock Inn. The inn became a center point for the town, and the Rockefellers' impact on the overall character of Woodstock was still obvious. Woodstock has been the recipient of many awards from publications such as *National Geographic*. In 2011 *Ladies Home Journal* named Woodstock "prettiest town in America."

Woodstock Village is an incorporated area of the town of Woodstock and in 1973 was listed on the National Register of Historic Places.

The district is 2,270 acres encompassing ninety-five buildings and sites that contribute historical significance to the area. The village green is used as a weekly farmer's market in summer and autumn. It's also a place for fairs, flea markets, plays, and concerts, and we found it to be a beautiful space to relax and take in the quaint and historical atmosphere. The green is bordered by homes of late Georgian, Federal, and Greek Revival style. The unusual character of this place enhances its picture-postcard look.

I knew I would age on this trip! It was June 10, my seventy-eighth birthday. I wished myself a "happy birthday" and treated myself to a high-cholesterol breakfast of bacon, sausage, toast, and juice. Janie wished me a happy birthday, and more greetings came in via e-mails and phone calls. It was only 8:00 a.m. and I was already having a blessed day.

Even in the short time we had been in Woodstock Janie and I had found many opportunities (suggested by our angel, Akankha) to become involved in the Woodstock community. One of those opportunities was through Hand in Hand, the creation of Lauren Oldenburg, a native of the village.

Lauren returned to Woodstock after many years in California. Her idea was to provide a meeting place where everyone could gather, have a meal, and enjoy fellowship regardless of circumstance—whether down-and-out or the richest person in town. That became the basis of Hand in Hand. Lauren encourages participation by all to promote a healthy, viable, thriving community through collaboration of individual voice and action.

Hand in Hand provides direct service or referrals for individual clients and community service agencies. It operates without prejudice regarding race, ethnic origin, physical or mental disability, age, gender, or sexual orientation.

Volunteers are the backbone of Hand in Hand. They collect and sort and distribute donated items; prepare and serve food;

speak about the organization to others; and serve on a board of directors or on committees to handle the many projects.

On our first visit to a Thursday evening event at Hand in Hand, the electricity was off. We learned it had been off for hours, but tables were lit with candles and the planned five-course meal was served.

Dinners are themed. For each meeting a poem is written; a guitarist and vocalist provide dinner music; and everyone is welcomed. Lauren, the instigator, has been doing this for seven years. She gathers food from grocers and restaurants that donate to the cause, and she plans a menu from what is donated. Her dedication and that of the volunteers who come every week amazes us. Janie and I volunteered to be a part of next Thursday's event.

Janie and I usually had trouble recalling how we'd gotten to such a point, but this was one of those times when we weren't speaking to one another. We're both prone to venting our frustrations, which can lead to one or the other of us stalking off to "do our own thing." This particular Sunday, I'd been to church, made lunch, laid in the sun for a short time, and taken a doze. I later got in the car and drove to town, where I walked and window-shopped. Nothing was open, but I got a sense of what each shop offered and how pleasant and quaint the town appeared—with flowers blooming everywhere and the river running through. As I strolled through the town, I was grateful for the ideal weather, a temperate seventy degrees, with a cool breeze, and sunny.

Janie and I had passed the hamlet of Taftsville in our comings and goings, and I decided to ride over and look around. Many small towns have interesting beginnings and Taftsville is no exception. Daniel Taft settled there in 1796. Within nine years he had built a home, dammed the river, and erected a sawmill and an ironworking shop that produced scythes and axes. Power for the mill and shop was drawn from the river.

Three of Daniel's sons joined his enterprise. They added a machine shop, foundry, and construction business. The Tafts built many of the beautiful brick-and-frame houses that line main street today. D. Taft and Sons built the Taftsville Country Store in 1840 to provide hardware, feed, and foodstuffs for the community.

The village post office is inside the Country Store. In 1875, it was moved, but it returned to the store in 1933. This landmark store on the National Registry of Historic Places still serves the community as a grocery, information and message center, lost pet retrieval service, billboard for local events, and gossip-central. Some of Vermont's unique commodities are sold there: jams, jellies, pancake mixes, fruit butters, coffees, fiddleheads, dilly beans, mustards, maple candy, salad dressings, sauces (hot and barbecue), dipping oils, and more.

A sign in the store reads: "If it's not made in Vermont, we don't carry it." The store is best known for its selection of Vermont cheeses, more than forty different cheeses including, but not limited to cheddar (from mild to extra sharp), flavored cheddar, Colby, Parmesan, gruyère, bleu, brie, Camembert, chèvre, fontina, and gouda. These cheeses are made from goat, cow, and sheep milk. Vermont's old standby cheese is Grafton Four Star, a four-year-old extra, extra sharp cheddar.

The Tafts have done business for years with the Kendall family, who make maple syrup. Vintage wines and a fine selection of cigars are also offered by the store. Lucky for me; the store was open seven days a week, making a Sunday afternoon a good time to visit. I even managed to speak with the proprietor, and enjoyed tasting many samples.

The Taftsville Covered Bridge was constructed in 1836 by Solomon Emmons to link Taftsville to communities and farms to the north and east. It is one of the longest covered bridges in Vermont, the oldest in Windsor County, fourth-oldest in the state, and was built with lumber cut at the Taft sawmill.

We were becoming more and more attached to this town, and, as always, it's the people who made the difference. Our angel, Akankha Perkins, asked us to meet her at the Farmer's Market near our house. We bought sandwiches for lunch and headed to Bridgewater where Akankha's friend Louise Denham lives. Louise is from Texas and Akankha thought Janie would enjoy the connection.

I know Louise wouldn't mind my telling her age (she's ninety-five) as she is a beautiful Southern belle—a gracious hostess with a quick mind and a gentle spirit. Louise lives in the home of her daughter Harriet (and Harriet's husband), a teacher and drama coach at a local high school. Harriet is on the art scene in a teaching capacity, and has been involved in many award-winning productions. Before leaving, Janie and I agreed to go with Louise to visit relatives who own a bed and breakfast in Windsor.

The 31st Annual Quechee Hot Air Balloon, Crafts, and Music Festival began Friday June 17 and ran for three days. We were eager to see the Balloon Glow—an event featuring balloons that are inflated and lighted, but tethered. Although scheduled for Friday night, it was postponed due to rain.

Quechee is very much like Woodstock with its interesting shops, historical homes and buildings, but smaller. On Saturday, knowing we had all afternoon to see the balloons, we stopped at the Simon Pearce glassblowing and pottery workshop. Pearce opened his first glassblowing workshop in 1971 in Kilkenny, Ireland. His design aesthetic and skills had evolved during time spent at Shanagarry Pottery, which was owned by his parents. He gained glassblowing experience while working in European glass houses, traveling, and studying at the Royal College of Arts in London. Simon wanted to create beautifully designed products—from premium quality materials, using time-honored techniques—intended for a lifetime of everyday use.

To gain independence from European business constraints and high energy costs, Simon moved his operation to Quechee, Vermont in 1981. He bought and restored an historic woolen mill on the Ottaquechee River, which would provide hydroelectric power for his glass furnaces and electricity for the entire facility.

Simon uses glass of a lead-free mixture of silica, lime, potash, and barium that comes in pellet form. The raw glass pellets are fed into the glass furnace where they are heated to approximately 2,400° degrees F. The heated end of a blowing pipe is placed into the molten glass. By turning the pipe, a glob of glass gathers, and interestingly, that glob is called a gather.

The glassblower brings the gather to his workbench where it is shaped, using wooden tools called blocks. Once the glass is symmetrically shaped, the glassblower blows down the pipe and forces an air bubble into the glass. When the piece is formed on the pipe, a second pipe with a small amount of glass—called a pontil iron—is attached to the bottom of the first piece. Now the whole piece is severed from the original blowpipe, and reheated in an oven called the glory hole. The rim of the piece is finished by hand.

When the piece is finished it is placed in a special oven called a lehr, which is set at 950 degrees F. The glass must be cooled very slowly to avoid cracking and to relieve any stress in the finished object. This process is called annealing, and takes six to eight hours. Each newly made piece is inspected and graded. If a structural flaw is found, the work is discarded.

The Simon Pearce complex includes workshop facilities and viewing rooms, retail store, and the mill restaurant, Glassblower Café. Opened in 1983, the café quickly gained public recognition and is now one of Vermont's most popular fine dining establishments. One feature of the restaurant is its award-winning wine list. The café is also known for using only the best ingredients, and preparing them carefully but simply. Janie and I loved this place.

We were seated by a window overlooking the waterfall and covered bridge. Original handmade dishes and impeccable service were equal to any place we'd ever been. A special part of the experience was meeting Deanna Heon, manager of the café. Naturally our conversation turned to our journey. Deanna was fascinated by what we were doing and recounted a recent two-week backpacking trip she'd made, by herself, in Italy. Deanna has traveled extensively in the U.S. and abroad. We talked and had our picture made with her. She is a beautiful girl. Janie and I invited her to the Thompson Center for our talk on Tuesday. Dessert, compliments of Deanna, was a delicious blackberry compote. We were reluctant to leave, but after watching demonstrations of glassblowing and looking at everything in the retail shop, we were ready to see the balloons.

My husband, Fletcher, and I visited Taos, New Mexico, once and were outside Angel Fire on our way home when we came across a sky full of hot air balloons in flight. Janie has also lived in Plano, Texas, which holds annual balloon festivals complete with balloon races and competitions. Balloons also occasionally flew right over Janie's apartment building. She and Mother once joined the chase as a balloon was landing. Janie said the huge, bright pink balloon was the head of a cat with protruding ears. She and Mother visited with the balloon owner. On any given day during balloon season, Janie said, balloons are visible all over the sky. But neither of us had ever seen a Balloon Glow.

Hundreds of people had gathered to watch what looked to be about twenty-five balloons. A team of workers is required for each balloon and a crew of chasers who follow the balloon and pick up its passengers and the balloon after its descent. The colors and designs on the balloons were beautiful and seemed more vibrant as they ascended against the backdrop of the clear blue sky. Weather conditions must be just right for safe flight.

Janie and I wanted to know how the balloon could lift off the ground, be safely maneuvered, and brought down again in the right location. I have since learned hot air balloons are an ingenious application of basic scientific principles. Hot air is lighter than cool air, and warmer air rises in cooler air. A balloon has three main parts: the envelope, the actual fabric body of the balloon which holds the air; the burner, the unit that heats the air and propels it up inside the envelope; and the basket, where pilot and passengers stand. The envelope has to be large because it takes such a large amount of heated air to lift it off the ground: To lift a thousand pounds of weight, 65,000 cubic feet of heated air is required. To keep the balloon in the air and rising, hot air must be propelled upward into the envelope by use of the burner.

Propane gas is used to heat the burner. The pilot fires the burner at regular intervals throughout the flight to ensure the balloon is stable. Hot air will not escape through the hole at the bottom of the envelope because, firstly, hot air rises, and secondly, buoyancy keeps it moving up. Opening the propane valve, to allow more flow to the burner, controls upward movement of the balloon. In turn the burner fires the flame up into the envelope.

The more the valve is opened, the bigger the flame, the faster the balloon rises. To descend, a parachute valve at the top of the envelope is used. A long cord running down through the middle of the envelope to the basket controls the valve. The pilot pulls on the cord, letting hot air escape and decreasing the inner air temperature of the balloon, slowing ascent. To move horizontally, the pilot maneuvers by changing the vertical position of the balloon. The wind blows in different directions at different altitudes, and the pilot ascends or descends to an appropriate level, riding with the wind, until he is in the desired position.

All of this information wasn't necessary to enjoy the balloons, but I enjoyed learning it. Janie said we are living proof that "travel broadens the mind." Though in our case, it was also broadening something else due to all the delicious food we'd consumed. And there was the problem of remembering all we'd learned.

A few more words on balloons. The first manned hot air balloon, designed by the Montgolfier brothers, ascended from the

Bois de Boulogne in Paris on November 21, 1783. In America, Jean-Pierre Blanchard made a flight January 10, 1793. His hydrogen-filled balloon lifted off from a prison yard in Philadelphia. I don't know the reason. The flight reached 5,800 feet and landed in Gloucester County, New Jersey. President George Washington was among the guests observing the takeoff.

The first military use of a balloon in Europe took place during the French Revolution, when the French used a tethered hydrogen balloon to observe movements of the Austrians in 1794. Balloons were used in America during the Civil War and during World War II in England.

Now, we're through with balloons. I promise.

Sharing with the group at Thompson Center meant that Janie and I each spoke about our adventure up to this point. We were pleased that the talk was well attended and many questions were asked at the end. Our neighbor, Barbara West, was there, and Deanna Heon from Simon Pearce's Glassblower Café. Audrey Richardson from the *Vermont Standard* called for an interview and came by to shoot our photograph for the paper.

So much happened at the Thompson Center, we could go on forever; dinner and a movie—*The King's Speech*—was an event we thoroughly enjoyed. The center even provided popcorn and soft drinks. All we had to do was sign up a couple of days in advance. Great fun.

Another special event was the celebration on Saturday, June 25th of the Center's twentieth anniversary of its founding. Although it had been raining, weather did not hamper the spirit of festivities. Hamburgers, hot dogs, watermelon, and desserts were served. A trio of musicians played bluegrass music. Later, a tour of the center was given, annd ice cream and cupcakes were offered. One of the guests was Robert Hagar, a former analyst and correspondent for *NBC News*.

Hagar started his career in radio before moving over to television and his stint in 1969 covering the Vietnam War. For thirty-five more years he was the face of NBC on the nightly news. Hagar is a delightful man, personable, handsome, charming, and we were pleased to meet and talk with him.

It was amazing how fast the pace picked up when we were getting to the end of our stay in a place. Our list would grow longer rather than shorter. In this instance, we didn't want to miss the opportunity to be with Louise Denham again on our planned trip to Windsor and the Snapdragon Inn owned by her relatives.

The Snapdragon Inn at 26 Main Street in Windsor was first known as the Skinner House, owned by John P. Skinner circa 1815. Skinner owned a stage line, headquartered in Windsor, that ran along the Connecticut River. Sometime in the 1820s William Maxwell Evarts purchased the property, which began a two-hundred-year period of ownership by the Evarts family line. Evarts was president of the Association of the Bar of the City of New York and chief counsel to President Andrew Johnson. Evarts' daughter and heir, Elizabeth Evarts, married Edward Perkins.

Their son, William Maxwell Perkins, became the iconic editor to famed authors Ernest Hemingway, Thomas Wolfe, F. Scott Fitzgerald, and Marjorie Kinnan Rawlings. A Perkins heir sold the inn to Perry and Jill Seale, and they in turn sold to Louise Denham's relatives, the current owners.

The family has renovated the old house to a nine-bedroom bed and breakfast with a living room, a couple of dining rooms, a library, and beautiful grounds—all right in the middle of the lovely and quaint town of Windsor.

We all took lunch at Windsor Station Restaurant, once an Amtrak depot with marble floors and outstanding woodwork. The ticket booths were still intact. I don't remember what we ate but I do recall being impressed with the food and tremendous size of the portions.

Being in a time crunch, we left Louise Denham with Sherrill Larsen, one of the owners of the station restaurant, to be delivered back to her home in Bridgewater. Janie and I rushed to our house to meet the reporter from a television station in Rutland, Vermont. Susie Steimle of WCAX was waiting in our driveway. She said she'd just gotten there. Susie conducted all aspects of the interview: staging, camera work, and the actual conversation.

That evening when the interview was aired we were at Thompson Center for dinner and a movie night, but we caught a later broadcast and thought we had done a good job getting our message across.

One of the special old sites in Woodstock is the historic Woodstock Inn. We'd driven by many times but felt we needed to be a little better dressed than our usual shorts. Bill, who has worked there for thirty-eight years, was eager to share his love of the Inn with us. He opened one of the rooms to show us how elegant and contemporary the Inn has grown to be.

A booklet titled "The Story of the Woodstock Inn" gives a bit of early history. To quote: "The French and Indian War was being resolved in Great Britain's favor and prospects for peace and settlement looked promising for the upper Connecticut River Valley. To encourage this, in 1761, King George III granted sixty town charters in this region to Governor Benning Wentworth of New Hampshire. One charter was for Woodstock."

An Ensign Richardson arrived that year, hoping to homestead, but found an impenetrable tangle of evergreen swamp. (Sounds like lower Florida or Louisiana.) No roads had been cut, and the only open land was a small abandoned Indian campsite located north of what the Iroquois called Wtatock Quitchey; now called the Ottaquechee River. Richardson immediately took leave from the hostile place to a more favorable location.

In 1765, a Harvard man, Timothy Knox, settled in Woodstock near what is now the Health and Fitness Center. As the story about Knox goes, he put himself in exile while suffering disappointment over a love affair. Knox was pushing for the wilderness of the Northwest. He followed the Connecticut River upstream, arriving at Quechee Valley, and stopped. The nearest settlements were Hartland and Hartford. We earlier wrote about James Sanderson who built a cabin in 1768. Knox was the only resident of Woodstock for three years prior to Sanderson's arrival.

A Captain Israel Richardson, in 1791, gave Woodstock land for a courthouse on the Green, the town's central square. He built a house for lawyers and other employees of the court two years later. The house was known as Richardson's Tavern and was on the site now occupied by the Woodstock Inn.

Today's Inn has 142 recently renovated rooms, nineteen of which have wood-burning fireplaces. Each room reflects Vermont's historic respect for nature and authenticity, with wood beam bed frames, neutral décor, and organic bath products. And added to this are features such as deluxe marble bathrooms, exquisite linens, warm blankets, and every modern convenience to make it a one-of-a-kind resort.

Regional recipes using locally grown food are the specialty of the four-diamond culinary team at the Inn. According to its website, the inn blends traditional style with sophisticated tastes, creating a full menu selection of savory side dishes, artisan breads, and decadent desserts. We thought to experience the food at the Inn's Red Rooster restaurant, but left knowing it was a little out of our price range. Enjoying the elegance and old-world charm of such a place would have been lovely.

Charles Kuralt mentioned many small towns in his book, *America*, and we wanted to visit them, if possible. One of those towns is Barnard, Vermont, in Windsor County. A couple of notable people were charmed by this small place, namely Sinclair Lewis, Nobel prize-winning novelist, short story writer, and playwright, and Carl Zuckmayer, German writer and playwright. The Barnard General Store is a landmark, and we were told by everyone to visit and have breakfast there. The store's slogan is, "The most food you'll ever eat on a paper plate." True! Everything was homemade and delicious. We were served so many pancakes that a separate paper plate was required.

Passing through the village of Strafford, we spied beautiful old houses and buildings and saw a couple of women working with horses at Huntington Farms. I know I have mentioned my husband Fletcher's love of horses and his horsemanship, but if I haven't, here's a day that Janie and I enjoyed and the reference to

Fletcher couldn't be helped as I am sure he was watching over and laughing with us all day.

At Huntington Farms we met the horse trainer, Deb, and a groom, Molly. By invitation we walked through the barns and were told that at least thirty foals were there. The colts were barely able to stand. Some of the mothers were friendly, and some weren't. Many other horses were in training and several college students worked at the farm as grooms. It all brought to mind the times when our children rode horses and participated in equestrian events.

Our reason for being in this neck of the woods was to locate the grave marker of a most famous horse, the Justin Morgan horse of Chelsea, Vermont. Kuralt had mentioned the horse in his book. Otherwise we wouldn't have known, nor would we have thought to ride around all day on dirt and gravel roads, up and down hills and over the river and through the woods to shoot a photo of the grave marker for the Morgan.

A sign in the town of Chelsea makes reference to the grave but offers no directions to find it. We turned off the main road, tried several different road offshoots, and were about to give up when—thank goodness—we saw a UPS truck. The driver said to follow him. He was going "almost there."

We reached the main road again but never saw the UPS truck. We took a left, and apparently he went right. After several miles we went back into town. Janie tried the general store/post office for new directions. The postmistress sent us right back where we'd been. Janie said the post office was most unusual, with pictures and green plants in the front window and a room with a couple of chairs, small table and a lamp, and an open book resting on the table. The room seemed to be the domain of a cat, appropriately named Zip Code. The actual post office was at the back of the room.

Having followed our latest directions and with the same results as before, we turned around. This was our third time to pass through town. A man mowing his lawn looked like a good prospect and we stopped to ask for directions again. He sent us back to the place we'd just come from. No doubt people in this small town wondered why two old ladies in a Buick Enclave were riding back and forth through town, now on our fourth trip.

At the main road again, we came to a fork in the road and stopped to consider which way to go, wishing OnStar could handle a request for a horse's grave marker—no street address. A car passed by, almost made his turn, and then apparently noticing our Alabama tag backed up to speak to us.

We talked a bit and learned he was from Huntsville, Alabama, and owned a house one mile from where we sat. He said, "Why don't you stop by our house and meet my wife, Carol?" We did. Imagine her surprise when we pulled into the driveway, got out of the car, and began calling, "Carol! Carol!" She came to the door and invited us in, offering refreshments. Carol was baking pies and they were tempting, but we still hadn't found the grave of the Morgan horse. With new directions, we offered our thanks to Ron and Carol Jurgens—great folks—and set off again. Ron's son lives right by the grave marker. We found it and got the photo we wanted.

Why did we spend our day in this pursuit? Because my husband, Fletcher, had mentioned the Morgan so many times in conversations about horses.

Justin Morgan was a singing schoolmaster in Randolph, Massachusetts, in 1791. He accepted a two-year-old bay colt as payment for a debt owed him. Morgan had the horse, named Figure, for thirty years. During that time the horse became legendary due to his ability to outwork, out run, out trot, and out walk any other horse in the area. Figure fathered countless sons and daughters, testament that he was the greatest breeding stallion of all time.

Popularity of the Morgan, as the breed was called, spread nation wide. Outstanding horses found in every generation added to Figure's lineage. During the Civil War, the 1st Vermont Cavalry was mounted exclusively on Morgans. Of the one thousand horses, only two hundred returned home, having served in seventy-five major conflicts.

The Morgan was reputed to be the best of the cavalry and artillery horses. The breed also earned its keep as a general-purpose frontier horse in hauling freight or passengers, trotting races, pulling doctor's buggies, delivering mail, or drawing the carriages of presidents and financiers.

The Morgan is noted for its small ears set above a broad forehead, large kind eyes, tapered muzzle, and expressive nostrils, an arched neck set on a well-angled shoulder, broad chest, short back, deep compact body, and legs with flat, dense bone. His proud bearing gives the Morgan a distinctive beauty that catches the eye. The stamina and spirit of the Morgan has contributed greatly to the formation of other American breeds: the Standardbred, Quarter Horse, Tennessee Walking Horse, and American Saddle Horse.

Well, we came, we saw, we conquered (so to speak). By the time we got back out to the main roads we were singing John

Photo Album

Lou, left, and Janie unpacked and ready to begin our year of revisiting Charles Kuralt's America

With Kevin Belton at The New Orleans Cooking School

Hack Bartholomew at Café Du Monde in New Orleans

Robert, Lou, Janie, Bob at Palm Court Jaze Café, New Orleans

Key Lime Pie Blue Heaven Restaurant, Key West, Florida

Magnolia Plantation, Charleston, South Carolina

Angel Oak, Charleston

Gedney Howe III,
Charleston, South Carolina

Warren Davis, Our Angel,
Blowing Rock, North Carolina

View from condo balcony in Blowing Rock, North Carolina

Swinging Bridge, Grandfather Mountain, North Carolina

View from Grandfather Mountain, Blowing Rock, North Carolina

Doris and Marshall Edwards in Blowing Rock

Brett, builder Rodger, artist daughter Rachel

Bed-Stuy Neighborhood, New York

Yankee Stadium, New York

Roy and David, Bed-Stuy neighbors in New York

Favorite scene in Woodstock, Vermont

Our house in Woodstock

Queechee Balloon Festival, Queechee, Vermont

Our cottage in Woodstock, Vermont

Mike Hillmann of Ely, Minnesota

Friends Angela Campbell and Gene Domich in Ely, Minnesota

Car and canoe, Ely, Minnesota

Pat Shannon, Twin Bridges, Montana

Landlords Marsha and Don Greenmore Twin Bridges, Montana

Ferry to Ketchikan, Alaska

Ketchikan, Alaska

Landlady Nicole Church and mother-in-law Jane, Ketchikan, Alaska

Local Ketchikan artist/sculptor/musician Dave Rubin

Creek Street Creek, Ketchikan, Alaska

Shirley, Marge, Nancy, Denice visiting Ketchikan

Typical adobe Taos, New Mexico

My Taos casita

Home, November 22, 2011, Chatom, Alabama

Denver's familiar song, *Take Me Home, Country Roads*. This was just another of those "crazy days" we enjoyed, but what a way to meet people and see the countryside.

Before going home, though, we decided to head over to Hanover, New Hampshire, and Dartmouth University. We were so close. It had been raining off and on all day, keeping us in the car rather than getting out to explore. We drove around, getting a good view of the campus, which is located on the Connecticut River and surrounded by the White Mountains—a beautiful, ideal environment for learning.

Dartmouth is a private Ivy League university with a liberal arts college, Geisel School of Medicine, Thayer School of Engineering, and Tuck School of Business. In arts and sciences there are nineteen graduate programs.

Established in 1769 by Congregational minister Eleazar Wheelock, Dartmouth is one of nine colonial colleges founded before the American Revolution and the smallest in the Ivy League. The total student body numbers 6,141 with an undergraduate enrollment of 4,248. Dartmouth alumni, including luminaries such as Daniel Webster, have been famously involved with the college. We thought the campus had the most beautiful scenery of any in the Ivy League.

Janie and I ended the day with a stop at Pizza Chef so we wouldn't have to deal with food when we got home. Breakfast at Bernard Country Store had been so filling that we hadn't been hungry all day. We could also truly say we had seen many of the country roads of Vermont this day, and some in New Hampshire as well. We had indulged ourselves in a grand day of sightseeing and fun, and felt so blessed.

Sunday, June 26, we attended Congregational Church to hear missionary speaker Brian Birdsall. I found it enlightening to hear Brian talk of his work with the Campus Crusade for Christ in Kiev, Russia. Brian's wife, a teacher and administrator at the school for children of Campus Crusade workers in Kiev, was away at school in South Carolina completing several degrees. Brian's daughter, Tory, a sophomore at Rice University in Houston, was spending summer with him in Woodstock, speaking at various churches. Many Dartmouth students attend this Congregational Church; in fact, when Brian was studying at Dartmouth College, he was responsible for leading many students to this church. That relationship continues today. Janie and I invited the two of them over for lunch and were delighted when they agreed.

We haven't said anything lately about household chores, but an invitation to friends at Hand in Hand and at church necessitated a bit of attention in that direction. I was in a spin about food, too. Since our guests were arriving at 10:30 a.m., we decided some breakfast food would be appropriate. Janie made a spinach dip and a fruit tray. I prepared cheese squares, sausage triangles, sand tarts, brownies, and coffee. We also offered nuts, chips, and fruit punch. We had such a good crowd and a good time. Peter Pickett was the only man, but it didn't seem to bother him. He was surrounded by our many female guests: Margarete Pierce, Ruth Beebee, Deanna Heon, Pam Butler, Diana Leskovar, Nancy Peterson, Margaret Thomas, Louise Denham,

Delia Vanek, Deanna Jones, and Peter's wife, Carol Pickett. We were disappointed that Akankha Perkins couldn't come—she was working—and our neighbor, Barbara West, came later.

On our last Thursday in Woodstock we visited Hand in Hand to tell everyone good-bye. Some of the ladies took us to lunch at Long Trail Brewery in Bridgewater on Friday. They had written a poem for us, which brought us to tears. Some of Lauren Oldenburg's steadfast helpers were at the lunch—Pru, Ann, Renett, Madeline, Tyler and Traver, and Pru's granddaughter, Jasmine. Jasmine had crocheted a necklace for Janie and me.

Back at our house we found that the owner, Scott Chisholm had arrived. He and his mom, Sandra, and two sons, Essah and Yessef, were picking up their camper trailer on the way to a Blue Grass Festival in Tunbridge. Essah and Yessef are such handsome boys, and we were delighted to have met them and Sandra.

If we could have, we would have gifted everyone we met in Woodstock. That not being possible, we gave a few thank-you happies to several friends and got ready to say a final good-bye.

June 30, and I was taking my last walk on the lovely country road. Normally I wouldn't see anyone when I was walking, but today I met Nancy Pejouhy, an eighth-grade math teacher who lives on Biscuit Hollow Road. Nancy was interested in our trip, and I gave her our blog address.

This was packing and traveling day. We're doing well with it, but Deanna Jones from the Thompson Center dropped by and made everything so much easier. Janie was especially grateful for the help since quite a few trips on the stairs were required. We insisted Deanna stay for lunch and help us clear leftovers of meat loaf and potato salad. Then we sent her on her way to get some rest on this, her day off.

I knew we would never get over this feeling of sadness upon leaving each place. The people and the environment become dear to us, and again we are reminded of the uniqueness of our journey, living for an entire month in eleven different locations. We are still amazed and thankful and feel blessed to continue enjoying our adventure. No doubt we will relive it for the rest of our lives.

OnStar gave a route to Boothbay Harbor, Maine, our next destination, that seemed to be taking us in the opposite direction. We were traveling due south on the Interstate. Janie called to ask questions, which got us rerouted onto country roads and took a couple of hours longer than anticipated. We arrived safely, but quite weary.

Again, our long-term accommodations would not be available for several days. We would make do at the Flagship Motel in Boothbay until then.

Chapter Seven
Boothbay Harbor, Maine
July 2011

FLETCHER AND I HAD been to Maine five times. On one occasion we just rode up the East Coast, looking with nothing in particular in mind. Outside of Jackson, Maine, we had car trouble and our Volvo was towed into town. The mechanic who worked on the car was also a pilot, which turned out to be quite fortunate for us. He would have to fly to Portland, Maine, for the part and asked Fletcher to fly with him. Fletcher was thrilled, for the flight offered a great view of the area he would have otherwise missed. We stayed in town several days, attended baseball games, and got to know some local people. Once the car was repaired, Fletcher and I drove on to Canada, then made a loop back home.

Our Baptist association in Alabama once made two mission trips to Maine, the men working on building projects while the women led vacation Bible school or prepared food. This would be quite a different stay.

Boothbay Harbor is a lovely town and easy to explore. The streets are lined with shops, restaurants, motels, and houses, but each is unique—no cookie-cutter places. On my first morning I walked downtown in the quiet, shops not yet open, little traffic, and enjoyed the scenery.

Janie and I planned to stop by the Chamber of Commerce today, which is next door to our motel, and get lots of brochures on things to see and do in the area. After that, we'd start with lunch at the Tugboat Inn and Restaurant on the waterfront in the heart of town.

The superstructure of the historic tugboat, *Maine*, is the heart of the Tugboat restaurant, which has been built around the boat. Five white-frame buildings with railed balconies and red roofs comprise the complex of rooms, marina, restaurant, and bar built hard against the bay. The sheltered marina offers slips for long-term docking and transient moorings. At the restaurant Janie ordered the lobster bisque, and after all our outings, she declared it the best bisque ever.

Today we would move into our house at Ocean Point, five miles from Boothbay. But first I walked; I went to the washateria where a young college student from Bulgaria was working for the summer. He was nice, polite, and kept the place spotlessly clean.

At Cottage Connections I picked up the key for our place and returned to the motel to reload the car. A quick stop at Radio Shack for a printer cord, a trip to the grocery store, and we were on our way to the cottage with its red siding and white trim, sitting on the edge of a high bank. The Atlantic Ocean lapped against the shore, which when you're in the house seemed directly below the windows—no bank at all. The panoramic view of the water was not hard to take.

Tom, an employee of Cottage Connections, came by to help unload the car and hook up our electronics. Most of the time we had to unplug the phone, then plug it into the computer in order to use the computer. That meant during computer time, we had no phone service. Cell phones only worked if we walked about a quarter mile from our house to an area referred to as "Three Trees." When someone asked for our cell phone number we chorused, "Three Trees."

The house was old, but everything worked. Our access was from the back and right into the kitchen. Off to the right was a little pantry, which held the refrigerator and cabinet storage; to the left, a full bath. Down several steps was the master bedroom (quite large), with a big closet and bay window that showcased the water. Upstairs again, the great room and dining area were furnished with a beautiful old oak table and chairs, desk, couch, rockers, chaise longue, built-in bookcases, and a fireplace. Lots of windows gave a view of the boat launch and swimming areas.

We were happy to be settled when the day was done, knowing tomorrow was Sunday, a day of rest.

The road by our house circled around the point, running so close to the house at points, I believe you could sit on the porch and touch cars as they passed. Flowers bloomed everywhere:

amidst the rocks leading down to the water, on porches, in pots cascading to the ground, in baskets hanging from trellises. Chairs and tables have been placed in tiny dirt plots between the rocks where the water laps close by, a breeze blowing most of the time.

It was the most picturesque setting imaginable.

We rounded a bend in the road a short distance from our house and there stood the most beautiful stone church. Services were held every Sunday during summer, with different speakers each week.

From 1899, church rituals were held in homes and the "casino," which was actually a community center. In 1917, the Janet M. Wilson Memorial Chapel was dedicated in memory of Lewis Wilson's wife.

For years the Unitarian Association owned the chapel. In 1985, a committed group of Ocean Pointers raised money to purchase the chapel, and established a charitable corporation to hold ownership. The interdenominational character of the chapel has always been maintained.

The first Sunday I attended the church, I kept hearing a drone-like sound, as if one of the organ stops was stuck. I wondered why Danny Beal, the organist who had provided music for the services for years, didn't turn off the organ. But when he moved away from the instrument the sound continued. It was then I realized the sound was a foghorn out on the water. It sounds every minute, without end, forever and ever, we were told.

During the month of July it was our privilege to hear the following ministers: Rev. Charles Carrick, chaplain, Wyoming Seminary of Kingston, Pennsylvania; Rev. Peter Panagore, First Radio Parish Church of America, Ocean Point, Maine; Rev. Wesley A.

Smith, First Baptist Church, Hamilton, New York; and Rev. Jack Fles, Episcopal Church, Dardiner, Maine.

Sunday, July 3, was a special day for at least two reasons. My oldest son, Robby, celebrated his fifty-seventh birthday. You can imagine how old that makes me. I called and congratulated him—the only way to look at a birthday because we know the alternative. I had already sent a card. When our children are okay, we are okay, and a phone call can make the difference when you are far away.

On my walk this morning, I met Joel Patrofsky, a young violinist and singer in a family group called Sky. Joel was at Ocean Point to attend the wedding of a friend. We chatted and had prayer together and went on our way. I later saw him at the church service with all of his friends.

One of our neighbors came over later in the afternoon and invited us to a cookout, which included neighbors in the closest homes nearby. We learned that most of our neighbors have been coming to Boothbay Harbor for much of their lives to stay in homes long owned by their families.

We enjoyed the event and the food and meeting so many good folks from the community: Leslie and Lannie Whitehouse; David and Allison Butterworth; and Dale, Randi, and Elizabeth (I don't recall their last name). But these were our closest neighbors: John, Susan, Julia, and Chris, friends of Randi's family; Mitch and Dawn Weiss who owned the Lobster Dock, which we had frequented several times; and Abby. We were warned that some locals would be shooting fireworks more than one night to celebrate the fourth of July holiday. The fireworks show planned in town was canceled due to fog.

The cover of Charles Kuralt's book, *America*, depicts a beautiful Maine coastline and lighthouse. Standing in our yard at Ocean Point, we could look in the direction of Pemaquid Point, only four miles away by water.

The drive to the point was lovely, traveling about one hour Down East, passing through Boothbay, Edgecomb, and North Edgecomb, east a few miles across the Damariscotta River at Newcastle, down the Damariscotta Peninsula through Bristol, Pemaquid, and New Harbor to the point.

At times like this I sometimes wished for a chauffeur, because you miss a lot when you're driving. Janie would have driven if I'd asked, but we both know I don't like to give up the wheel.

Despite all that, I could see the scenery was spectacular.

Designs caused by years of waves pounding the boulders have been etched into rock formations along the shoreline, leaving the impression the stone has been hand-painted. The sound of the ocean is deafening. We notice there's no seaweed—just beautiful clear blue water as far as the eye can see.

Janie and I inched our way on foot down the rocks to the very location where Kuralt sat for his book cover photo. A couple walked by, the man carrying a camera. We asked him to take our photo and he did. Another serendipity!

Russ Webster is a retired newspaper reporter and photographer, now writing a book on photography and teaching classes on the subject. He and his wife, Joan, had been roaming the country for seven years in their fifth wheel, a recreational vehicle. Their camper was parked not far from our house on Ocean Point. See how the Lord places people in your path.

John Quincy Adams, our sixth president, commissioned the Pemaquid Point Light Station in 1827. Due to use of saltwater in the mortar mix, the lighthouse crumbled and had to be rebuilt in 1835; this time only fresh water was used for the mortar. The original light was lit with candles and an Argand-Lewis parabolic reflector. The beam was visible for two miles. Augustin Fresnel invented a superior method of focusing light in the early 1850s. The original Fresnel lens still serves the Pemaquid Light. It is one of only six Fresnel lenses still in use in Maine.

Fisherman's Museum at Pemaquid was once the lightkeeper's house, built in 1857. Artifacts of lighthouse and maritime history are displayed in the museum, which is owned by the U.S. Coast Guard and licensed by the American Lighthouse Foundation. It has been added to the National Register of Historic Places. Janie and I hope to make the cover for our book in the exact same spot.

Meanwhile there were happenings at home. One of my daughters, Kay, telephoned to tell me of the death of a friend. Edith Mae Plemmons Wilcox died July 5. I wrote her family, "I can't imagine our worlds without Ms. Edith, a contributor and supporter of everything good about Chatom and surrounding areas." Janie also received an e-mail informing her of the passing of one of her friends since middle school, Carol Smyer Jones from Fairhope, Alabama. Their friendship had held up all those many years.

Everywhere we looked in Maine, the scenery took our breath away—flowers and more flowers made riding along the highway going into town a treat to the eyes. We checked on some things (like how to get our mail), looked at houses to rent (a matter of curiosity), and landed at Lobster Dock for lunch. Remember we'd met the owner, Mitch, at the neighborhood cookout.

Lobster Dock, as its name implies, is right on the water. There are several levels of tables and booths for seating, but you order at a counter. Mitch had been featured in a *Throwdown with Bobby Flay* on the Food Network Channel in a show on preparation of lobster rolls. I don't think Mitch won the contest, but his lobster rolls and everything else we ordered were wonderful.

Janie and I were now anticipating the arrival of our sister, Shirley, and her partner, Marge. They'd be here by the fourteenth, and we'd purchased tickets for the play, *Nunsense*, on Thursday evening and the Carousel Dinner Theater for Friday night.

Janie and I had had another big set-to. Each of us had grown weary of her constant pain and the inability to do anything about it. We had gotten referrals to doctors from our neighbors, but being tourists, it was all but impossible to get something set up as far as injections or pain pills. Unable to withstand more than a few minutes of any activity, Janie was taking Tylenol, but it isn't effective against the level of pain she was experiencing, which continued to get worse. Time resting in bed with a heating pad brought some relief. Having Shirley and Marge here would, we hope, lessen the tension somewhat, giving each of us time with other people.

Janie and I spoke to the Rev. Peter Panagore as we left church on Sunday. He asked about our visit to the point and when I mentioned Kuralt, the reverend said, "You have to meet Robert Mitchell." At the time I had no idea who Mitchell was, but was thrilled to learn he had created the cover photo for Kuralt's book. Rev. Panagore gave us Mitchell's phone number, and we called immediately. His daughter answered and said he would surely want to call and meet us. He did, and we set up a time to meet at our home. Oh my goodness! We were excited. We couldn't stop thinking and planning for his visit.

Life on the coast of Maine is all about the water. In his book, Charles Kuralt mentioned Herb and Doris Smith and a sail Kuralt took on their sixty-five-foot schooner *Eastwind*. An ad described the two-hour voyage aboard Boothbay Harbor's largest charter schooner as "giving you time to relax, see the coastline, lighthouses, working lobstermen, wildlife, and remote islands accessible only by boat." We called and made reservations for an evening sail.

Herb and Doris Smith have built five schooners named *Appledore*. The name was chosen by Herb as a tribute to his wife, Doris. He first saw her when, as a teenager, he sailed by Appledore Island and noticed her standing in the doorway of her home. She waved. Doris and Herb have sailed around the world twice with their three children on schooners they built by hand. *Eastwind* is a sister ship to the *Appledores*. The Smiths wrote two books about their world voyages: *Sailing Three Oceans* and *Dreams of Natural Places*.

The weather was perfect for our evening sail. Herb and Doris worked together, naming the islands, pointing out lighthouses, and sharing stories of their life at sea. Artha Harriman, a musician who lives in California, was on the boat with us and serenaded with his harmonica. Artha writes music for movies. He mentioned his latest one, but my note-taking fails me as to the name.

At one point, Herb declared, "Next stop, Portugal." Our response, "Sail on!" At that moment no one cared if we ever turned back. The Smiths were entertaining, down to earth, and so happy with their life. Another round-the-world sail is in their future. Herb said he feels the restlessness starting.

Charles Kuralt always stayed at Brown's Wharf Inn of Boothbay Harbor. We had called and made an appointment to interview the owners, Ken and Joan Brown. The Inn was Kuralt's favored destination, someone said, because of habit, affection, and familiarity. Kuralt always said he stayed there for fear of what Ken Brown would say if he tried to go elsewhere. In talking to Ken and Doris, we realized again that Kuralt was a people person, kind and considerate, endlessly curious about people and the things they loved. When asked if Kuralt had a particular room at the Inn, the Browns agreed he had probably stayed in every room.

The gigantic statue of The Old Lobster Fisherman wearing his bright yellow sou'wester makes missing Brown's Wharf Inn highly unlikely. Flower boxes with bright red blooms lined the balconies of the weathered gray two-story building. A private deck for relaxation allows a panoramic view of the harbor. Brown's restaurant has been around for more than fifty years, serving lobster and other seafood fresh from local waters. Guests can fish from the dock and tie up their boats at the private marina.

We hoped to return for a meal and more time with the Browns. That didn't work out, but we left with another glimpse into the life of Kuralt and what he personally meant to people.

Finally, it was Tuesday, and Robert Mitchell was coming. Janie and I had prepared goodies and even dusted and vacuumed a little downstairs.

I must say that Robert Mitchell proved to be one of the most interesting and delightful persons we had met on our trip, and you know that is saying something special. He is a handsome man, and we felt as if we had known him forever.

Mitchell brought us a calendar featuring his work, as well as notecards and postcards. As a child, Robert Mitchell was fascinated by the street photography of Henri Cartier-Bresson published in *Life* and *Look* magazines. Cartier-Bresson's unique style of photojournalism was coined "the decisive moment." Mitchell's photography is different from Bresson's, yet also extraordinary.

Our time with Robert Mitchell passed too quickly, and we did not get a picture of him because we hoped to meet again with him and his family during this stay. Regretfully, that did not happen, but he generously gave us some very helpful ideas about writing our book. We did ask Robert if he would photograph us at Pemaquid Point for our cover photo.

Never bashful, we didn't mind asking, and were anxious for

his response. Wouldn't it be amazing? At the very least, we hoped to see Robert Mitchell again one day.

As always, our neighbors were helpful and supportive of the quest Janie and I were making. David Butterworth, whom we met at the cookout, brought a card belonging to a reporter from a local newspaper, and we made the call to set up an interview for next week.

Shirley and Marge had arrived, having flown in to Portland, Maine, and rented a car for the drive to Boothbay Harbor. They settled in, and after a quick snack we prepared to attend the musical comedy, *Nunsense*, at Boothbay Playhouse on Wiscasset Road.

The playhouse got its start on the old Jasper Wyman farm on Route 27, which was purchased in 1937 by H. Osgood Lacount and his son, Sherwood Keith, from Somerville, Massachusetts. The Lacounts began construction of the theater in April of that year and opened in July with the Eugene O'Neill play *Ah, Wilderness*. Although begun as a summer theater, the playhouse soon gained a reputation as one of the finest in New England. The Lacounts built seats for three hundred and theatrical features unusual for the time, such as fly space, a pin rail, an elaborate trapdoor section in the stage, and large doors at the rear that could be rolled back allowing the outdoors to become part of the scenery.

Many young actors spent a summer at the playhouse before launching careers on stage, in television, and in film. Two notables are Christopher Reeve of Superman fame and Tom Hulse who starred as Mozart in the film *Amadeus*. Maeve McGuire went on to a long career in television soap operas. Polly Holliday from Jasper, Alabama, started at the playhouse, then caught the imagination of the public with her saucy portrayal of a waitress named Flo in the 1970s sitcom *Alice*. Holliday has since appeared in countless movies, television shows, and on the Broadway stage.

In 2005 the playhouse underwent a change of ownership, to Dean and Susan Domeyer. Renovations began, adding a permanent stage with wing space on both sides of the stage, tiered seating, and a new green room and dressing rooms.

This was my second time to see the musical *Nunsense*. Both productions and the cast rivaled anything on Broadway. Janie had first seen it in Birmingham performed by a local non-professional group as good as Broadway, she said. Dan Goggin, who wrote the music and lyrics of *Nunsense*, arrived in New York City as a young singer. He'd made his debut in the 1963 production of *Luther*, which starred Albert Finney. During the run of *Luther*, Goggin and another cast member formed a singing duo. Someone in the show gave Goggin a mannequin of a Dominican brother, a gag relating to the play. Goggin transformed the figure into a nun whose acerbic quips with a clerical slant became material for a series of greeting cards. From that he wrote the cabaret show, then a full-length musical. The original off-Broadway production opened in 1983 and ran 3,672 performances.

Goggin's musical is about the five Little Sisters of Hoboken, survivors of a one-time missionary order that ran a leper colony on an island south of France. It is discovered that Sister Julia has accidentally killed the other fifty-two residents of the convent with her tainted *vichyssoise* during a bingo session with a group of Maryknolls. In a vision, Mother Superior is told to start a greeting card company, which will raise funds for the burials. The cards are an enormous success. Thinking there's plenty of money, the Reverend Mother buys a VCR and camcorder for the convent, leaving inadequate funds for the last four burials. The deceased nuns are stored on ice in the deep freeze and a variety show is organized to raise more money. All the characters present solo-star performances, madcap dance routines, and an audience quiz. Even on this second viewing, we found the show to be one of the most entertaining we've ever seen.

Shirley and Marge were a little tired after their trip from Birmingham, settling in, and then the musical. It didn't take long for us to say good-night to one another.

On Friday, we took Shirley and Marge to Lobster Dock for lunch and then just rode around looking at the town and deciding what to do while they're here. We were already scheduled for the Carousel Dinner Theater. Five wonderfully talented young people performed selections from Neil Diamond's *Sweet Caroline*, followed by a Hit Parade Revue of songs from 1954. The evening was different from the previous night, yet equally entertaining.

Janie didn't go with us to the dinner theater. She has been less and less able to keep going for any length of time. When we returned home she was waiting up for us though, and we recounted what she had missed.

While in Maine, Shirley wanted to eat seafood, which we did at Lobsterman's Wharf, Lobster Dock, Ocean Point Inn (my favorite), Barnacle's on Monhegan Island, as well as back at our own Schell's kitchen, which featured Ham and Egg Pie, one of the favorite dishes Mother used to make for Daddy. I always try to make it just as she did. Apparently I succeeded because the girls said it was very, very (I added an extra very) good. I certainly valued Marge's opinion because she is herself an excellent cook—I would even say a "gourmet cook."

We decided to visit Monhegan Island on Saturday and made our reservations, knowing it would be a long, busy day. It was something we didn't want to miss. The small rocky island is ten miles from the mainland, scarcely a mile in area and only accessible by boat. Our trip was another of those perfect-weather-outing excursions. We left Pier 8 in Boothbay Harbor on the Balmy Days II at 9:30 a.m. and didn't return until 4:00 p.m. The trip on the sixty-five-foot boat took one-and-a-half hours to cover the twelve nautical miles from Boothbay.

Monhegan is no amusement park. All property belongs to the local Monhegan Land Trust. No personal cars are allowed, only several pickup trucks used to cart luggage and supplies from the ferry landing over the unpaved roads. The trucks have right of way. Pedestrians must move to let them pass.

For an overnight stay, reservations are necessary. Summer months are busy; no camping is allowed. Dogs must be on a leash. The most important rule is probably that you'd better be at the wharf at the appointed ferry departure time. Except for restaurants and shops, there are only two public toilet facilities and two public telephones on the island. A light jacket is recommended even in summer as the island is exposed to the open Atlantic.

Monhegan Island was known to Native Americans as a prime fishing area long before Captain John Smith's visit in 1614. Its economy is still dominated by fishing and lobstering. Even in modern times, the year-round population seldom exceeds sixty-five.

The Monhegan Historical and Cultural Museum, also called Lighthouse Museum, is one of the most popular places for visitors, but I was the only one of our party to walk up the steep gravel road to see it. Janie and Marge each used a cane, and Shirley's knees wouldn't take the strain. All my walking had paid off, making me our designated walker. The view from the top took my breath away. From the high bluff the vista sweeps across a marsh, an historic island hotel, Manana Island, and the sea beyond.

Walking is the chief tourist activity on the island. Seventeen miles of trails meander the one-and-a-half mile long stretch, which is only half a mile wide. The trails are often steep and strenuous and climb wooded areas and over rocky ledges to the highest ocean cliffs on the Maine coastline. Ted Edison, a summer resident, founded Monhegan Associates in 1954 to preserve and protect the wild lands of the island and its "simple, friendly way of life."

At Lobster Cove on the island's south end, the wreck of the *D. T. Sheridan* lies scattered across the rocks. Sheridan was a tugboat, built in 1939, and wrecked in November 1948 while towing barges in a dense fog.

Harbor seals are often found near Pebble Beach and whales are sighted in their movement from north to south. The island is on a flyway and becomes the resting place for migrating birds. In every direction, views are magnificent, and that includes looking up at the unbelievable colors of sunrise and sunset. Stars in the heavens glisten and shine in this sky undiminished by ground light and urban pollutants. Even the Northern Lights are evident toward the end of summer.

We meandered through some of the shops in the village featuring work by Rockwell Kent and other island artists. Shirley bought a couple of paintings for herself, and Marge purchased a beautiful scene of the Maine coastline for Janie, who couldn't make the walk. Monhegan has been a summer haven for artists for more than a hundred years.

An interesting part of our return sail was going all the way around the island where we viewed the cliffs from the sea and spotted seals as we rounded certain points. The highest cliff is a hundred and seventy-five feet.

From the ferry, we walked to the little café Barnacles. We were quite weary, and I don't recall what we ate, only that we remarked it was very good. Despite our fatigue, the day was so worth the effort to see this most special, unique, and beautiful place.

Ocean Point where we were living was idyllic. The landscape changes as tides rise and fall. Many mornings were heavy with fog and we could barely see out the windows; around noon the light changes producing a beautiful summer afternoon; and at night the slight cooling off in evening contributes to indescribable sunsets. Like our mood swings, there was something different every hour. I often woke early in the morning to the sound of engines of shrimp and lobster boats idling, starting, idling. And then the tour boats are about all day long. Lobster boats come so close to shore we could watch them empty their traps and drop them back into the water. Evening brought quiet. When walking Shore Road I could see five lighthouses in the distance, and hear the ever-present foghorn. Ocean Point is not just picturesque, but a laid back, old-fashioned, restful-looking place.

Mealtime again and Janie, Shirley, Marge, and I were treating ourselves to dinner at Ocean Point Restaurant. Reservations were for 7:30, and we'd asked to be seated at the windows to catch the sunset. The menu was extensive. I tried stuffed haddock with a shrimp sauce on top, the house salad, and finished with *crème brulee* for dessert. Dinner was delicious and the sunset spectacular. We couldn't have fit one more activity into the day. After a game of cards we called it a night, not needing to be rocked to sleep.

It's Sunday, July 17, and after church with Shirley and Marge, we sat down with Janie to discuss what we had been dreading to talk about: Janie going home. She hadn't been able to make it to church this morning and was even now recuperating from our activities yesterday. Janie's need to make this decision had long been obvious to Janie and me, and it didn't take Shirley and Marge long to figure out that it would be best for all. Janie's constant pain had only become worse in the past weeks. She needed to return home to Austin for treatment she could not get while traveling. I hated it, for all of us, because Janie and I fully intended to complete the trip as a unit.

At Lobsterman's Wharf Restaurant we enjoyed our last dinner together. The appetizer of crab cakes was even better than the entrée. It was a good evening, recounting all we'd done and those activities we'd particularly savored along the way.

After checking possibilities for shipping Janie's belongings home, we find that the U.S. Post Office offered the cheapest method. A ticket for Janie was booked for the trip from Portland, Maine, to Austin, Texas, coinciding with Shirley and Marge's flight back to Birmingham. They would go to the airport together. Despite careful planning, a mix-up at the airport caused Janie to have to make three plane changes before arriving home in the evening. My daughters, Kay and Ellene, were coming in Saturday. I could hardly wait.

It was difficult to explain how it felt now that I was alone in Boothbay Harbor, Maine, with four-and-a-half months remaining on the journey. What should I do? Maybe I thought for a second about going home, but that was all I allowed myself. I had told Janie that I intended to continue the trip alone, and she had said that she never imagined I would do otherwise. I knew I had to finish what I'd set out to do, and barring any terrible mishaps, I could do it by myself. And I knew I was not really alone. I had depended on the Lord thus far, and that wouldn't change. I would, in fact, depend on Him even more. I wouldn't feel all that alone, even though I was.

I woke very early the next day, and it dawned on me that I could absolutely choose what I wanted to do. I took several boxes of Janie's belongings to the post office. My next priority was the newspaper interview scheduled with Lisa Kristoff, assistant editor of *Boothbay Register*. We chatted for two hours. I served sherbet with toasted coconut and pecans and cookies, and enjoyed meeting and sharing with her. Her subsequent article was great.

In one of the many conversations with people in Boothbay Harbor, someone had mentioned Mary Lou Teel, and I recognized her name. She and her husband, Peter Freundlich, are noted in Charles Kuralt's book. They worked for many years with Kuralt on *CBS Sunday Morning*. Peter had since died, but I took a chance and telephoned their summer home in Boothbay. Mary Lou answered and agreed to an interview the next morning.

Teel's lovely old waterside home is a converted barn, the perfect house in the perfect place, purchased in 1985 when she started working for CBS. Teel is now a writer/producer at *CBS Sunday Morning*. I was excited to talk with her in person, and she was just as delightful as I thought she would be. Mary Lou is another person who really knew Charles Kuralt.

She spoke highly of his personality, his work ethic, his love of people, and his ability to see the best in people and then work closely with them.

We talked some about the journey Janie and I had taken; she thought it inspiring. Teel's advice about the book and the fact that we were not writers per se was, "Just write the book," then see what happens. I was inspired by Mary Lou Teel's interest in our project, and her advice.

At home, whitecaps were on the waves. Wind and light fog made everything hazy. My chores, washing and ironing and shopping, were done. I rested and enjoyed the view and atmosphere—a perfect way to end the day.

I spoke to Shirley and Janie, both home safe but spent. Janie has a doctor's appointment for next week. She was relieved to be home, and free of the walking and riding that had aggravated her situation. At the same time she was heartbroken not to have completed what we started together. A health problem such as hers was the only obstacle that would have made Janie give up.

I had begun to think about accommodations for Ely, Minnesota, my next stop. But for now the focus was my daughters, Kay and Ellene, and their arrival. The morning had brought a few rain sprinkles, and the weather had turned a bit cooler. I tried to stay busy, killing time until my girls arrived. At 1:00 a.m., they came in, tired because they had set out at 7:30 a.m. the previous day. We talked a while, and then, the bed felt so good.

Time with my girls started with Sunday church. I knew they would appreciate the old chapel around the bend. The Rev. Jack Fles, minister of the Episcopal Church in Gardiner, Maine, was guest speaker and his message was as good as I thought it would be.

We took lunch at Lobster Dock and spent the afternoon wandering in and out of village shops, stopping for coffee at Moose Café. One of the more interesting boutiques was Mung Bean at 37 Townsend Avenue, a private company categorized under Artcraft and Carvings, established in 1974. Still run by the brother-and-sister team who founded it, the store specializes in Maine-made and American-made handcrafts—wood, tinware, pottery, jewelry, collectibles, and toys—unique and affordable.

Dinner at Ocean Point ended another full day. I went to bed early and have no idea when the girls finally fell sleep.

I worried now that when I mentioned Janie, it would seem our months together were all bad. No, that time was good, but just happened to include problems we couldn't correct and had not anticipated. Janie had made all our original contact calls up until the time we were in Maine. She made calls reaching out to strangers asking for information, interviews, and reservations. She was also the navigator when traveling and our techie when stationary. Janie was also very appreciative of my cooking. She helped immensely in getting this venture successfully on the road.

What I am pointing out is that now, it was so different. I was totally in charge of what to do, see, visit, and I had to do it all without feeling guilty, knowing Janie would have loved to be there. If only she could have been.

When we'd last spoken since her return to Austin, Janie had said she felt a great sense of relief to no longer be in the car for hours—the worst possible thing for her health—working up courage and energy to do things that needed to be done. She said she was aware she'd been slowing me down, but she also had truly wanted to continue the trip, and had been especially excited about Alaska. Bear with me. This change is part of the journey.

Kay, Ellene, and I decided to partake of the Clambake at Cabbage Island. For seventeen years, the Moore family—spouses, siblings, children, nieces and nephews—have run the operation. Reservations are required to attend a clambake, offered seven days a week from June to September. A local boat owner runs participants to the island in Linekin Bay. Wayne Moore purchased Cabbage Island in 1986 and restarted the clambake tradition. We cruised for forty-five minutes on the Bennie Alice to narrated facts and folklore about the area, and enjoyed close up views of historic lighthouses, magnificent homes on the rocky cliffs, marine wildlife, and lobstermen working their traps.

Once on the island, exploration was encouraged as well as other activities: fishing from the dock, horseshoes, volleyball, badminton, watching fishermen haul in their traps, as well as just sitting and relaxing, enjoying the peace and quiet.

In case of inclement weather, there was a guest building constructed in 1900 that seats a hundred and seventy-five. A huge fireplace offered warmth if needed, and rain gear and umbrellas were available in case of a shower.

The clambake itself was authentic Downeast. Clams and lobsters cooked in seaweed, steamed from top to bottom, and covered with tarpaulins and rocks to capture all the flavor and sweetness of the meats. The meal included a cup of traditional New England chowder, two luscious bright red lobsters, tender white steamed clams wrapped in foil, sweet golden corn on the cob, an egg, onion, and potatoes. Dessert was blueberry cake from the famous recipe by Ruth Leavitt. We dined for an hour, walked slowly around the island, almost dozed when we sat down, and were so sated, we didn't even want to talk to one another on the boat ride home. It was that kind of day—slow, easy, relaxing, excellent food, and people who were pleasant and eager to please.

Kay and Ellene wanted to order lobster to ship home. We found a place that could accommodate them. Then we ate again at Tugboat Inn and Restaurant, and made our way to Coastal Maine Botanical Gardens. After sixteen years of planning, the gardens opened June 13, 2007. Since that time they have become one of Maine's top attractions and one of the few waterfront botanical gardens in the U.S. The natural landscape is dramatic and compelling, with a mile of walking trail alongside a saltwater river.

Our favorite section, Lerner Garden of the Five Senses, is

nearly one acre employing a variety of elements to accomplish wayfinding—sensory cues by which a person with a disability can navigate in the garden landscape. A circle of random river stones invites bare feet to explore. The heady aroma of lavender, spicy peonies, and sweet roses prick the nostrils. Velvety lamb's ears are planted on a low stone wall, perfect for fingers running along the surface. A gurgling fountain cascades down a granite wall. Dan and Lyn Lerner of Pennsylvania, known philanthropists, donated more than one million dollars to the garden project that was the dream of Mollie Moore. While in England on a garden research trip, Ms. Moore lost her sight due to pneumococcal meningitis. A friend told her about sensory gardens, prompting her mission to incorporate the idea into the gardens of Boothbay. More than seven thousand plants, each appealing to one of the five senses, have transformed what was once a bare lot. The girls and I also enjoyed the Children's Garden with its themes from children's literature with a Maine connection. This garden and Garden of the Five Senses really brought out the child in us.

Late in the afternoon, we drove to Southport. Fog began to roll in across the water, and the air became cool. We passed homes that were a charming mix, some beautiful, some ragged and unkempt, but always the view of the water and boats remained compelling.

I hated to see my girls leave, and I just hoped they had had as good a time as I had. They later reported their flight home was shorter and easier than the trip up.

And now I began to think about leaving on Friday, calculating distance, where to stop at night, and learning a little about Ely,

Minnesota, my next destination. The Rand-McNally calculator told me it was 1,716.7 miles to Ely. This would be my first solo drive, a little different, and I was planning three days of travel.

I moved through my usual leaving-town chores: washing clothes, putting the house in order, donating canned goods to the church, checking the car—under the hood and filling the tank with gas—and then I was ready to say my good-byes, the part I always dreaded.

I put OnStar in control and on my first day made six hundred miles, staying in Fredonia, New York. After a good night's rest, I was ready to drive another long day to Racine, Wisconsin.

The last few hours on my third day were a little nerve-wracking. The road was two-lane and nothing but woods, and woods, and more woods. I wondered, Have I taken a wrong turn and ended up back in Washington County, Alabama? Those were some of the most apprehensive moments of the trip for me. In the end, I was anxious, but there was no need. OnStar would have alerted me with, "You have left the planned route. We will continue when you return to the planned route."

Finally, a sign appeared, leaning right: Ely.

What a welcome sight! I might have said something like, "Thank you, Lord," or "finally." Quite a few miles later, I eased into town.

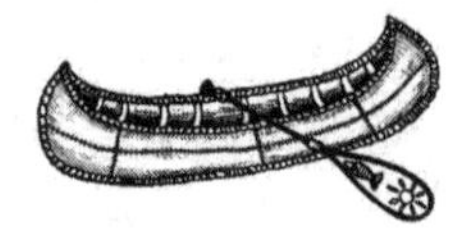

Chapter Eight
Ely, Minnesota
August 2011

AT FIRST GLANCE, Ely (pronounced *ee-lee*) seemed a typical small town, population 3,460, with one main street running through it but looking a bit shabby. The one street is lined with businesses related to the great outdoors and exploration of nearby wilderness areas—outfitters and outdoor clothing stores—alongside the usual business offices found in a small town.

Today Ely is best known as the entry point to Boundary Waters Canoe Area Wilderness and home to International Wolf Center and the North American Bear Center. Resorts, lodges, camps, and lake areas surrounding Ely draw people from near and far, raising population numbers to 7,000 at times.

Minnesota is known as the Land of 10,000 Lakes. The word, *minnesota*, is Dakota for "clear water." With all the parks and businesses and references to water in Ely, it was no surprise to learn from locals that "you're not a true Elyite unless you have a canoe atop your vehicle." Right then I became determined to have a photo made of me with a canoe on the roof of my car.

According to the Chamber of Commerce brochure, Ely features unique shops, good places to eat, friendly people, Tuesday night "live" music, the Dorothy Molter Museum, and the wilderness centers mentioned earlier. And, of course, there's fishing, clean lakes, and canoeing. Ely is the largest "jumping off" place for the Boundary Waters Canoe Area Wilderness and claims to do more wilderness canoe outfitting than any other town or city in the world.

One thing I immediately loved about Ely was the wide streets, two lanes of traffic with a lane on each side for parking and enough room for making U-turns without having to maneuver or back up. It's a welcome change after some of the parking experiences in other places, New York City for example. I hadn't checked the legality of U-turns here, but I had seen others make them so I assumed it must be legal. And I'd seen only two police cars in town . . .

It seemed strange not to have secured a place to stay since that had been our pattern the whole trip, but I wanted to have a look first. There were many possibilities in the outlying areas—resorts, lodges, camps. But because I am alone I preferred to be in town. I found a room at Budget Host Motel right on the main street. The owners, Roger and Debbie, were very kind and willing to work with me even though I could not say how long I would be there while looking for more appropriate lodging.

Having settled in, my first concern was the computer not

working. I checked with Debbie at the office for advice. She mentioned a young man named Brian T. Schurter, an attorney from Urbana, Illinois, who had been coming there for many years. He'd had car problems and his family had returned home while he stayed to await repair of the vehicle. Brian offered to check my computer. I took it to the office and Brian gave it a look. Nothing worked. We agreed to let it wait until the next day. Neither of us had eaten so we walked together to a restaurant, probably a good mile. I kept up with him, even walking mostly uphill. We enjoyed a good meal, and I'm sure I talked his ear off. You always wonder if you'll see someone like that again.

Next day, the computer was still uppermost on my mind. Someone mentioned the go-to computer guy in town, Dave. I walked to his shop and Dave agreed to come to the motel after lunch and check my equipment. Meantime, I contacted several realty companies, looking for a house to rent. One name kept recurring: Angela Campbell, who had e-mailed me and agreed to meet me for lunch.

When the Lord places a special angel in your path, you know immediately. Angela is a beautiful lady—a born-again Christian, a working woman, divorced with two grown children—and after talking for a few minutes, I knew she was beautiful on the inside as well. We learned all about one another within an hour, and Angela offered me a room at her own home just one block off the main street. She would be at work all day, she said, and I would have the house to myself. It's a beautiful four-bedroom, spacious and tastefully furnished. But I wasn't ready to commit to anything yet, not sure what I wanted. We decided to look together for something reasonable for me.

Back at the motel, Dave, the computer guy, checked my machine and discovered the problem was with a connection in the office. His discovery was helpful to me and to Debbie, the motel owner. She was not aware of a problem with the motel's electronic connections. Dave refused payment for his service, but later I gave him a gift certificate to the local ice cream parlor.

Angela Campbell and I met again for supper at Rockwood, a popular downtown restaurant at 302 E. Sheridan Street, the main thoroughfare. Built with lots of wood paneling and beams and rock walls, the restaurant had a cozy cabin feel; it is decorated with memorabilia of fishing, skiing, mining, and hunting in the North Woods. The menu offered several takes on walleye, a fish closely related to the European pikeperch and native to most of Canada and the northern United States. It is also the state fish of Minnesota and sometimes called walleyed pike or jack salmon. The name walleye comes from the large staring eyes of the fish. If I'd eaten walleye before, I didn't recall. Its texture is much like catfish, but I don't remember what it tasted like; the flavor was not distinctive enough to compare or recall.

A new day. Angela phoned, as we're going to meet regarding some rental possibilities and then later go to the Wilderness Outpost about thirty miles out of town. First we walked the area near Angela's house where we saw several houses for sale. One particular place had my name written all over it. We met with the agent, Jan Erluch, who said she would contact the owners, Ward and Muffin Nelson. The house looked perfect to me: ideal location, furnished with all I need, a home away from home.

I rented the wonderful 1920s Craftsman-style house—the type sold in a kit in the Sears Roebuck catalog in the early part of the twentieth century—that Jan Erluch had showed me. It sat two blocks off Sheridan, near everything important—the hospital, grocery (which even had someone to load groceries into the car), restaurants, post office, police station, and churches. The street was lined with old trees, quiet, peaceful, and sooo pretty.

Muffin and Ward—I hope we're on a first-name basis since I had been entrusted with their home—had moved from this house to a home on Burntside Lake but left furniture to accommodate their daughter and family who sometimes stayed here. Muffin came by to pick up some personal items, and Kevin, Angela's helper and friend, was with her and helped me move in. Thank you, Lord. This was the eighth move on my journey, but I'm not tired of it. The rent for this house was so reasonable that when Muffin told me the amount I kind of gasped. Her response? "Oh, is it too much?" Does the Lord provide?

Muffin's husband, Ward, came by amidst all the moving in and arranging. I was happy to meet this personable man who I found to be immediately likeable, as was Muffin. Ward Nelson had retired after thirty-six years with IBM, working the last few years from his home. While standing in the yard talking to Ward, Mike Hillman, a remarkable man prominently mentioned in Kuralt's book, stopped by. I was thrilled to meet Hillman, and will speak more of him later.

I'm off to the Wilderness Outpost facility with Angela to meet about thirty other people who make up the "Tuesday Group." First there was lunch, then a tour of the outpost's new administration building. The outpost has a staff of one hundred and seventy-five. At any one time, ten different groups are on the water, outfitted with canoes, food, clothing, and anything else that might be needed for an unforgettable camping experience in this wild and beautiful place.

The Boundary Waters Canoe Area Wilderness is 1,900,000 acres, a destination for canoeing and fishing, and Minnesota's top tourist attraction. It lies within the Superior National Forest of northeastern Minnesota, under administration of the U.S. Forestry Service, attracting visitors from around the globe, who come for the canoeing, backpacking, fishing, and dog sledding and stay at the 2,200 backcountry campsites, most of which are accessible only by water. About seventy-five percent of the area is reserved for nonmotorized boat travel. Portage trails connect most lakes and rivers, resulting in more than 1,000 miles of canoe routes. I wasn't sure what portage meant, and was informed it is the practice of carrying watercraft and cargo overland between two bodies of water, sometimes to avoid river obstacles. Minnesota's many rivers and lakes allow travel continuously, with portaging, across the vast wilderness.

After touring the facility, Angela and I rode to "the end of the road." Whether it was the end of Snow Lake or Johnson Lake, I don't know, but we could go no further. At the Outpost I had met Terry Jackson, a freelance writer for the *Ely Echo*. Terry was interested in my trip and asked if we might set up an interview. Naturally, I was thrilled. We made a date and Terry conducted the interview and shot photos. Later he asked to return for more pictures. Maybe he'd had a hard time finding a decent photo to use? All teasing aside, I was pleased with his article and the picture he published in the *Ely Echo*.

Angela Campbell is a busy woman. In addition to her other activities, she manages Elywear, a clothing store whose owners are from Colombia, South America. The owners visit the store often and hire college students from Colombia to intern during the summer. There are many instances like this in Ely, which contribute to the town's unique cultural flavor.

Angela was keeping me scheduled with things to do and people to meet. With her help, I'd booked an appointment for a haircut, just across the street from Elywear. Again, someone I'd never seen before gave me a cut I ended up quite pleased with. Now, Angela and I were attending an open house for Twin Metals.

More than four billion tons of copper, nickel, platinum, palladium, gold, and other metal resources can be found in northern Minnesota, the largest known undeveloped deposit of strategic metals in the world.

Twin Metals was formed in 2010, to develop and operate an underground mining project in northern Minnesota. Revitalizing this century-old mining industry in the state will create large numbers of construction, engineering, exploration, and long-term mining jobs for generations of Minnesotans. Twin Metals has declared its commitment to protect the environment, using sound practices in every phase of the plan. This is no quick study, hurry-up proposition.

Twin Metals is now entering year four of baseline studies and pre-feasibility analysis. Its efforts could provide economic diversification to the region, state, and nation for decades. I do hope to follow the developments.

As always, there were housekeeping chores to be done, and I also took a little time to arrange my belongings.

The house I'd rented was wonderful. I loved everything about it—from the location, amount of space, and huge basement to the Internet access, Wi-Fi, and kitchen. I felt perfectly at ease and at home already.

Sometimes I forgot I was the sole caretaker of my car. I found a service station that would change oil, rotate tires, and check filters, hoses, and all that other car stuff. The car and I were now good for the next phase. I'd never pumped gas before this trip. Had never wanted to, and would always arrange for someone else to do it—or for the attendant to do the honors. It was just one of many odd things about me, I guess. But small-town America could be wonderfully accommodating.

I church-hopped my first Sunday in Ely. Grace Lutheran was one block from my house with services at 9:30 a.m., and diagonally across from my house was First Presbyterian with services at 11:00 a.m. I visited both, and found the messages to be good and the people friendly. I especially enjoyed the music at each church.

My mind might have wandered while receiving instruction for communion, because I did take the wrong cup at the Lutheran church, drinking the wine instead of grape juice. Lesson learned; I'd listen more carefully next time, but those communion cups are quite small, and I was sure I hadn't weaved, wobbled, or swayed while walking to the next church. The absence of young couples and children was evident at both services. It was summer, and perhaps people were away on vacation. I hoped that was the reason.

Kuralt's name worked magic when mentioned. People loved to talk about him, especially if they'd known him personally.

Kuralt bought a radio station in Ely back in the 1950s that was on the verge of ruin. He is reported to have said, "A town needed a voice." Yet in this area he is known best for his love of fishing, canoeing, and the wilderness.

I found several quotes in news articles and magazines relating to Kuralt, or Ely. In June 1955, the *Orlando Sentinel* wrote, "Retired CBS newsman Charles Kuralt has bought a radio station, WELY, in Ely, Minnesota, saying it will give him another good reason to return to one of his favorite places, in the heart of the Boundary Waters Canoe Area Wilderness."

Another quote came from Kuralt himself: "On the map, Ely appears to be at the end of the road. For people who love wilderness and beauty and solitude, on the contrary, it's at the center of the world." *National Geographic Traveler* named Ely one of the "50 places of a Lifetime to Visit," saying, "If it is absolute solitude you want, you only have to paddle far enough."

The highest point in Minnesota, at 2,301 feet, is Eagle Mountain in the Boundary Waters Canoe Area Wilderness. Except for Indian pictographs on some of the rocks, footprints on some portages, or perhaps signs of old campfires on some islands, there is no sign that human beings have been in the area. No motors, airplanes, generators, cans, or bottles are permitted, and it's unlawful to cut down a tree, or even to cut off a bough or chip away bark. Groups of more than ten canoeists must split up and go in different directions. All these precautions are taken to preserve and protect what is enjoyed by many.

You certainly cannot walk into the area, hop into a canoe, and push off. Basic things, such as proper permits, reservations if overnighting, and fees, are required for a visit. Advance planning is the key. An outfitter can supply equipment, maps, and food, as well as tips and preparation for a custom-designed trip for any ambition or ability. Within an outfitter's expertise is a short relaxing week with emphasis on leisurely fishing, or a challenging two-week adventure covering miles of territory. Their knowledge ensures a trip that will be enjoyed with a sense of confidence.

Visits with family while so far from home have helped reaffirm my determination to complete this journey, and given me the love and reassurance to persevere. The children of my oldest sister, now deceased, are scattered from Cypress, California, to Aledo, Texas, to Kennesaw, Georgia. We seldom get together as a family, so I was thrilled to receive a call from my niece, Jo Anne, in California. She would be in Bozeman, Montana, in late August and would spend several days with me in Twin Bridges. She and Janie had been planning this for some time. A week or so later, an e-mail from my nephew, John Schell in McLean, Virginia, told me he would be in Bozeman on September 9 after hiking in the Grand Tetons with friends. I'm excited about both visits.

Some days it was difficult to make up my mind to get out—I'd have rather stayed in and read or done nothing. Then the realization would surface that time was limited. I'd only so many days to visit, inquire, and soak up the uniqueness of a place. And that's what I tried to remember: each place is so unique.

I wanted to tour Vermillion Community College, sometimes called Boundary Waters College. The school takes advantage of its location to offer classes in Natural Resource Management, Business Management and Tourism; Protection, Preservation, and Recreation; as well as Liberal Arts and Sciences. I met and talked with Tommy Bennett, recruiting coordinator. Six hundred students are enrolled in the two-year programs, while "some stay three years," he said. Residential dorms are available, a difference from most two-year schools. Students come from all over the world, and why not? The campus is quite lovely, with a unique curriculum. I was impressed.

Even with two churches near my house, I looked for a Baptist church. I learned that the Ely Baptist Church had changed its name to Ledgerock Community Church. The reason, someone said, was the need for compromise: a concern that "Baptist" in the name might keep some people from attending. The service was contemporary with guitars, harmonica, accordion, and keyboard music; and video to enhance the message. The mission statement read, "To live empowered by God's Spirit to reach people for Christ"—hopefully the purpose of every church.

August 9 was a busy day and not an unusual one. I joined the Tuesday Group at Grand Ely Lodge Resort and Conference Center and was introduced by Terry Jackson. It was another opportunity to meet people and enjoy a beautiful setting and excellent food.

After a quick visit with Angela Campbell at Elywear, I stopped by the Chamber of Commerce. Trudy, whom I had talked with on the phone, was away doing hostess duty at an old mine, which is the Ely Arts and Heritage Center at Pioneer Mine Complex. Ely Greenstone Public Art manages the center. The old mine operated underground from 1888 to 1967, producing 42 million tons of Bessemer-grade iron ore over the space of two world wars and the industrialization of America. Two buildings renovated in the 1990s are open to the public. The Shaft House has a walking tour, with exhibits explaining the old machinery and the way it was used in the mining process. Throughout summer and fall, classes in oil painting, a children's art camp, a juried art show, and receptions and tours are available. In 1978, the mine was placed on the National Register of Historic Places.

I completed my busy day by calling Bill Campbell, Kuralt's fishing buddy and Angela's former husband, to arrange an interview. Then I picked up Angela and we attended a Lia Sophia jewelry party with some of Angela's friends. Finally, I returned home and was in bed by 10:00 p.m. This type of day repeated itself many times as I would meet someone who suggested meeting someone else, and on and on, with me trying to make contacts but finding it impossible to follow up on all of them.

Early one Monday morning, Angela and I drove to Grand Marais, Minnesota, a small town on the north shore of Lake Superior, between the Sawtooth Mountains and the lake. *Grand marais* is French for great marsh. In early fur-trading times a marsh was twenty acres or less in area. This marsh is nearly at the level of Lake Superior and situated at the head of the little bay and harbor leading to the village settlement. It is one of the entry points to Boundary Waters Canoe Area Wilderness via Gunflint Trail, which starts in the middle of town and heads up and back into the woods. The trail is sixty-five miles of blacktop winding through beautiful woods, past lakes and cabins, outfitters, even resorts and guides, as well as deer, moose, and bear. You're advised to keep your right foot on the pedal.

Road access to Grand Marais is by Minnesota Highway 61; it is the only way in or out by car and the only paved road in Cook County. Grand Marais does have an airport, but no scheduled service. You can, of course, boat in via Lake Superior when it isn't frozen.

Sixty-one heads northeast from Grand Marais following the shore of Lake Superior and is known as North Shore Scenic Drive. Coming from Ely, it was one of the most beautiful drives I'd ever seen. I oohed and aahed until I couldn't do it anymore. We pulled off the road several times at scenic overlooks, and took pictures at a waterfall where people were swimming and sunning on the beach. Unlike the white sands of the Alabama Gulf Coast, the beach here was brown sand and rocky; but nevertheless, a beach.

Angela and I enjoyed walking around Grand Marais, in and out of stores, and as usual Angela knew people there. The small town is a vibrant artistic community with distinctive small businesses and a diverse group of citizens. Many restaurants and shops are only open seasonally, and a call ahead may keep you from being disappointed.

Over lunch at Angry Trout Café on the north shore, Angela and I watched sailboats and floatplanes on the lake. The restaurant is a former commercial-fishing shanty perched on the edge of the water. Only locally grown produce is served, along with hand-harvested wild rice and fresh fish from Lake Superior. Our food was excellent.

One appealing enterprise in Grand Marais is the North House Folk School, a non-profit supported through membership. The school is a gathering place for community activities, live music and dances, potlucks, films, festivals, ski swaps, boat auctions, outdoor baking in firebrick ovens, and other simple important stuff. A range of one hundred and twenty courses from basketry to northern ecology to woodworking are taught, and the courses may run half a day or two weeks. All classes have one thing in common: in each there is meaningful satisfaction that comes from creating items using the hands, heart, and mind. A humorous note: you can literally bury yourself in your work here. The Build Your Own Casket class is one of the school's most popular.

I would have loved to drive to Duluth to see the city, but in Grand Marais, we were at least two hours from Ely and it was already mid-afternoon. Our perfect day was not spoiled though, with the sun shining so brightly and temperature-perfect light-sweater weather. I couldn't help feeling a little guilty knowing that in Alabama the days and nights were sweltering.

The International Wolf Center and the North American Bear Center are on opposite ends of Ely. Both are considered must-sees. The International Wolf Center advances the survival of wolf populations by teaching about wolves and their relationship to wild lands, and the role of humans in the future of wolves. In response to controversy, the center pledges to provide information to educate the public. To help people make decisions about wolf populations, up-to-date and accurate information is needed. One issue being studied by the Center is human tolerance of the wolf. The Center values high-quality education to foster interest and understanding of wolves and wolf issues.

Learning opportunities at the Center included observing the resident wolf pack and a tour of the wolves and humans exhibit on hunting and feeding behaviors. There are videos, lectures, and demonstrations. You can even go on evening "howling" expeditions.

The North American Bear Center is home to three captive black bears. Ted, a male born in 1997, weighs 860.5 pounds and is perhaps the largest black bear in Minnesota. The prettiest bear in the state, according to the Bear Center, is Honey, a female born in 1996. Lucky was born in the wilds of Wisconsin and taken by people as a pet. They soon realized he was too much to handle and wanted to release him. Wisconsin Department of Natural Resources said that could not happen. Lucky was about to be killed when officials inquired if the North American Bear Center would take him on. He arrived at NABC in 2007, weighing ten pounds. Visitors at the Center named him Lucky.

First-time visitors to the Bear Center express surprise upon entering the welcoming interior with its walls of natural wood, murals, and huge mounted bears in life-like poses. A wall of windows overlooks the bear enclosure with its pond and waterfalls. Background sounds of bears foraging, cubs nursing, and bird songs fill the air. The educational goal of the Bear Center is to replace myths (about bears) with reality.

Bears have been demonized for centuries, mainly because of

exaggerated perceptions of danger. Misinformation leads to eradication campaigns using bounties, poison, trapping and shooting. The eight species of bear worldwide are now listed as vulnerable, threatened, or endangered in all, or portions of, their ranges. Humans are occupying remote habitats that once ensured protection and isolation for bears, and the attitudes of those people will determine the future of bear populations.

Videos of wild bears are available at the Bear Center and allow people to learn from the bears themselves. There is an interpretive nature trail and a gift shop, too. Its sign reads: Welcome to the Bear Necessities Gift Shop.

The Front Porch Coffee and Tea Company at 343 East Sheridan Street is a gathering place for locals and visitors in Ely. Coffee and fresh-baked goods are offered all day long. I met there with Gerald Tyler, and we were invited to join a table of eight men to visit. Gerald and a Minnesota cattleman have been involved in a notice-of-intent to sue the federal government over the ruling of the Minnesota gray wolf as an endangered species. The Minnesota wolf is considered a separate species from other wolves in the forty-eight states, and is a "recovered" species. A new ruling by the government could put the wolf under state management, which it is believed would ensure the long-term survival of the Minnesota species.

Charles Kuralt is both well-liked and remembered as an admirable man in Ely. At the local Chamber of Commerce I met with Lynda Fryer, administrative director of the Chamber and Visitor Center. The room was full of people seeking plans for hiking, portaging, and camping; Lynda unhurriedly helped them all with information, materials, and advice. Her sense of humor and quick smile are certainly an asset to the Chamber.

I was interested in what Lynda would have to say about Kuralt. She spoke, as many have, of how much Kuralt liked visiting Ely, and how he valued his privacy. Pictures of Kuralt lined the wall of the Chamber office. Kuralt said many times that this was his kind of town. He genuinely liked people, and we decided neither of us had found anyone who didn't like him.

As mentioned earlier, Bill Campbell, an attorney and Angela Campbell's former husband, was Kuralt's fishing buddy and adviser. Bill was responsible for negotiations and legal work required for Kuralt to buy the Ely radio station. Bill and Kuralt probably made forty fishing trips together to Twin Bridges, Montana. I shared with Bill my plans to visit Montana next, and we discussed routes, places to live, and things to do. I appreciated Bill's generosity in talking with me and enjoyed his speaking voice, which rivaled Kuralt's. Another busy day ended with an invitation to Angela's for supper and an Arbonne party—makeup and skin care products. It was a fun evening.

Ward and Muffin Nelson (who own the house I'm renting) have invited me to supper at their cabin on Burntside Lake. Muffin gave me excellent directions, which I didn't take long to mess up. My husband, Fletcher, always said I had the poorest sense of direction, as no matter what direction I took I thought I was facing north. He was right. I drove out of Ely going past the Bear Center instead of the Wolf Center, as Muffin had directed. What was supposed to be nine miles turned into a much longer drive. I called Muffin and she got me back on track. I could get to the cabin either way, but I'd taken the longer route. It was a beautiful drive through the woods. When I arrived I learned that plans had changed. We would be going to Ward's mom's house by boat, and would pass Burntside Lodge, a resort they wanted me to see.

Burntside Lodge is a complex of twenty-three log cabins with wood floors and knotty pine interiors, most of which were built in the 1920s. The place began as a hunting camp, Brownell Outing Company, one of the first outfitters in the area. It opened in 1914 with one log structure. Ray and Nancy LaMontagne purchased the camp in 1941 and had managed it for forty-one years. The resort remains under direction of the LaMontagne family whose philosophy is, "preserving the past while facing the future."

Burntside Lodge is listed by the U.S. Department of Interior on the National Register of Historic Places. The lodge is considered historically significant because it is the earliest full-scale commercial resort operation in this part of the country. It also contains the largest collection of log resort buildings of high integrity in northern Saint Louis County.

Local craftsmen constructed the buildings using native materials—"a remarkable architectural achievement in an outstanding state of preservation," states the Department of Interior. The prestigious resort has been written up in *Fodor's 1000 Places You Must See Before You Die*, *Gourmet* and *Wine Spectator* magazines, Country's *Best Log Homes*, and other feature publications. Any further description I might offer of the resort and scenery would be inadequate. My first thought was, "Please, leave me here."

The ride to Ward's mom's house was lengthy, but spectacular. We saw a huge bald eagle nest in the trees. While I'm not a "water person," I liked seeing everything from that vantage point.

At the Nelson family home I met Ward's mother and Aunt Dib, her daughter and husband, Ward's sister-in-law, Nancy, and son Ryan and his girlfriend. They made me feel like family. We had a wonderful dinner of grilled steak, potatoes, salad, drinks, and a tasty fruit tart for dessert. Surely the Lodge cuisine could not have been better.

My return trip home went without incident, no scenic side jaunts or wrong turns, and I even managed to take the shorter route. I hope I'd expressed to all involved how much I enjoyed the evening.

I was still church-hopping, going to Grace Lutheran at 9:30 a.m. and then the Presbyterian Church at 11:00, and loving it. On this particular morning, August 21, 2011, I was truly impressed with a special program. Several women in the church presented beautifully written narratives that began with the birth of John the Baptist in Luke and included the birth, death, burial, and resurrection of Jesus Christ. One of the church ladies had written the narratives, and she had selected scriptures to read, if desired, that documented and reinforced the dialogues; as well as hymns appropriate to the scriptures. Minimal costuming was used, just enough to portray the character each lady assumed. I found the service moving, a reminder of what Jesus Christ did for each of us. I was pleased too to meet Mike Rouse, the pianist, who leads the music each Sunday and is truly talented. Shouldn't we feel we've missed something each Sunday we fail to attend?

I had met Mike Hillman while moving into my house here in Ely, but this was the first chance we'd had to sit and talk. Mike is well educated, a storyteller of the oral tradition—a headliner at the Minnesota Storytelling Festival. He has been an iron miner, resort manager, and historian, and he doesn't mind letting you know right away how much he cares for the well-being of Ely and the preservation of the elements that make Ely so special. Mike is also a musician, actor, guide, and teacher, but most of all Mike is a writer. One of his three published books is *Livin' At The End of The Road, Stories of Old Ely and the Lake Country.*

Every person I met in Ely, when I explained why I was there, said, "You've got to meet Mike Hillman."

Mike's great-grandfather was one of a party of eight men who came to Ely by canoe in 1883 and found the richest deposit of iron ore in the world. The mining lasted eighty years, enriching families like the Rockefellers and the Carnegies, but not the miners themselves. When the mining ended, many of those men became trappers and fishermen.

The Wilderness Act, a bill passed by the eighty-eighth Congress in 1964, was conceived "to establish a National Preservation System for the permanent good of the whole people . . ." It also ended most of the trapping and fishing industry.

Mike said if he could turn the clock back to the 1950s, he would, because there was a freedom then without restrictions—a paradise (in Ely). Most of the men Mike knew when he was growing up stayed in Ely for the same reasons Mike stays now. "It's my place," he said.

Mike seemed content with his place in the world, and certainly is his own person. Wiry and bearded, he rides his bicycle everywhere, was married once. Two hours with Mike passed quickly. We learned he is the Head Howler of the Wolf Center. Tourists like to go out at night and hear the wolves howl. Mike volunteered to become Leather Lungs Hillman, howling up wolves for the tourists. Charles Kuralt described Hillman as a tenacious and able man of worth who could do anything he set his mind to, even it was something he'd never done before. I had to agree. My take on Mike, "He's a treasure of a person."

Gene Domich and Geri Fisher have been friends of Angela Campbell for many years. Gene is a retired engineer who worked at one time in Alabama, now lives in California, but returns to Ely each summer where he lives on family property at Burntside Lake. I don't know how Angela and Geri met, but everyone knows Angela.

The four of us went to dinner at Rockwood and then crossed the street to the Front Porch parking lot to listen to Pat Surface and the Boundary Water Boys. Pat's award-winning music label is Spiritwood. Pat Surface is six-feet, eight-inches tall and a former all-star basketball player, but his first love has always been music. Adopted at age two by the LaPlants, a formidable musical family in Saint Paul, Minnesota, Pat grew up surrounded by music.

Seven musicians including himself make up the Boundary Water Boys, a troubadour/balladeer style of soulful vocals and string instruments: guitar, violin, dobro, bass fiddle, steel guitar, and mandolin. Two of the musicians are LaPlant brothers and another is a cousin. Several hundred people sat outside to listen to this regular summer entertainment in Ely. I did get someone to photograph me with the very tall Pat Surface. We looked like Mutt and Jeff. What a fun evening! Before it ended, Gene Domich invited me to his summer home for a canoe ride one day.

I have said I must have a photo of me in a canoe. Gene gave me good directions to his home, and I managed to follow them, arriving without taking any side trips. Gene showed me his renovated houseboat, a beautiful dock, and a boathouse used as an entertainment area. We walked the property his family had purchased many years ago. Then, Gene put a canoe in the water, and I climbed in for instruction on how to hold the paddle so I would look authentic. Gene shot a photo of me paddling the canoe.

We took a "yellow boat" ride to another island where Gene filled water jugs with fresh, cold spring water. He spends his summers clearing ground on his property and refurbishing the home. The location is remote, on a point with beautiful views all around, heavily wooded; yet in a boat or vehicle you could reach "civilization" in minutes.

My outing was delightful, and I thanked Gene for devoting an afternoon to an old lady and at the end, fulfilling her wish for a picture paddling a canoe. All my folks at home know I'd never do anything connected with water sports, but everything I'd done lately has been on or focused on water. Well, I was in Minnesota, and this was an adventure.

The landscape of northeast Minnesota would look different today if not for the efforts of Harvard-educated Chicago lawyer Frank Hubachek. Frank spent his boyhood holidays in northern Minnesota and discovered at a young age his need to experience nature in unspoiled, unfenced settings. Frank came from a family of means, and while that might imply to some an unfamiliarity with getting his hands dirty or an indifference to the need for economic progress to sometimes take a backseat to preservation, Hubachek proved all that wrong. An outspoken advocate and fighter for preservation, he persevered even when threatened with arson and violence against his family, even when the opposition pressured his business clients to shun him and when the success of his efforts would have meant giving up his beloved camp complex on Basswood Lake. A man of integrity, energy, generosity, humility, and foresight, Hubachek created the Wilderness Research Center, and funds from his ongoing endowment impact the Quetico-Superior region to this day.

I was invited to meet Bunny and Dale Wiersema, who have been caretakers of the University of Minnesota Remote Station, Wilderness Research Center, for twenty years. Cheryle Douchat, whom I'd met at church, invited me to meet them. The research facility was originally owned by the Hubacheks, but went to the university after the death of Mr. Hubachek. Two long-term research efforts distinguished the early years of the center—an effort to develop a white pine hybrid resistant to the pine blister rust that devastated white pine populations, and early studies that revealed the surprising benefits of fire to the ecology of the forest.

The research center, three-hundred acres and twenty-seven buildings, is not open to the public because of the sensitive nature of many of their experiments. I felt privileged for the opportunity to tour it. Because of changes in center ownership, much of the quaint signage and artifacts from the Hubachek era are disappearing. But with Bunny and Cheryle, I enjoyed poking around and in and out of the cottages at the complex. Cheryle's father was involved in construction of many of the buildings. Quaint cabins and the beautiful lodge still contain memorabilia of the Hubachek family.

So many of the people who have made an impact on our country and abroad are from small town USA, yet I continue to be surprised by that for some reason. Asked if I had met my neighbor, Simon Bourgin, I had to say, "No." Once again I hear that familiar phrase, "Well, he's someone you should meet." Our houses face one another on our corners, and I had seen Mr. Bourgin on his front porch in a wheel chair. I began to inquire about him.

Seems Bourgin's career was primarily as a journalist. His first job was as Washington correspondent for the Foreign Policy Association covering Congress and Capitol Hill on war and peace issues. During World War II, he was assigned to the Ninth Air Force as an information officer for the fighter-bomber group operating on grass strips in England and France.

While on assignment in the Balkans for *Stars and Stripes*, the soldier's newspaper, Bourgin saw a society falling apart in Hungary, the Red Army confronting Americans in Vienna, and the self-liberated Yugoslavs establishing communism. Bourgin was asked to join the staff of *Life* magazine after he'd expanded one of his *Stars and Stripes* reports into a *Life Reports* article. Once out of uniform, Bourgin became the Vienna correspondent for *Life* and made daily radio broadcasts across the Iron Curtain during the Cold War.

Ten years later, Bourgin returned to the United States as West Coast correspondent for *Newsweek*, then joined the Rand Corporation—the pioneering national security "think tank"—as assistant to the president. His next position was science adviser to Edward R. Murrow at the U.S. Information Agency. From there, Bourgin moved to the State Department to become senior adviser to the United Nation's conference on Science and Technology for Development. In 1968, when Astronaut Frank Borman wondered what to say from space on the dark side of the moon to an audience of one billion on Christmas Eve, Simon Bourgin came up with the opening lines of the Book of Genesis, describing the creation of the world. Bourgin's final assignment in government was at the Nuclear Regulatory Commission as its deputy press secretary.

When I visited Bourgin, I was delighted to find the tall, handsome, elder gentleman eager to talk and visit. Our conversation began with his warning, "I may be talking to you and forget what I'm saying, or fade away." But, he laughingly promised, "I'll be back." And that was the way our conversation went. I could easily imagine what he must have been like years earlier. Bourgin was ninety-seven years old when I met him. His career had been varied and apparently satisfying. He remarked that he felt he'd never left Ely. Bourgin is an extraordinary man, and I knew I will never forget him.

Late in his life and at the urging of friends in Ely, Bourgin wrote (with some assistance from a journalist) a book about his life: *Simon Bourgin: The Odyssey That Began in Ely*. That book is available through the Ely-Winton Historical Society.

Ward and Muffin Nelson, my landlords, had invited me to the Ely Rotary Club Annual Auction. Ward is the outgoing president and came by with a ticket for me for the dinner. The dining area of Grand Ely Lodge was packed with several hundred people. I was seated with Ward and Muffin and three other couples. The Ely Rotary was celebrating ninety years of service and friendship in the north woods.

In 2009, this club finalized incorporation with Rotary International, operating under a new set of by-laws and certification with the IRS as a charitable organization. Informing the citizenship, fostering safety and community pride in parks and public places, scholarships for students, penny jars to fight hunger, and tonight's auction count among the many good works of Rotary. The evening was full of laughter, a good meal, and interesting bidding. I bought a package deal: a haircut, car wash, ice cream, and dinner for two at Smitty's on Snowbank Lake—a distance out of town but said to be a scenic drive. I never got to Smitty's, but left the certificate for Angela Campbell and Gene Domich.

During the evening I couldn't help but think about my hometown's Annual Library Auction that raises thousands of dollars every year through the hard work of many dedicated people.

For fifty-six years, Dorothy Molter lived alone on the Isle of Pines on Knife Lake, fifteen miles and five portages from the nearest road. Dorothy was born in Pennsylvania and raised in Chicago, but she became a legend in Minnesota's Boundary Waters Canoe Area Wilderness.

I'd been fascinated with the story of Dorothy Molter, who was called the Root Beer Lady or Knife Lake Dorothy. A licensed nurse, Dorothy first came to the Isle of Pines in 1930 as a vacationer with her family. At that time the Isle of Pines was a fishing resort. After visiting again in 1931, Dorothy became a regular visitor. Bill Berglund, owner of the resort, recognized Dorothy's toughness and love of the north woods. He hired her and, as he thought she would be, Dorothy was the perfect employee. Berglund's health was failing. He offered room and board for Dorothy in exchange for her nursing skills, and he promised to will the resort to Dorothy at his death. When Berglund died, Dorothy remained on the island.

The two books I read about Dorothy said she'd garnered the nickname Nightingale of the North Woods because of her background in nursing, and soon became a first responder. She was often the only source of medical assistance in the area. Outfitters would point to her island on the map and tell their clients, "If you run into trouble, head to Dorothy's."

Dorothy's isolation, and her status as a single woman in an area traditionally populated by men, eventually attracted attention. She received thousands of visitors over the years, including canoeists, tourists and anglers, reporters from national magazines, and even a movie star or two. The *Saturday Evening Post* once published an article about Dorothy entitled, "The Loneliest Woman in America." Dorothy said she was hardly lonely. At times she had more company than she knew what to do with.

Dorothy lived without electricity, telephone, or other utilities. She used propane and a battery-powered two-way radio. Her cabin was heated with a wood stove. She operated Isle of Pines Resort from 1948 to 1975. The Wilderness Act caused Dorothy's property to be condemned by the U.S. government. She was told to leave. Dorothy's friends petitioned the government on her behalf. Because of their efforts, a lifetime tenancy was granted. However, many travel restrictions were implemented, making it impossible for Dorothy to transport heavy goods to the resort—for example, the soda pop that she offered to visitors. Dorothy tried making her own root beer, which she brewed using the clean clear Knife Lake water. She cooled the soda with ice cut from the lake in winter and stored it in her old-fashioned icehouse.

The popularity of Dorothy's root beer, and the publicity stemming from her public dispute with the Forest Service, made her a celebrity of the North Woods and brought droves of canoeists to Knife Lake each summer. Dorothy needed assistance to keep up with the demand. Friends and family began to help produce the beer. Her great-nephew Steve apprenticed and stayed on the island, learning to make the root beer. Between 1976 and 1986, the year of Dorothy's death, they brewed an average of ten thousand bottles of root beer each summer. Dorothy died of a heart attack at the age of seventy-nine while hauling a load of wood for her barrel stove.

Dorothy's family held a memorial in Midlothian, Illinois, but few of her friends from Ely could attend. Those same friends wanted a service in her honor to be held at her place on Knife Lake. Snowmobiles had been banned in the area for several years, and a trip to Knife Lake was impossible without them. A group of locals put forward a request to the U.S. Forestry Service to lift the ban for one day to venerate this great woman. Public support was so great that once again the USFS deviated from protocol and allowed the service. The snowmobile authorization applied only to a marked trail for use between the hours of 9:00 a.m. and 4:00 p.m. on the designated date, with no allowance for side trips.

Dorothy's property was also the center of one last fight. According to the terms of Dorothy's agreement with the forest service, the islands would be returned to their natural state when she ceased living there. That meant no additional facilities could be added and existing buildings had to be removed. A Property Disposal Plan was already in place. Again, Dorothy's friends campaigned on her behalf to save her cabins and preserve her memory. Jean Larson, director of the Ely Chamber of Commerce at the time, contacted the forestry service about salvaging Dorothy's cabins. John Pegors, regional director for Minnesota Pollution Control Agency, approved the application for an open-burn permit requested by the Kawishiwi District Office of the Forest Service.

Stipulations from the Forest Service on removal required completion by April 15, 1987, and accomplished without use of snowmobiles. Work crews were transported by previously planned and approved flights to and from Knife Lake. Dorothy's "angels" had only forty-eight days to remove the cabins. They weren't just working against the clock, but fighting weather as well.

Every piece of evidence of habitation was extracted, including the perennials Dorothy had planted over the years. Following the removal of Dorothy's cabins, all remaining structures on the Isle of Pines were burned, returning the islands as much as possible to their natural state of wildness. The average paddler would notice little evidence that the island had ever been inhabited or that a courageous woman had lived there the last fifty-six years of her life.

Finally, on May 6, 1993, what would have been Dorothy Molter's eighty-sixth birthday, her "angels" celebrated the culmination of six years of labor and toil with the grand opening of the Dorothy Molter Museum, a permanent monument to the Root Beer Lady of Knife Lake.

Ward and Muffin Nelson had invited me to a corn party (that may not have been the official name). We were greeted in the front yard of a beautiful home by a papier mâché ear of corn, large enough for a six-foot-tall man to stand by at equal height. We each autographed the ear of corn and then had our photo taken with it. The party menu consisted of all things corn and corny: cornbread, corn dogs, corn soup, corn salad, candy corn, and corn-on-the-cob. Games were played, all relating to corn. A mystery corn man who had to be identified with corny clues mingled with the guests, many of whom had dressed in keeping with the corn theme. It was the most interesting and original party I'd ever attended.

My time in Ely was getting short, and I was feeling the urgency that comes each month when it became time to move to another place. Yet, there was more to do. My sister, Shirley, who lives in Birmingham, is a social worker with hospice. She and one of the hospice physicians were talking about my trip when Shirley said I was in Minnesota. Dr. Elizabeth Kvale asked, "Where?" and Shirley answered, "Ely."

"My mom is in Tower, Minnesota, where she's spending the summer," Dr. Kvale said. "We've spent summers there most of our lives." Tower is only twenty miles from Ely, and, of course, that prompted a visit. I called Elizabeth's mother, Janice, and we agreed to meet for lunch at Sulu's Café in Tower. By profession a nurse, Janice has taught at the University of Texas and is a writer of short stories and articles. Janice gave me a resource online to find writing tips. Once again, I couldn't help but be amazed at all my special encounters that seemed to come from nowhere, but which have been the making of this trip. Serendipities.

Remember Iron Mike Hillman? I had an opportunity to cook supper for him one night and enjoy another visit. Mike came by on a subsequent day with an autographed copy of his book: *Ely Lives, Her People, Her Stories*. He wished me well with my writing, and I extracted his promise to take the leftovers from my refrigerator. It's what friends are for.

Meanwhile, I gathered loose ends, the final things I had listed to do. That included inviting Ward and Muffin Nelson to lunch after church, a high priority. They'd been most kind and generous with invitations and introductions, and I was more than grateful. I was able to say good-bye to people at church that morning, also.

Ely holds a walkathon, an American Cancer Society Relay for

Life Walk, in Whiteside Park. Hometown USA is amazing. I was reminded of similar activities in my hometown of Chatom, Alabama, all through the year. Ely is no different, with its high school band playing, food booths, entertainment and other activities, and hundreds of walkers. Rain dampened the luminaries but not the spirit of those manning tents with information or the walkers, for this was a worthy effort.

Leaving Ely without a photo with a canoe on top of my car was also not an option. I was determined. A week ago I had stopped by Piragis Northwoods Company, Canoe Trip Outfitters and was told that I had only to come by. They would see that I got that picture.

Michelle, the manager, took me around to the back of the Piragis complex where assistants, Christina and Jamie, easily picked up a canoe and put it on top of my car. They shot the photo and my wish was fulfilled. Janie and I had concluded early on in our journey that the only way to know about something was to ask. You would get one of two answers, Yes or No. That's why I now have a picture of myself standing by my car with a canoe on top. Thank you, Michelle, Christina, and Jamie.

My thoughts turned to Ketchikan, Alaska, and the safest way to get there. Ketchikan is my October destination. Motel reservations had been made since early spring, thanks to Janie. I called Nicole, who would be my landlord there, for advice. She recommended I take the ferry from Bellingham, Washington—a thirty-two hour trip—rather than drive to Prince Rupert, British Columbia, and take a ferry from there—five hours. Nicole's concerns were many: driving alone on less traveled roads; weather, as it would be October and unpredictable; and the need to schedule the ferry, which operates only twice a week to Ketchikan. I was making decisions and reservations. And I appreciated Nicole's concern for my safety.

It's my last evening in Ely. Angela and I were walking to the Oriental Orchid for Chinese takeout when a friend of hers named Sure drove up in his Jeep and stopped. "Let's go for a ride and show Lou the greenstone," he said. Angela and I climbed in for what ended up being a fast ride—it felt like ninety miles per hour—with our hair blowing in the wind. Finally Sure came to a stop at a huge stone, a piece of what is known as Ely greenstone.

Greenstone is a basaltic lava with grey-green to yellow-green coloring derived from the presence of chlorite. A metamorphic rock, it indicates volcanic origin followed by periods of intense heat and pressure. The Ely rock was probably buried deep and later exposed by erosion. Pillow structure in Ely greenstone suggests lava, which hardened underwater. It is believed that the Superior Uplands—highlands of northeast Minnesota and northern Wisconsin—were in Precambrian times (3.5 billion to 600 million years ago) an arc of offshore islands. A similar greenstone is found in New Zealand, also known as New Zealand nephrite or New Zealand jade, prized by the Maori for its hardness and beauty. This was another must-see in Ely, and it was most unusual.

Angela and I eventually got our Chinese food, and chatted with local businesswoman JoAnn O'Reilly while we ate. JoAnn is president and chief executive officer of Razor Edge Systems, a family-owned business that makes sharpening tools. John and Rose Juranitch founded the business, starting with only five hundred dollars and help from the entire family, including their five children. All pitched in working the assembly line in their basement and manning booths at sports shows where the sharpening products were sold in the 1970s. The company is committed to not just meeting but exceeding customer expectations, and it is known for its outstanding service and having the highest standard in sharpening tools. The website states they are "privileged to operate in God's country—Ely." What interesting people, the Juranitch family and JoAnn O'Reilly!

When I first drove into Ely my perception was that the town appeared a bit shabby. My, how my opinion changed. Not that anything had been done since I arrived to beautify the town, but just being there, seeing what makes Ely the special place it is, and realizing how hard the people work to make it a number one town, changed my perspective. It is a town that is difficult to describe. Ely doesn't put on airs. It just is what it is: A small town sometimes struggling to staying alive, but showing off its natural beauty; abundance of pure water, game fish and wildlife; scenery unlike any other place; and many, many talented, resourceful, celebrated people. I liked Ely. Looking through the magazine *Ely Summer Times*, I saw an ad for the International Wolf Center that read, "What happens in Ely stays with you forever." I felt that way. My stay in Ely would be with me forever. So far I had said that about each place I'd visited on the trip, and I was still amazed how true it rang. I am the most blessed and fortunate person.

It concerned me that I had not been adequately putting into words how I felt about all I'd seen and done so far, but I hoped and prayed my book about the trip would in some way touch people's hearts, thank those who had shared with me along the way, and be an encouragement to those who self-limit what they think they can do.

My last morning in Ely I met Angela for breakfast at Britton's Café, which advertises local flavor in both food and clientele. Breakfast was hearty: eggs, sausage, bacon, biscuit, pancake—a meal to keep me going down the road.

As usual, I left Ely a little later than originally planned, as I didn't really want to leave. I drove around town one last time. I have mentioned here a lot of people in writing about Ely, but there are many more I failed to name, only because of space constraints. I can truthfully say that every person I met in Ely made an impression, and I won't forget the faces or circumstances of each. I will always wish that I had kept better notes.

With that, I connected to OnStar and was on the road again. I wouldn't be surprised to learn that every time I started OnStar somewhere, someone could be heard saying, "Here's that crazy lady from Alabama again. You deal with her."

The phrase "You have left the planned route" had been worn out. But it's nothing personal, and the OnStar advisers are always gracious when I need help. Anyway, I was entirely dependent on their directions, and remained confident OnStar would get me safely to Twin Bridges, Montana.

Chapter Nine
Twin Bridges, Montana
September 2011

MY FIRST DAY OUT of Ely as I neared Bismarck, North Dakota, I called a dear friend from Chatom, Alabama (my hometown, in case you've forgotten). I had hoped to see Martha "Dits" Nelson and thought perhaps she would invite me to stay overnight. After several calls and receiving no answer, I kept driving. When I did stop there was no room at the inn, or at any inn for at least a hundred miles in any direction.

Since traveling alone I had not made a single reservation for my road trips, mainly because I didn't know the distance I'd travel in a day. This time I did not finding lodging so easily. At one motel the clerk spent time calling other motels and finally said the closest reservation was fifty miles away and not on my route; the clerk did find rooms available at the Prairie Knights Casino and Resort Indian Reservation. With little choice, I took it.

FEMA and National Guard personnel were out in force in the

area I drove, due to historic flooding in North Dakota, according to one newspaper. Fires had preceded the flooding. I saw flooded areas on my way to the casino, but no roads were closed.

I only saw the lobby, but the casino appeared to be a beautiful resort. My room was huge. I had already eaten, so I went to bed immediately. Next morning was like driving in another world. There was an eerie look to everything—smoky and foggy. I could not see my car or any other, and had to follow the taillights of the car in front of me to find the main road and get my bearings.

After that unusual start the day was good, and I drove to Livingston, Montana, arriving late, late afternoon. My niece from California, Jo Anne, was visiting a couple of retired teachers in Bozeman—Pat and Fred Cornelious. I called them the next day, arriving later to pick up Jo Anne. We visited a bit, and Fred spent time on his computer looking up ferry schedules for the Alaska part of my trip. I would see them again. They had gotten me a ticket for the upcoming Maya Angelou lecture at Montana State University.

Jo Anne and I were now on our way to Twin Bridges, Montana. Neither of us had been there before, and we were excited, completely ready for the next adventure, and already awed by the beautiful scenery.

King's Motel and Flatline Outfitters sits right on Main Street in Twin Bridges. The motel is owned and operated by Marsha and Don Greenmore; the outfitter, by their son, Matt. Southwest Montana is known for great fly fishing. On Flatline Outfitters website, fishermen are warned: "Your nerves better be steady, my friend, because these fish don't tolerate mistakes." In a review on the King's Motel website, a client claiming to be accustomed to five-star accommodations gave King's six stars. My room was completely adequate, but when Marsha Greenmore saw how much stuff I had with me she offered me another. Jo Anne and I agreed we both would be more comfortable with extra space, yet we could still be together for everything else we wanted to do.

Twin Bridges is essentially a one-street town, less than a mile long, with most of the businesses on Main Street. Several shops had closed for the winter season, but the basics were there: grocery, post office, banks, auto repair, several bars, real estate agents, a weaving shop, museum, and a gift shop with locally made crafts. Four or five restaurants, churches, and a small medical clinic rounded out the commercial district. I could easily walk everywhere I might need to go.

Jo Anne and I were on the sidewalk near the grocery when a young couple stopped and asked if the car with an Alabama tag belonged to us. I wondered if we looked like we were from Alabama, whatever that might mean. A chat ensued, and we were introduced to Matt Hill from Birmingham, Alabama, and his wife, Suzanne. Matt is a loan officer with the First Madison Valley Bank in Ennis, and Suzanne works with the Ennis, Montana newspaper, *Madisonian News*.

Upon returning to King's Motel, Jo Anne and I met Don Greenmore, the owner, and his son Matt of the outfitter next door.

Matt's wife is a pharmacist in Dillon, and we would meet her later. I refer to King's Motel as a mom-and-pop operation because it is evident the Greenmores personally put in much work to make it the most comfortable and hospitable of accommodations.

Twenty miles from Twin Bridges is Dillon, Montana, in Beaverhead County in the southwest corner of the state. Deep basins separate the towering mountain ranges. Dillon is home to the Beaverhead River, a "blue ribbon" fly-fishing river. The headquarters of Beaverhead-Deer Lodge National Forest; the University of Montana, Western Campus; the Dillon Field Office of the Bureau of Land Management; and the National Franchise Office of Great Harvest Bread Company are all in the small community of Dillon, the major trading area for more than 13,000 people in two counties. Dillon also forms the center of the Outfitter-Guide Fishing service, the reason many people come to the area.

Montana's biggest weekend takes place in Dillon at the Beaverhead County Fair. Jo Anne and I decided to visit the fair after walking around town, window shopping, and eating lunch at a great little café called Strawberry. The fair is *big*! Every kind of livestock imaginable was shown, including fifty rabbits. Exhibits included needlework, canning, photography, woodworking, serious art displays, baked goods, flower arrangements, and leather items. In addition, a rodeo and a carnival offered entertainment. Our five dollar donation was hardly enough to pay for the enjoyment we had.

The centuries-old tradition of hospitality in the American West likely began with the meeting of the explorers Lewis and

Clark and the Shoshone Indians at Camp Fortunate. That receptivity, often found in hostile environments, continues today in Dillon and surrounding communities.

The wide open landscape encircled with mountain peaks more than ten-thousand-feet high gives credence to Montana's unofficial nickname, Big Sky Country. The area offered much to see and do.

Our next foray was to the beautiful, small town of Ennis about twenty-six miles southeast of Twin Bridges. Ennis is quaint, an old town banked by meadows, streams, glacial lakes, and mining camps. Three mountain ranges, the Madison, Gravelly, and Tobacco Root surround Ennis, population nearly nine hundred, with a main street of only two blocks. We're in the heart of the best fly fishing in the country and have arrived during the Fly Fishing Festival. It was Saturday and the bank wasn't open for business, but the lobby offered hospitality because of the festival. Matt Hill, whom we had met in Twin Bridges, was there. We were introduced to Mary Oliver, vice president of the bank, who was quite interested in our story.

Asking locals to suggest a place to eat almost always got us to a good meal—in this case we were sent to the G Bar Saloon for lunch. I hadn't thought about football at all, but it was Saturday and when we entered the bar and glanced up at the television, I noticed Auburn University (in Alabama) playing Utah. It was a close game, thrilling, with only two minutes left to determine a winner. Final score: Auburn 41, Utah 38. Lunch was great, and the game exciting. And who should call at this time but one of my children. I had to tell them I was in a saloon, and I had caught the football game.

Our servers were all young people who had cornered the market on western hospitality. Knowing how to accommodate visitors is noticeable all about town.

Even though I'm not into fishing, Jo Anne and I looked around at fishing stuff while browsing the shops and the festival, which is a project of the Madison River Foundation. We enjoyed the live music, raffles, and angling celebrities; casting clinics and competitions; fly-tying demonstrations and instruction; exhibits, auctions, and chili cookouts. It was a fun time and quite a different experience.

And another serendipity occurred. At a Farmer's Market on the edge of Ennis, we stopped and fell into conversation with Ken and Penny Hall who had lived in Taos, New Mexico. I said, "Oh, I'll be there for the month of November." They asked where I was staying, and I admitted to having no plan. Ken immediately wrote down the name of a realtor, Sue Westbrook, at Taos Blue.

Our return route to Twin Bridges took us through Virginia City, the oldest town in Montana and capital of the territory before it became a state. Virginia City is a well preserved Victorian gold-mining town of one hundred and fifty year-round residents. More than one hundred historic buildings complete with artifacts and furnishings populate the town.

For tourists, there are stagecoach rides, live theater shows, historic lodging, and unique shops such as an old-fashioned bakery and candy store. It was easy to imagine characters of the Old

West walking down the same boardwalks where we strolled—vigilantes, rowdy miners, women of ill repute, and likely some respectable folks, too.

Nevada City, with its fourteen original historic buildings, is just one-and-a-half miles away from Virginia City. A collection of more than one hundred historic buildings, saved from locations all over the state, has been transplanted in a three- or four-block area of Nevada City. It is now a backdrop for living history weekends during the summer months.

The Nevada City Music Hall is a museum of historic music machines, Gavioli organs and player pianos. Gavioli and Cie were a Franco-Italian organ-building company in Europe. The founder of the company, Giacomo Gavioli, made (as a hobby) automatic-player music machines in the form of bird organs and flute clocks. That hobby led him to building larger instruments. The collection of these instruments displayed in Nevada City is the largest in the world. Both Virginia City and Nevada City took us back in time. It was hard to leave and return to the real world.

Jo Anne's time with me was limited, and we worked to cram in as much as possible. We left the fair in Dillon without seeing any of the evening's activities, headed home, and made reservations for dinner at the Old Hotel, once called Twin Bridges Hotel, built in 1879. The inn is a beautifully renovated historic three-story brick building at the corner of Fifth and Main, retaining all the charm of its original hardwood floors, staircases, doors, and architecture. The restaurant cuisine provided by Paula and Bill is defined as a fusion of Pacific Rim and European. On its website, glowing customer reviews describe dishes of bison, or lamb, scampi, game hens stuffed with goat cheese, homemade breads, and homemade ice cream. The menu changes weekly with an emphasis on fresh, seasonal, and local products. We found the food and service impeccable. It reminded me of August in New Orleans.

I called the realtor in Taos, New Mexico, that had been recommended to me earlier in the day and secured reservations for my own casita at Taos Lodging. I was now booked for the rest of my trip. Ain't God good?

Jo Anne and I had such a pleasant reunion; I hated to see her leave. She is calm, easy-going, well-traveled, and, of course, kin, not company. We skipped church in order to get to the airport in Belgrade on time. After driving the hour-and-a-half from Twin Bridges and checking in, we enjoyed a leisurely breakfast in the airport restaurant. Jo Anne and I said our good-byes, not knowing when we might be together again.

My walking route traveled through the county fairgrounds alongside the Beaverhead River. The fairground facility has many barns, sheds, stables, stalls, show arenas with bleachers, a playground for kids, and the town's softball fields, also with bleachers. All of it, beautifully maintained. My route took me about three miles, and I saw few walkers, or dogs, or horses, bikes, or skate boarders. Few people are out at 6:30 or 7:00 a.m.

My nephew, John Schell, said he would be in Bozeman on the ninth, leaving on the tenth, and I was invited to the home of his host family, Steve and Jean Schnee, for dinner. I was excited to see John and meet his hiking buddies. John is a lawyer, husband, father of three sons, an all-around great person, and a hiker of many years. His buddies—Steve, Clark, Modi, and Steven—had been friends forever, and on this trip they hiked in Yellowstone and the Tetons. Several members of our host's family were invited too: Steve and Jean's two daughters, a son-in-law and baby, and Steven's wife, Linda.

Despite having spent their afternoon at a funeral for a friend of the family, Steve and Jean welcomed us with a wonderfully prepared meal. Dinner included appetizers (large pastry shells filled with chunks of celery, cucumber, chickpeas, and ham), a cheese tray with crackers and cherry tomatoes, and, of course, beverages. Dinner entrees of barbecued ribs and chicken breasts were served with roasted new potatoes and a veggie tray of mushrooms, asparagus, and peppers. A green salad, fruit bowl, and bread rounded out the meal. Somehow I failed to make note of the dessert after having eaten that wonderful meal.

Meeting John's friends and hearing about their hiking experiences made the evening memorable. But the night wasn't over for me as I had reservations in Livingston at a Best Western Motel where I'd stayed on my way to Twin Bridges. I wanted to get closer to the G Bar M Ranch in Clyde Park.

Years ago when my youngest daughter, Ellene, was a teenager, Fletcher and I and eight other girls from the Girl's Auxiliary, a branch of the Women's Missionary Union, traveled to the G Bar M Ranch. Our GA leader and host for the trip, Cindy Craig, had once worked summers as a ranch hand. Kay Odom, a nurse and Cindy's sister-in-law, also accompanied us. When we were at the ranch that December years ago, everything was covered in snow, and it was a drive of at least thirteen miles on dirt roads. But this time I found it easily. Explaining who I was took a bit more effort because the owners of the ranch had died. The current owner-manager was only eight years old when we were last there.

G Bar M Ranch is three thousand acres of working/guest ranch, which means the operation is a horse and cattle ranch where guests are invited to share in the lifestyle. Guests are welcome to help with all day-to-day activities. Mike and Mary, the current owners, were preparing a lunch for "the quilting ladies," and I did not tarry. I left with a heavy heart, remembering that wonderful December of long ago and all that has changed since.

The sign said: "Ruby Valley Parish, Church of the Valley, Ministers: All the People." I liked that, naming the ministers as "all" of us. From the looks of the bulletin and the many service organizations listed in the church brochure, it was a true statement for this small town. The church crowd was quite small, only one young person, but the spirit of those attending was not dampened by the lack of numbers. I met almost everyone during the coffee-and-cake social after the service, and it seemed evident all were excited to be there.

A senior center lunch get-together was held at the Wagon Wheel restaurant on Tuesdays and Fridays, with an occasional speaker, but always food and visiting, for only five dollars. Someone said, "You need to sit by Walt Shular," and so I did. Walt had once taken Charles Kuralt fishing, and he spoke of that, but the best part of meeting Walt was enjoying the banter between Walt and Harold Smail. Their back-and-forth quips were worthy of any stand-up comic's, and kept me laughing.

After lunch, I changed clothes and gears, and left for Bozeman to attend a lecture by the late Dr. Maya Angelou, author and former poet laureate of the United States.

Bozeman is described as a place with big-city amenities and a small-town feel. Population in 2010 was 37,280, making Bozeman the fourth largest city in the state of Montana. The city is named after John M. Bozeman, who established the Bozeman Trail, an overland route connecting the gold rush territory of Montana to the Oregon Trail. John Bozeman led the first group of two thousand settlers on the trail in 1864.

Bozeman today is home to Montana State University and blessed with an eclectic mix of ranchers, artists, professors, ski enthusiasts, and entrepreneurs, many drawn to the world-class outdoor recreation to be found in the area. A slice of old-fashioned Americana, Bozeman was designated an All-American City in 2001 by the National Civic League, an award recognizing a city whose citizens work together to identify and tackle community-wide challenges and achieve uncommon positive results.

I met Fred and Pat Cornelious at their apartment, and we went to Montana State University Brick Breedan Fieldhouse for Maya Angelou's lecture. The crowd was huge, and we were in the balcony, but with good seats.

I had not realized Dr. Angelou had become so frail even then, not in her looks but in her need for assistance to walk onto the stage. I have always loved her speaking voice, but had to listen very closely to catch all the nuances. She was quite the teaser and joker in her delivery. It was a beautiful hour, a reminder of the influence we each have in life's journey. Her message that night came from the Book of Genesis, and the account of how God put the rainbow in the sky. She reminded us that each of us has many rainbows and that we can become the hope and encouragement needed by someone else.

Dr. Angelou was born in 1928 in Saint Louis, Missouri—a poet, memoirist, actress, and important figure in the American Civil Rights Movement. Over the course of her life, she wrote seven autobiographies, essays, children's books, plays, and screenplays. She was in great demand on the college campus lecture circuit for decades, and seating often sold out long before the actual event, as was the case for the lecture we attended.

In Dr. Angelou's first book, the memoir *I Know Why the Caged Bird Sings*, she recounts the first seventeen years of her troubled life. At age three after her parents' divorce, she and her four-year-old brother were sent to Stamps, Arkansas, to live with their father's mother. Angelou was raped. Her attacker was jailed for one day, released, and found kicked to death four days later.

The trauma caused Angelou to become mute, a condition that lasted five years. She once said of that time, "I thought if I spoke, my mouth would just issue out something that would kill people randomly, so it was better not to talk."

Universities, literary organizations, government agencies, and groups galore have honored Angelou. More than ten honorary degrees were bestowed on this remarkable woman before she died on May 28, 2014.

It was a lovely and rare evening. I enjoyed seeing Fred and Pat again, and I thanked them for including me in the outing. An added bonus of the night was getting to walk around the

MSU campus before the lecture—a beautiful setting. I was back over the mountain and home by 11:00 p.m.

When President Thomas Jefferson dispatched Meriwether Lewis and William Clark to find a water route across the uncharted West, he realized his dream for exploration of the lands acquired in the Louisiana Purchase of 1803.

Jefferson expected Lewis and Clark to encounter woolly mammoths, erupting volcanoes, and a mountain of pure salt, but what they found instead was no less surprising: three hundred species unknown to science, nearly fifty Native American tribes, and the Rocky Mountains.

In May 1804, Lewis and Clark and forty-five other men set out in a fifty-five-foot keelboat and two pirogues. They were commissioned to map the land, to hold diplomatic councils with native peoples, and to study and record everything regarding plants, animals, minerals, soils, and native ways of life.

In the winter of 1804-05, the explorers arrived near the Hidatsa Indian villages where they built a fort and would spend the winter months. Several trappers who they thought might be able to interpret and guide the expedition of the Missouri River in the springtime were interviewed. The two explorers agreed to hire Toussaint Charbonneau, a Quebecan trapper married to a young Shoshone girl, Sacagawea.

I had not read anything about, or even thought about the Lewis and Clark expedition since elementary school. When I walked in the park in the mornings I would passed a statue of Sacagawea, who played an important role in the legend of Lewis and Clark. I also made a trip to the Twin Bridges library and checked out several books on the expedition and Sacagawea. Should you have time, I would recommend it. It was good to read and learn more about her later life and especially about her children.

While at the library, I also checked out *Charles and Me*, written by Pat Shannon, Charles Kuralt's mistress for thirty years.

In each place I've visited, when people learned I would be in Twin Bridges, Montana, following Kuralt's journey, they asked, "Are you going to see Pat Shannon?" My answer was always, "If the opportunity presents itself."

First I read the book, *Charles and Me*. I visited Weaver's Studio, owned by Norman Frankland in Twin Bridges, knowing Ms. Shannon had a connection there. Frankland weaves beautiful rugs. He said Pat Shannon usually came to his studio several times a week. Twin Bridges is small town USA. When I decided to call Pat, because time was getting short, she said she knew I was in town. We agreed we both would love getting together and chose to meet at a renovated schoolhouse moved to a site by the Big Hole River.

One cannot escape history in this place. The Big Hole River was a part of Jefferson's Louisiana Purchase. Lewis and Clark mapped the land traveling up the Jefferson River to where it forks at what is now Twin Bridges. The northerly fork of the river, which Lewis and Clark named Wisdom River, is now known as Big Hole River.

Pat Shannon is a gracious, interesting woman, slight in stature, with a ready smile, graying hair, and easy to talk to. She was interested in my journey. We chatted, took pictures, and planned another meeting, but I ran out of time before we could reunite again. I do want Pat to know that my time with her was special to me.

I quote from the copy on the book jacket of *Charles and Me*: "In this candid memoir, Pat Shannon writes of her relationship with America's well loved news correspondent, Charles Kuralt. They met in Reno, Nevada, in 1968. Charles was in his second marriage. Pat was divorced with three children. Charles never divorced. They never married. Private and protected, the companionship of almost thirty years escaped attention until Charles' death in 1997. *Charles and Me* tells of the life they built for themselves and the children, far from celebrity's glare." Pat Shannon and I sat in the old schoolhouse Kuralt had had moved to Big Hole and renovated to use as his study.

Kuralt built the little North Carolina cabin on the Big Hole River, on ninety acres he'd purchased. For twenty-two years beginning in 1976, the Big Hole belonged to Charles and Pat during the month of September.

Then the abandoned Pageville schoolhouse, built in the 1880s and sitting next to the highway, seemed a terrible waste. After moving it to the riverside, Kuralt spent a year renovating the old building with its graying boards and carpenter Gothic.

Inside, the building was teak and mahogany and marble. Ornate double doors with leaded glass and brass fittings opened to the entrance hall and mahogany staircase. A massive partner's desk from a London antique shop was added to befit this elegant gentleman's library, and a yellow silk rug from China outlined a reading corner.

Bookshelves were in abundance, lining the room with its tall ceiling, and a porch overlooked the beautiful river and tree lined banks. Within walking distance and in sight of the library was the little cabin Kuralt had built.

I loved this description from Pat's book of the surrounding land and vegetation: "The hills are dappled with buckbrush and scrub pine. Low growing bitterroot hugs the dry rocky soil, heralding the Big Hole spring with fragile pink blossoms. Subdued most of the year, spiny plains cactus, our prickly pear, calls attention to itself in the early summer with waxy yellow blooms. In late summer fragrant gray-green sagebrush offers clusters of tiny silver flowerets to anyone walking by. It is a muted landscape made lovely by the changing waters and frequent dazzling sun. And the cabin sits down in the bottom of this narrow fertile strip bordering the river. Tall, weathered cottonwoods spread canopies of shade, and shrubby willows form dense thickets in the hollows and along the creek. The meadow grasses are a mix of alfalfa, rye, barley, and wild iris. It's about as close to heaven as a dry fly fisherman can get."

I treasured this look into Kuralt's life and getting to know the woman he shared it with for almost thirty years. A true love story.

The Twin Bridges Historical Society museum is open from Memorial Day to Labor Day; however appointments can be arranged out of season. I met with Joy Day, a member of the historical association and an agent with Novich Insurance Agency. Joy set a meeting for me with Bill Nicholls, a bright, articulate, ninety-two-year-old historian.

Bill's grandparents, Owen and Sarah Thomas, homesteaded on the Lower Ruby River in 1882. Ed, Bill's father, took over the one-hundred-and-sixty-acre ranch in 1919. He said they got electricity in 1922 and lost the ranch in 1927. Bill served in the

Navy, worked in a plant for the Atomic Energy Commission for twenty years, and then hired on as a custodian for Montana State University for ten years more.

The museum is housed in the Reid Building, built in 1917, located on Main Street. Bill took me through the entire building and probably mentioned everything in there: old mining equipment, geological specimens, old photos, vintage clothing, and an exhibit about Benny Reynolds, a Rodeo Hall of Famer. Bill now shares his special knowledge of Twin Bridges with everyone.

Marsha Greenmore, owner of the motel where I was staying, invited me one day to accompany her to Bozeman where she had an appointment and planned to do some shopping. I agreed. We stopped off in Ennis and had a wonderful breakfast at Yesterday's Restaurant and Soda Fountain inside Ennis Pharmacy. The place was like one of those "yesterday's" soda fountains. Marsha drove a different route to Bozeman, showing me new scenery to enjoy—mountains, rolling hills, and lakes—just beautiful.

After Marsha's appointment, we indulged in a manicure and a pedicure, and I had my hair trimmed. We wandered a mall and several big box stores, and finished with an early supper at a Mexican restaurant, a favorite place for Marsha and her husband, Don. The atmosphere and food were delightful. This was my fourth time in Bozeman, and I was liking it more and more. I loved that downtown was the center of everything; that it still buzzed, unlike the main streets of many small cities today.

It was still September and I was still in Montana. A typical morning walk unfolded almost like a slide show and at times it moved me to tears with its beauty. It was as if I had a remote I could change at will: clouds moving quickly across the sky one moment, sunshine giving the mountaintops a different look the next, cool breezes blowing one minute, then the next being able to see long, long distances on a clear day. Several mornings recorded a temperature in the upper twenties. Hated to think about leaving all this, except—leaving meant I would soon be in Alaska.

It is always interesting to visit a gallery that displays the work of local artists. In Twin Bridges, River's Edge Gallery showcases paintings, weavings, sculpture, pottery, jewelry, and quilting. Classes and lectures are offered too. I regret that I didn't write down the name of the lady manning the gallery when I visited because she was both gracious and attentive.

Since this area is all about fishing, I had heard about Glenn Brackett before my arrival. Glenn is internationally famous for his carefully made bamboo rods, and I called and set up an interview. As Kuralt says in his book, Glenn works while he talks.

Small in stature, with a bearded face, a smile that makes you automatically smile back, and twinkly eyes, Glenn was an approachable man in his overalls. In size and demeanor, he was almost elfin—an exceptionally talented and interesting elf.

Many years ago when Glenn first came to the area, he and a partner started the R.L. Winston Rod Company, which made graphite fishing rods. About six years ago Glenn sold his interest in the company in order to concentrate on the bamboo rod. He formed Sweetgrass Rod Company and travels to China, near Canton, twice a year to select a particular species of bamboo. The bamboo is shipped to Twin Bridges, where Glenn stores it, letting it age for a year or two. According to Glenn, matching, cutting, tempering, gluing, and finishing the strips of bamboo is an art. All bamboo rods have a hollow core, which makes the pole lighter and gives more action, but requires a lot more work. Glenn said it usually takes a fisherman ten to fifteen years of fishing before he's ready for a bamboo rod. Glenn's rods never break, and get better with age.

Sweetgrass Company makes square rods, four-strip rods, five-strip rods, even eight-strip, but most are six-strip rods. I was told the rods being cut the day of my visit would be ready in a year. During that time they would hang in a heated cabinet with string tied tightly around them, and a four-pound weight hanging on the tip sections. At the end of one year, the string would be removed, the rods scraped, sanded, wrapped and varnished, the reel seat put on and they'd be ready to be sold—internationally.

Glenn's crew is expert in the many different steps and overall process of making the rods. They call themselves the "Boo Boy" team. All are fishermen. The Boo Boys feel that being a fisherman is key to understanding what makes a rod fish and cast well. Jerry Kustich has been part of the team for twenty-five years. He can usually be found in a stream testing everything from flies to waders, and different bamboo designs. Jerry is an advocate for public access to Montana's rivers, a devoted environmentalist, author, and fishing ambassador. He lectures on and represents the ideals for which all serious fly anglers stand. Other members of the Boo Boy team—Mike Watson, Dave Delisi, Dana Escott, Wade Lambert, Jason Fox, and Sam Drunkman—make up eighty years of collective rod-building experience.

Jerry Kustich wasn't in the building during my visit, but I called to arrange an interview with him later. He autographed a copy of his book, *At the River's Edge, Lessons Learned in a Life of Fly Fishing*. A full-time fisherman, Jerry reflects in his book on the wisdom he's gained from fishing, wisdom that keeps him in touch with living life fully and keeping body and soul together. In the book's foreword, Glenn wrote, "Jerry has been my right hand for many years."

Glenn Brackett is said to be an inspiration in his local community as well as in his shop, and sees it as his sacred duty to preserve his legacy by teaching others the many lessons involved in building bamboo rods. From the Sweetwater Rod Company brochure I gleaned: "We hope that what we do brings you peace. And that our work will help you feel nature more deeply, imagine more than exists beyond what you can see, and experience the little things like the pleasure of seeing a mayfly tail as it twitches. That it will somehow lead to finding the wilderness within through the wilderness outside, point to the discovery of streams that flow into the ocean of possibilities, and free you to 'just be.' Ultimately, our hope is to inspire our supporters to help others discover the mystery, wonder, and magic encompassed by the fly-fishing journey. Sincerely, the Boo Boys."

Glenn's signature rods include: eight-sided configured rods, hollow-fluted, two-to-three-piece rods, every line weight and length available, leather case, and scrimshaw seat—all rods made from start to finish by Glenn Brackett. They are personalized and serialized, and Glenn limits the number sold to ten per year. The price is $3,900.00. Glenn will personally take your calls.

Marsha Greenmore and I found another opportunity to spend time together, other than seeing one another around the motel. We made a trip to Butte, about forty-five miles from Twin

Bridges. Marsha had coupons for a great sale at Herberger's department store, which is much like what I'm familiar with in the South at Belk's. We shopped and enjoyed lunch, walked about, and were home before dark. Marsha was delightful to be around. And accommodating. I was sure her experiences meeting and pleasing the many people who visit Twin Bridges have enhanced her abilities in hospitality.

This was to be my last day in Twin Bridges, and Marsha was helping me load my car. Because of ferry schedules to Ketchikan, Alaska, my stay in Twin Bridges had to be shortened. I would leave this place with the same regrets I had in leaving the previous eight locations on my journey. Twin Bridges proved such an unusual place with much to offer, and the people have been gracious and kind. My stay was made pleasant and unforgettable because of Marsha and Don Greenmore and many others I met there.

Cruise ships to Ketchikan, Alaska, stop their schedules the last day of September. Ferry schedules change from daily landings to twice-a-week sailings. This changed my plans. I would go to Bellingham, Washington, rather than Prince Rupert, British Columbia, on the advice of my landlady in Alaska.

By land and sea, the total distance from Twin Bridges, Montana, to Ketchikan, Alaska, is 1,537.2 miles.

Leaving Twin Bridges on Interstate 90, I stopped for lunch in Wallace, Idaho, a town of about 940 people, listed on the National Register of Historic Places. Wallace claims to be the Silver Capital of the World. Within minutes of town are year-round recreational activities: ski areas, snowmobile trails, and unlimited riding possibilities for ATVs, motorcycles, and jeeps, as well as places for fishing, hunting, and golf. The town also hosts many festivals offering entertainment for locals and visitors. After looking around I was back on the road, arriving in Moses Lake, Washington, by 4:00 p.m.

My schedule had me arriving a day early for the ferry. Marsha had said that the drive would be scenic, especially around Coeur d'Alene, Idaho. She was right! I didn't want to rush. I arrived in Bellingham by early afternoon, found a Best Western motel, and rode to the ferry terminal ensuring that I would easily find it the next day. I decided to go ahead and purchase my tickets, avoiding a line the next day. The ticket agent said to bring plenty of reading material, snacks, and walking shoes. It would be a welcome change to let someone else get me from Point A to Point B. And I looked forward to knowing what to expect on the return trip.

Chapter Ten
Ketchikan, Alaska
September/October 2011

BEFORE GETTING IN line to board the ferry, I spent time walking around the Fairhaven Historic District of Bellingham, Washington. Fairhaven has the look and feel of a seaside village, but with easy freeway access to shopping, dining, and employment opportunities in Bellingham. The red brick buildings, quaint shops, and streetside cafes have been carefully maintained, preserving their old-world charm. Fairhaven was once an independent and thriving logging town with a large cannery that processed salmon to be sold all over the world.

In 1903 Fairhaven and Bellingham merged with two other nearby cities to form what is now the city of Bellingham, ranked one of the best places in the United States in which to retire.

Once I got in line for the ferry, there was nothing to do but wait. My information said I should be in line two hours before boarding time or run the risk of losing reserved space on the ferry. Couldn't let that happen. I believe in doing what is suggested when on a schedule like mine.

There was noticeable security about: police everywhere, sniffer dogs, and the Coast Guard. After my car was given a check, I boarded at 4:15 p.m. The car was secured and I went to my cabin. It had a set of bunk beds, closet, desk space, and a bath with shower. All I needed, plus a porthole to look out. I was very comfortable. I walked about the ferry a little to get my bearings and attended a safety meeting at 6:00 p.m. Instead of a big meal in the dining room, I chose to eat at the snack shop: chowder and crackers, salad, and Jell-O. Good, and easy.

The government of the State of Alaska, through the Alaska Marine Highway System, operates the ferry on which I was traveling. I had no idea the Alaska Marine Highway System was so extensive. There are ferries of all sizes and routes, hundreds of employees, and hundreds of thousands of passengers.

I was reminded too that Alaska is a big place with 656,425 square miles of rugged wilderness, scenic beauty, and abundant wildlife. Unlike the Lower Forty-Eight, many Alaskan communities are not accessible by land-based roads, requiring travel by sea or air. The Alaska Marine Highway makes up a large part of the state's highway system, and is a route so special it has been designated a National Scenic Byway and All-American Road, the only marine route so recognized. This prestigious honorific signifies a road that possesses multiple intrinsic qualities and contains one-of-a-kind features not existing elsewhere.

The AMHS with its eleven-ship fleet serves a 3,500-mile route and thirty-three ports. The ships move some 320,000 passengers and 97,000 vehicles annually. My ferry, the *MV Columbia*, can carry 499 passengers and 134 twenty-foot vehicles. Forty-five four-berth cabins and fifty-nine two-berth cabins were available, including three cabins compliant with the Americans with Disabilities Act. All staterooms aboard had private bath facilities. In other words, I was on a cruise ship and I had brought my car along with me. Many amenities are available on the ferry: full-service dining or a café, cocktail lounge, movie theater, gift shop, and a video arcade. On the cabin and boat decks are ice and vending machines. Also to be found on board: lockers, showers, and a coin-operated laundry.

One of the more interesting things about the ferry was that you could walk aboard with your backpack and sleep in the solarium, even set up a tent on deck, or sleep in a comfortable recliner chair in the solarium, and still enjoy all the advantages of the trip.

Another unique option: bring a vehicle, whether bicycle, car, motor home, or kayak. Car-deck space sold out quickly. Early advance reservations were advised. The cost of a vehicle does not include the driver. Any vehicle that can be driven or towed legally on a highway may be transported on a ferry. Fare for a car was determined by overall length and width. Should you incorrectly estimate dimensions, you could be charged additional fees and even be moved to a later sailing. Just to be sure, I got out my car manual and copied its specifications. My Buick Enclave measured 201.8 inches long, 79.0 inches wide, and 72.5 inches high, with a wheel base of 118.0 inches. Fuel tank capacity, twenty-two gallons. Chances were, had I not taken the ferry, I never would have known this. Do you know that much about *your* car?

During the safety meeting, I kept hearing the person mention "crossings." We would experience three of them, two rather short ones of thirty to forty-five minutes, and a longer one of at least two hours or more depending on the weather. A "crossing" is when the ferry is on the Pacific Ocean with no island or land mass to buffet the wind and waves. We were advised during crossings, especially if prone to seasickness, to find a place in one of the solariums and stay put. Which I did. I had a good book to read. The first two crossings were barely noticeable, but the longer one was a little rough. I was pleased with the way I handled it, considering that I'm not a good swimmer. In fact, I'd classify myself as a nonswimmer, but I believe I could save myself if needed.

Arriving in Ketchikan about 7:30 a.m., I took the only main road and drove about four miles to the Black Bear Inn on North Tongass Highway. I didn't see any activity, and not wanting to disturb anyone I went back to town, found a great grocery store and shopped for essentials. After gassing the car, I returned to the inn. Nicole Church was there to meet me. One of the fun parts of this trip has been meeting my new landlords in each place. Nicole is from California, where she met her husband, James, who is from Ketchikan. I liked them already. The first thing I learned about them was they are intent on making their accommodations more than acceptable to their renters.

Even on first sight, I find it hard to believe anyone would not like this place. Black Bear Inn is listed as Ketchikan's finest bed and breakfast and vacation rental. It's described as unique, affordable, personal, and private. My apartment was spacious and luxurious with a corner gas-log fireplace, which made it so cozy, especially on rainy days. There was a beautiful bath, utility closet with washer and dryer, shelving, a huge bedroom with two queen beds, chest of drawers in each bed nook, night tables, closet, and television in the living room and bedrooms.

Clocks, radios, nightlights, and basic great lighting were to be found in all the rooms, something lacking in so many places. The furnishings were appropriate for the setting: a wooded landscape on an embankment at water's edge overlooking the Pacific Ocean. Outside the inn was a covered cooking area and a spa. If I were interested, fishing and tour packages were available. You understand now when I say that Nicole and James wanted their guests to be comfortable, and pleased.

Today is Monday, September 26, and it's raining. Tuesday—more rain. Wednesday—rain. Thursday—rain. Friday—sunshine? "What about all the snow and ice?" people often asked when learning I would be going to Alaska. By Alaskan standards, Ketchikan's weather is mild. The median temperature in January is 33.3 degrees F. In July, it's 57.8. Rain falls 224 to 228 days annually, and the longest stretch without measurable rain is about twenty-three days.

Dave Kiffer, Ketchikan's mayor and a fourth-generation Ketchikan resident, is a freelance writer, musician, and teacher of music whose humorous and local historical stories can be viewed on the *sitnews.us* website. In the official publication *Historic Ketchikan, OUR TOWN, Discover Ketchikan Alaska*, Dave once wrote an article entitled, "Somewhere Under the Rainbow." In it, Dave wrote, "If it's precipitation, Ketchikan's got it. Eskimos have numerous words for snow and ice, and we have many euphemisms for, well, 'liquid sunshine.' Maybe calling it liquid sunshine is a sign of our optimism amid Southeast Water Torture. After all, it grows our trees, hosts our fish, runs our hydroelectric generators, and fills our lakes. But there is a painful truth to the story of the boy who was asked by a visitor how long it had been raining. 'I don't know,' he said. 'I'm only five years old.'

"There are wetter places on earth—but hardly anyone chooses to live there," Kiffer wrote. "When rain is the common currency, it's not remarkable that it comes in so many denominations—some days a nickel's mist or two bits' drizzle. More often, it's a steady, month-long downpour, and the rain gauge rises faster than the national debt. The saving grace is that rain doesn't stop life here." How true.

People in Ketchikan say that if you can't see the top of Deer Mountain, it's raining, and if you can see the top of the mountain, it's about to rain. No pun intended, but this doesn't dampen the spirits of the residents or visitors.

Ketchikan is an ideal city for strolling the waterfront, walking the board sidewalks, and visiting the many quaint shops to look at or buy native crafts, jewelry, and basketry. In spring and summer, you can watch the salmon run Ketchikan Creek, which flows through town; you can stand in awe of totem poles on the streets or lawns of Victorian homes; or watch the town turn lively when tourists debark from cruise ships during the summer months—as many as ten thousand in a season. When evening comes, the ships move on to the next port and Ketchikan is left with its twelve thousand permanent residents.

Ketchikan would seem to be in the world's least likely spot for a city. One's first impression is that the city is built on stilts, half over the water and half on the steep mountainside. Located on the island of Revillagigedo, known as Revilla to locals, its buildings are jammed against a mountain thick with trees and strung along the ocean waterfront. Ketchikan has twenty-six miles of road but is nowhere more than ten blocks wide. Many nicknames have been applied to the place: First City of Alaska, Salmon Capital of the World, Birthplace of the Alaskan Pulp Industry, and Totem Land.

Naturally I preferred to make a good impression on my landlords, but what did I do on the first sunshiny day when I might have been out and about? I caused the smoke alarm to go off. I had something in the oven and the extra heat caused the alarm. I was immediately reminded of a similar episode in New Orleans with Janie. Quickly, I turned on the fans, opened doors. The alarm only sounded for a few seconds but it seemed like an hour.

Later in the day I took garbage down and put it in the wrong place. I had to be told again what to do with it. And even later the very same day, I locked myself out of the apartment and had to locate Nicole to open it for me.

Three strikes and you're out, they say, and I wondered if that would be the case for me at Black Bear Inn. Nicole had to have been quite perturbed with me that day, but thankfully she got over it, and we became the best of friends.

I did hate to disturb Nicole. She had a daily routine, quite a busy one, much like Marsha in Twin Bridges. Nicole does all the cleaning and upkeep. And I had seen the laundry room of the inn piled high with linens to be washed. She also vacuums and puts everything back in order after a renter leaves. James works at several other businesses they own in Ketchikan, so Nicole chooses to do what is necessary at the inn to ensure it's all done right and on time.

One day I walked into one of the rooms and found a dismantled desk on the floor, waiting to be reassembled. I asked Nicole about it. She said that when she'd asked one of her clients if everything was satisfactory with the room, he said it really needed a desk. Immediately she ordered one. All the rooms at the inn are beautifully furnished with this kind of attention to detail.

October 1, 2011, I'd been in Ketchikan for one week, but not really doing anything. Today, I was officially beginning my month here. When Nicole said she had tickets for the 4th Annual Awards Dinner and Auction, "Women of Distinction," I knew it would be an opportunity to meet a lot of people. At our table were eight: Nicole and me, Choc Shafer, Agnes Moran (a candidate for City Councilwoman), Lois and Lloyd Gossman, Ellen Bishop, and Anne Lucas (one of the founders of the program, Women in Safe Homes). WISH is a non-profit organization providing advocacy for adult and child victims of domestic violence and sexual assault. Confidential crisis intervention and shelter is offered, and access to help through a twenty-four-hour, toll-free crisis line. The shelter serves Ketchikan, Saxman, Prince of Wales Island, Metlakatla, Wrangell, Petersburg, and Hyder.

The Women of Distinction celebration affirmed the extraordinary effort and commitment women have shown for community. The friend or family member or organization that had nominated them introduced their one of the five honorees. For each participant, a musical selection was presented, and then the honoree spoke. It was quite evident why each had been chosen. A special performance by the Ketchikan Inter-tribal Drummers, dancers wearing native dress, was given for one honoree.

Prior to the program we were entertained with music from Tears of Fancy, which seemed Celtic in origin with flute, guitar, and lute. The sound was not familiar to me, but it was very distinctive. I gazed around the Ted Ferry Civic Center in admiration of the decorations and auction items displayed. Very little extra sitting or standing room remained. I estimated that three hundred people were in attendance and enjoying a beautifully prepared prime-rib dinner.

I attended church at Gateway Baptist on my first Sunday in Ketchikan. John W. Hudson, pastor, was an attendee of Bob Jones University in Greenville, South Carolina. He and his family have been in Ketchikan for fifteen years. Pastor Hudson preached a great sermon. Everyone was friendly and the music was good, but the attendance small. The bulletin reported that the highest number present for morning worship in September had been fifty. Yet a full program of activities and opportunities for service were offered. Their statement read, "The friendly church that is standing by the gate and pointing the way to Jesus Christ." The message today relayed that conviction.

It has been said that all roads lead to Walmart. I had found one. Not a superstore but a mall with Walmart and McDonald's, which was full each time I visited. There were hundreds of other shops to browse in around town. Nicole has said she would help me sort out those that shouldn't be missed, as well as other attractions, and the best seafood restaurants. Seafood—that's what my sister, Shirley, would want when she arrived.

My walking trail ran beside the main highway. Most of it right by the water's edge. It went through a neighborhood with barking dogs. On the water side was every kind of boat imaginable, docked float planes, and houses in all sizes and shapes and types—some on huge lots and some crammed into the tiniest space. The route was about three miles round trip. I hadn't timed it yet, but already knew finding a time when it wasn't raining would be the greatest challenge.

My sister, Shirley, and her partner, Marge, had visited Janie and me in New York City and in Boothbay Harbor. Now it was October 5, and they were arriving today with their friends (and now my very dear friends as well) Nancy Underhill and Denise Knight. I met them at the ferry. The airport is on Gravina Island. To get to Ketchikan, you have to take a ferry across the sound—only an eighth of a mile. The only other way to Ketchikan is by boat or plane. Remember the Congressional scandal some years ago about funding for the so-called Bridge to Nowhere? That would have been the bridge connecting Gravina Island to Ketchikan, but it was never built.

Ketchikan's first commercial air connection to Seattle and the Lower 48 opened in August 1938 when Pan American Airlines brought in floating Clipper aircraft for test flights. Flight Service Station Staff estimate that twenty helicopters and about one hundred aircraft on wheels, or floats, are based in Ketchikan. Alaska Airlines brings in several flights a day, north- and south-bound, through the Ketchikan airport. The Alaskan sky is particularly busy in July when as many as sixteen thousand communications are made with flyers, compared to February when the number might be closer to thirty-five hundred contacts.

I had not thought about how five people were going to fit into my vehicle when I headed out to pick up Shirley and her party. Before leaving home I had removed the back seats to make space for my stuff. At her insistence, Shirley rode on a little box with a cushion on top, wedged between the two seats just behind the front row of seats. She didn't seem to mind. After all, the island is only thirty-some miles long. Shirley said the seat was quite comfortable, until I braked suddenly, sending her plunging forward. That didn't happen too often on the way home, to which Shirley's comment was, "Thank goodness."

My guests were weary after their long flight from Birmingham, Alabama, and having been up since 3:00 a.m. They were glad to eat a light supper and relax a bit before bed. I fixed a tomato-based chicken and bean soup, pasta salad, and sandwiches of ham, cheese, and pineapple on an English muffin; I topped it off with a light dessert. It sounds like a lot, but it really wasn't.

Shirley and Marge were settled in my apartment, and they loved it. Nancy and Denise were sharing a room with bath but seemed pleased with their accommodations. We spoke briefly about getting more rooms to give Shirley and Marge space but concluded the apartment was big enough for the three of us. And it would give us more time together.

With accommodations settled, we discussed what each of us wanted to see and do. The first thing mentioned was totem poles. There were three different sites we could visit, and even some totems to be seen in private yards and on business streets. We decided that we would ride first to the end of the island.

Information as to the length of Revilla is conflicting—one source indicates the island is twenty miles long, another thirty-six. From the visitor's bureau, I found a resource saying that from the Bureau the island runs 13.2 miles south to road's end, and from the same point going north, it's 18.2 miles to road's end, making a total distance of 31.4 miles from end to end.

Driving south is the most scenic, with lush forests and spectacular coastline views. We were surrounded by mountains, and saw several waterfalls right beside the road. Bald eagles sat on logs in a cove, and we saw a water otter, on the water of course. Many old ramshackle buildings added to the quaintness of the area. There were several miles of bumpy, gravel road before reaching a sign that announced, The End. Did I mention it was raining? The rain actually added to the beauty of the landscape, and we all were prepared with appropriate rainwear, so it didn't matter to us.

With perfect timing, we drove back into town and stopped for lunch at Annabelle's, the famous Keg and Chowder Restaurant on Front Street. Décor and furnishings were circa 1920s, giving an air of elegance to the rooms: white linen tablecloths and napkins, old silverware, china dishes, tapestry-covered high-back chairs—fabric seats for the booths, chandeliers, mirrors, and period paintings and wall paper.

We all started with clam chowder—Annabelle's recipe also dates to the 1920s—then we ate crab cakes, giving them rave reviews. Other appetizers: Coffman Cove oysters steamed piping hot and served with warm garlic butter. Our entrees: comfort-food chicken and bacon macaroni and cheese, breaded and fried chicken in a rich mascarpone cheese sauce, bacon tossed with rotini pasta, seafood sandwiches—a halibut BLT, seasoned and grilled, seafood tacos, and buffalo salad. Dessert was Carrot Cake made at Annabelle's and four inches tall. It reminded me of the Key Lime Pie at Blue Heaven in Key West, Florida. Our food was only a sample of offerings on the menu. Everything was tasty, leaving us wishing for a bite from every dish on the menu. We all would love to have eaten here again.

Totem poles are not religious objects and have never been worshipped. While the figures on a pole might be easily recognizable, the pole's significance or meaning can only be known if one knows the purpose and occasion for which it was created, as well as the individuals, groups, or stories associated with it. Totem poles are carved to honor important individuals, commemorate significant events, and to proclaim the lineage and social standing of their owners. Traditionally, this information was introduced when the pole was raised and then passed down orally from one generation to another.

The Totem Heritage Center on Deermount Street in Ketchikan houses a priceless collection of nineteenth-century totem poles and other carvings. The relics were retrieved from the Tlingit (the first T is pronounced as K) villages on Tongass and Village islands and from the Haida village of Old Kasan on Prince Wales Island.

Villagers moved to Ketchikan and other towns at the beginning of the twentieth century in order to be near schools and churches, as well as the canneries, mines, and sawmills that offered employment. Totems were left behind and were soon overgrown by forests and eroded by weather.

With the permission of native elders, the Alaska State Museum and the Alaska Native Brotherhood carried out the retrieval of historic totem poles. The elders also provided valuable cultural and historical information about the poles. Technical assistance came from the Smithsonian Institution and U.S. Forest Service.

During the heyday of totem-pole carving, between the middle

and end of the twentieth century, native artists on the Northwest Coast produced the poles that are now on display in the Heritage Center. Those poles were preserved as they were found, severely weathered, many with the original paint and much of the original detail intact, testament to the skill and sophistication of their carvers.

Because of their tangible references to people, events, and legends that figure in oral histories of northwest coast natives, totem poles have great cultural and historical importance. Unfortunately, much information has been lost with the passage of time.

In 1938, the U.S. Forest Service began a program aimed at salvaging and reconstructing the large cedar totems. Using Civilian Conservation Corps funds to hire skilled carvers from the older native population, two things took place: young artisans learned the art of carving totem poles, and the totems that had been left in the woods to go back to the earth were either repaired or duplicated. Fragments of the old totems were laid beside freshly cut cedar logs and every attempt was made to copy them traditionally. Tools for carving were handmade, modeled on older tools used before the coming of Europeans. The project helped save Tlingit and Haida culture that essentially had been lost.

We noticed a picture of Charles Kuralt hanging on a wall of the Heritage Center, commemorating his visit and his interest in the center and its work.

Ketchikan has many retail shops and art galleries; restaurants and lodging; transportation services such as buses, ferries, rental cars, water taxis, float planes, and charter fishing boats; guided tours and museums; and, for the tourist's ease, public restrooms, phones, and cash machines. From May to September the influx of tourists is huge. I was visiting on the off season and many of the businesses were closed, but there were enough open to feel acquainted with Ketchikan, and I was happy to be an October visitor. Everything was just right.

Shirley and Marge and their friends and I enjoyed a visit to Tongass Trading Center, which offered every kind of clothing and gear for Ketchikan weather. We browsed the store looking at curios, Alaskan jewelry, souvenirs and figurines, even salmon, and especially those things native to Alaska and made locally. What fun we had. Everyone was agreeable, so easy, and we enjoyed having time together.

One day we rode to the other end of the island, the north end. It was not as picturesque as the southern drive. More businesses and homes filled the landscape, but the view along the water was beautiful, as were the dense woods. Once again we rode in a misting rain. I now have a picture of The End, both north and south. I just hoped I labeled them.

On our way back to town, we visited Totem Bight State Park and its totems and clan house. When Alaska became a state in 1959, the land at Totem Bight—once called Mud Bight—passed from the federal government to the State of Alaska. The site was added to the National Register of Historic Places in 1970. The clan house, also called a community house, at Totem Bight could have housed thirty to fifty people. Inside was one large room with a central fireplace, surrounded by a planked platform, and walls and floors that had been made smooth using a hand adze. Occupants of a clan house were usually several families of the same lineage, each family being allotted its own space, but all sharing a common fire. Housewares, treasured items, and blankets were stored under removable floorboards. Food items were hung from the beams and rafters. Members belonging to the house would have been presided over by a house speaker, or head of house, of the same lineage.

The Tlingit and Haida are subdivided into two matrilineal groups, the Eagles and Ravens, called moieties. The carved house posts supporting the beams inside the clan house symbolize the exploits of Duktooth, a man of Raven moiety. Duktooth wears a weasel-skin hat and shows his strength by tearing a sea lion in two. Designs on the front of a clan house are rare, occurring only in cases of great wealth.

Other clans might interpret the totem poles in the park, depicting stories and events, in different ways. To understand the totem poles, a deeper knowledge of native people and their history is necessary. Since there was no written language, the totems are silent storytellers, meant to help the native people remember. The largest collection of totem poles in the world can be found in Ketchikan.

Nicole Church of Black Bear Inn met us for lunch at The Point, which is considered a local destination. The Point has an art gallery, bead store, yarn shop, and a coffee bar. Whether meeting for business or personal pursuits, or for knitting or beading lessons, the inn has a stunning view of the waterfront and serves wonderful fresh-baked cookies, soups, salads, and sandwich lunches. When we visited, artist and musician David Rubin was playing with his Potlatch Band—which included accordion, drums, fiddle, mandolin, and guitar. The band performs lots of oldies and was having so much fun the members' laughter was contagious. We could have sat and listened for hours.

Being in southeastern Alaska, Ketchikan is a region of glacier-cut fjords and islands covered with dense rainforests; it is called the Alaska Panhandle. The primary industries are tourism, fishing, and logging. The Panhandle includes Tongass National Forest, Glacier Bay National Park, Admiralty Island National Monument, and Misty Fjords National Monument—all served by the Alaska Marine Highway.

Alaska's famous Inside Passage is a coastal route for ocean-going ships, a network of passages threaded through islands on the Pacific coast of North America from southeast Alaska, through western British Columbia, to northwest Washington. Using the passage allows ships to avoid bad weather in the open ocean, and is a means to visit isolated communities along the way. It is heavily trafficked by cruise ships, freighters, tugs with tows, fishing craft, and ships of the Alaska Marine Highway system.

The Passage winds through Tongass National Forest, the world's largest coastal temperate rainforest and one of the last in the world. Whether you realize it or not, you're visiting the Tongass National Forest around Ketchikan when you cruise its shores, hike local trails, or fly into a remote lake or camp and picnic at a recreation area. You can travel the five hundred miles from Ketchikan to Yakutat and never leave Tongass National Forest. Vast expanses of untouched wilderness ensure fish and wildlife have the space, food, and shelter they need to thrive. One of the most beautiful places on earth, the temperate rainforest environment is also one of the most biologically productive places. With its old growth trees and world-renowned populations of wild salmon, brown (grizzly) bears, wolves, eagles, and whales, the Tongass offers a smorgasbord of nature to visitors.

Wild salmon are a primary link between the forest and the sea. They spawn in forest streams, swim to sea, and return full of nutrients to nourish the forest's soil and wildlife. Almost seventy-five percent of southeast Alaska's salmon are located in the streams of intact (no roads) old growth forests of the Tongass.

In the Lower 48 you are never more than twenty miles from a road. The Tongass hosts more than 11,000 miles of coastline, roughly the distance from northern Alaska to the southern tip of South America; 17 million acres of vast, untrammeled area support the grandest wildlife and most daring adventurers. The bear population amounts to one bear per square mile, and one bear will eat up to thirty-five pounds of fish, berries, and other food per day—the equivalent to seventy-five Big Macs a day.

Before coming to the Tongass, I hadn't thought about the fact that the Tongass is "my forest." I realized that I needed to do what I could to ensure that my forest is protected, that it will continue to provide the same opportunities and experiences tomorrow as it does today. One of the best ways to protect it is to stay informed and (I love this one even more) eat wild Alaska salmon! That would support Alaska's hard-working fishing families and encourage conservation of healthy rivers and sustainable Tongass fisheries. One particular slogan got my attention: "It's one of the greatest rainforests in the world, and it belongs to you."

While entertaining guests, I always want to sample as many restaurants as possible. One we had yet to try was Narrows Inn and Restaurant on North Tongass Highway. Narrows is a waterfront resort. You realize by now that much of Ketchikan is on the water, Revillagigedo Island (where Ketchikan sits) being separated from Gravina Island by the strip of water called Tongass Narrows. The restaurant was another beautiful setting in which to enjoy good food and ambience, and we met and visited with owners, Pam and Don Thornlow. Hard as we tried not to, we always ate and ate and suffered the consequences later. It was impossible to resist beautiful food in an equally beautiful atmosphere.

Shirley and Marge, and our friends and I, all love watching Alabama football. On Saturday I made a tailgate supper of barbecued ribs, potato salad, baked beans, and dessert. It was fun to view the homecoming game with Vanderbilt, eat again, work some with my computer and pictures (with Denise helping), and most of all, enjoy visiting.

Nancy and Denise were scheduled to leave early Sunday. They wouldn't allow me to accompany them on the ferry over to the airport, so we said our good-byes at the hotel. I hated to see them leave. I know they felt as I did. We had had a great time and probably couldn't have crammed anything else into our days.

Shirley and Marge would remain until Tuesday. After Nancy and Denise's departure we dressed for church services at First Lutheran. It's October 9, the Seventeenth Sunday after Pentecost. Like every Sunday, whatever church I'm attending, the pastor has prepared a message just for me—the one I need to hear—and this

Sunday was no exception. The old church held a good crowd, and I am happy to say that some children were there. An upbeat pastor, communion, coffee hour after church, and a credo, "Called by Christ to Invite, Equip, and Send," are worth mentioning.

I was trying my first salmon in Ketchikan at The Landing, directly across the street from the cruise ship docks. I had eaten salmon somewhere else that was rather tasteless and had hesitated to order it again. This salmon was so good, along with clam chowder, salad, and a stuffed potato. My refrigerator was full of doggy bags I'd taken home (even with no dog) and they were usually finished off!

Souvenirs from each place remained an important part of my journey. From lunch we went to Tongass Trading Triangle for a look around. It's a store with everything you could want. The second floor is nothing but ladies' wear. Then, home to supper, cards, and bed. We didn't actually do a lot that day, but we had an early start. Nancy and Denise called to say they had arrived home safely.

At this point in my journal I had started counting down the number of days left on the trip—forty-one.

Saxman Native Village Totem Park, about 2.5 miles south of Ketchikan, is one more totem sight to mention. The park displays poles and clan houses, as well as artisans' work on contemporary poles, and you can watch as they work. Nathan Jackson, considered the foremost Tlingit artist, is on site during the summer months. Saxman Village also features scheduled performances by traditional native dancers.

Another totem carver is Woody Anderson at Crazy Wolf Studio on Mission Street. Woody graciously consented to talk to us about his work. He comes to the area every day, walks around, and prays for his people, his town, and the country as well. Woody is a City Council member for the Saxman community, and he shared some of the good things about Saxman as well as some of their woes. Thank you, Woody.

The owners of Crazy Wolf Studio are Ken and Monica Decker. Ken is a master drum maker, of the type used by Southeast Alaska natives at ceremonies today, and those of the past. Ken uses Sitka blacktail-deer skins and Alaskan yellow cedar for the drums. They are all hand painted by him.

Ken is known as a Tsimshian artist. The Tsimshians were separated by language and culture from other Alaskan natives, and lived in North West British Columbia along the Nass and Skeena rivers. Ken is a Ketchikan native. We appreciated his eagerness to answer questions and talk about his work.

Decision time. Should Shirley, Marge, and I take the tram one hundred and thirty feet up the hill to Cape Fox Lodge, or should we drive? We drove. The lodge, situated on a high hill, overlooks downtown Ketchikan, the Tongass Narrows, and Ketchikan marina.

My first thought about the lodge was, I didn't want to leave. The building has huge beams and timbers, stone walls, and fireplaces. A special feature is an unusual collection of native art unlike any other in the world and beautifully displayed. A totem mural carved by Nathan Jackson is on the second-floor mezzanine; the Council of the Clans totems by Tlingit carver, Lee Wallace, face the front of the lodge. In the lobby and on the second floor balcony is a collection of Alaska Native artifacts.

The lodge can accommodate groups of up to one hundred and fifty people, and the Ted Ferry Civic Center next door handles as few as five, or as many as five hundred. All the amenities expected of a resort are available to guests. You can tell we were impressed, and we haven't even eaten in Heen Kahidi restaurant. That was our next stop.

From Heen Kahidi we could see Creek Street in downtown Ketchikan and homes that have only steps leading to them. The spectacular view would make anything taste good. As it was, Shirley finally ordered her king crab, over a pound of meat. She couldn't eat it all—so I got the leftovers.

We lingered a long time after dinner, soaking up the atmosphere and chatting with the lodge manager, William O'Brien, from Detroit, Michigan. You can tell we're into people, and I cannot imagine the manager of this place being anyone other than the very accommodating and eager-to-please person William is.

On our return to Black Bear Inn, we briefly wondered where the local meeting of Overeaters Anonymous might be. We didn't go out again the rest of the day, but visited and packed for Shirley and Marge who would leave the next day.

I insisted on driving to the airport via the ferry to deliver Shirley and Marge for their flight. It was raining, and I knew it would be easier for Marge, and I also wanted to see the airport.

After check-in, I couldn't follow, so I came home and once again, I was by myself.

Ketchikan Gateway Borough has declared 2011 the Year of the Artist. This unique recognition by the mayor and borough assembly brings attention to the many ways creative people contribute to Ketchikan's livability, its economic vitality, and its prominence as a year-round tourist destination. Several community organizations keep local arts in the forefront: Ketchikan Public Art Works, the Performing Arts Center, First City Players (forty-six years old), Ketchikan Theater Ballet (in its fifty-first year), and the Monthly Grind, a coffeehouse with regular local entertainment that has run from September through May for more than twenty years. The town also supports groups of quilters, singers, instrumentalists, writers, and even bagpipers.

Dave Rubin is an artist I met in Ketchikan who is the real deal, a truly unique and multi-talented artist, humble, with an infectious smile and persona. I mentioned Dave earlier, as head of Potlatch Band at The Point. Acting on the suggestion of a friend, Dave arrived in Ketchikan in 1983, with his folk rock band, Tattoo. New York City bred, Rubin had started painting during childhood, then studied at the Art Students League and the Reilly League of Artists in New York. He is also a saxophonist, guitarist, and songwriter. It has been said that for a couple of decades, Rubin was as likely to show up with his paintbrush as with a horn or a six-string.

The Southeast Alaska Discovery Center holds some of Dave Rubin's portraits of native elders and young leaders. He likes painting landscapes as well, and has illustrated a children's book, *Kitaq Goes Ice Fishing*. A remarkable statuary sculpted by Rubin represents the many diverse occupations of Ketchikan's pioneers. With the assistance of other artists, the bronzed figures of the monument include a miner, fisherman, logger; a native woman elder, an aviator, and a pioneer teacher; and Chief Johnson, a native leader and keen trader wise in the ways of Western property rights. The Rock was unveiled on the dock, Berth 2, July 4, 2010.

One day after Dave's lunch music session, he and I visited The Rock and chatted about his ideas in developing the work, getting city approval and financing, and securing a location to install the sculpture. Those details made seeing and admiring the work all the more vivid to me. After shooting pictures there on the dock, we went to Southeast Alaska Discovery Center. It was closed, but again, a door opened because Dave knew the director. We were allowed inside. I viewed Dave's paintings and toured the center.

"Discovery" says it all because the Discovery Center, with its exhibits, presentations, and information resources, is an introduction to the natural and cultural history of southeast Alaska. Exhibits relate to ecosystems, native traditions, Alaska's rainforest and natural resources, and of course, totems. Thank you, Director James Grof, for allowing me to visit the center with Dave.

Walking around town was easy and there was much to see. Ketchikan Creek flows clear and year-round through the town, fed by rainfall, springs, and snowpack. In summer, you could watch salmon by the thousands spawn in the gravel beds of the creek where they were born years before.

The Creek Street area was a red-light district in 1903 when the City Council ordered bordellos moved across the creek from the town's site. More than thirty bawdy houses lined the creek over the years. Ketchikan's famous madam in the heyday of Creek

Street, Dolly Arthur, painted her house yellow. Called Dolly's House, it is still open for tours. The house has been preserved much as she left it, with furnishings that are now antiques, and her own special contribution—its garish décor.

During prohibition, some houses became speakeasies; rowboats slipped in on nighttime high tides and liquor was delivered through trapdoors. Prostitutes operated upstairs in houses along the Creek. One of those houses, No. 5, was called the Star Building, a dance hall and "emporium of feminine delights," run by a large woman nicknamed Black Mary. Mary had a head for business and at one time employed Dolly Arthur before Dolly opened her own place at No. 24 Creek Street. The Star Building was so-called because of a small, lighted star made from naked light bulbs that glimmered high on its east gable. When Mary added on to the building, another star of dark wood was inlaid into the maple dance floor of the hall. The Star became the jewel of the red light district, and is on the National Register of Historic Places.

My walk went by Water Warehouse, once known as the Woodshop and built as a warehouse for Citizens Light, Power, and Water. Built in 1912, it's one of Ketchikan's oldest remaining commercial buildings. The view platform looks over the creek. The Old New York Hotel, built in 1924, remains in business, but not as a bordello—its previous occupation. The original building had eighteen rooms and one bath. In the bathtub a sign declared: "Baths on Saturday only." The manager gave me a peek at one of the rooms with its period furnishings, but modern amenities. So quaint.

Scanlon Art Gallery, 318 Mission Street, has been considered Alaska's major art center since 1972; it sits beneath the Ketchikan arch, which reads, "Welcome to Alaska's 1st City." The gallery showcases original paintings, fine art prints and books, posters, and sculpture. The owner, a friend of Nicole Church from Black

Bear Inn, would have spent hours with me had I had the time.

My walking tour also took me to Parnassus Book Store, in the process of moving to a new location on Stedman Street, but still open for business. Owner Maggie Freitag said in a published interview that the name Parnassus is from a mountain in Greek mythology. Author Ann Patchett in Nashville, Tennessee, recently opened another bookstore named Parnassus. Maggie has received many phone calls due to the use of the name her store has had since its opening in 1985. Parnassus Book Store was started by Lillian Ference, known to locals as Ms. Lillian and described as "everyone's Jewish grandmother."

I had finally gathered my nerve to ride the tram up the hill to Cape Fox Lodge where Shirley and Marge and I had enjoyed a meal. I wanted to know if anyone on staff had worked there when Charles Kuralt was in Ketchikan. Someone suggested that Executive Chef Craig Royball might have been. I was given his phone number and called to arrange a meeting.

Royball said the lodge manager at the time of Kuralt's visit was Licha Kellyking, now living in Missouri. I called Licha and we chatted about Kuralt. She said what I hear every time I speak to any person who met or knew Kuralt: he was a gentleman, a people-person, one of the nicest people you would ever want to meet. I would always be indebted to the amazing network of folks who so willing shared their personal knowledge of the man.

Why does Ketchikan have a tunnel with a street running around the side of it, and houses on top of it? It's all because of an immovable object, a shoulder of schist that plunged into the water more than a century ago. The time of the fall is unknown, but the rock divided Downtown from Newtown and was referred to as Knob Hill. Downtown had the deeper water and docks to service ocean vessels. Newtown had a small boat harbor. But for both sides of town, the rock shoulder jutting out into the water was a barrier to commerce. To get from one side of town to the other required a boat, or taking the Skyline trail across the top of the knob. In 1902, the city council voted to build a ten-foot sidewalk from the intersection of Grant and Front streets to Newtown, about 1200 feet.

The ten-foot-wide plank sidewalk was adequate for horse-drawn carts and foot traffic. By 1916 the sidewalk was improved to accommodate motorcars, but Ketchikan grew too large for its "planks." The pulp mill was coming, traffic would increase, and Model T's weren't the biggest rigs on the road anymore. A more grown-up Ketchikan was demanding circumvention of the rock. The question was whether to blast down the big rock or tunnel through. The tunnel was the choice, much to the delight of those residents with homes built smack on top of the boulder.

The tunnel became the new way to Newtown in 1954. A singular claim at the time was that the tunnel was the only one in the world that could be driven through . . . driven around . . . and driven over.

I don't know how Nicole Church could possibly energy-wise, time-wise, or any-wise be as involved as she is with her guests at Black Bear Inn, but she is. She had gone above and beyond the call of duty to ensure that I meet people. She had shared her friends and invited me to community events, which never would have been possible without her. Nicole, I hope you know I will always be grateful for the many opportunities you made possible for me.

One such event was the 16th Annual Alaska Day Auction at the Ted Ferry Civic Center, which benefitted Holy Name Catholic School. I estimated a crowd of more than three hundred. More than sixty sponsors, many cash donors, parishioners, and community members were there donating their time to make the fund-raiser a success. The center was beautifully decorated. Live and silent auctions took place; eighty-one items plus add-ons were held up for sale. We stayed through item sixty-one. Nicole said that any given year the auction cleared between $75,000 and $80,000. I never asked the amount made that night, but the evening was a beautiful show of community spirit and support.

Earlier in the month I had met Agnes Moran at the WISH auction. Agnes offered to take me for a ride up the mountains in an area where she often walks. The day we set out it was raining, but that is no longer a consideration, and her vehicle was four-wheel drive. We could almost see the mountaintop through the mist. The waterfalls were visible and the sun peeked through making trees glisten with drops of water. There was hardly a sound as we progressed, stopping several times to walk to the edge of Harriet Hunt Lake, and then to the end of the road. All that remained was to hike up Brown Mountain.

We made a rest stop at Agnes's home overlooking the water, its big picture windows in the living/dining room showcasing the lake. It's hard to imagine ever wanting to leave such a beautiful home, but Agnes does. She is an active borough council member, serves on many boards and committees, and is a wife and mother. Being a Ketchikan native, Agnes is attuned to the needs and wants of her unique community. What a pleasure it was to have spent this time with Agnes.

Nicole Church invited me to go with her to Family and Friends Dinner at Pioneer Home. Jane Church, Nicole's mother-in-law, is a resident there. Jane is in her early nineties, alert, and quite conversational. We talked about everything. The home was decorated for Halloween.

Boy Scouts from a local troop served the five-course meal. They were quite handsome in their uniforms and well instructed in how to wait tables, or perhaps they had done it before. A water glass did not fall half empty before one of the Scouts was at the table to fill it again. If they were working to earn a badge, then they really did just that.

Dave Rubin and his band provided entertainment, and again, I could see why he was so popular and well-liked. Dave shares his talent and time for many different causes.

I always compared any elder-care home I visited to the Washington County Hospital and Nursing Home in my hometown of Chatom, Alabama. Chatom's was top-notch because of the capable management by Director Doug Tanner and his dedicated staff. I rated Pioneer Home very high on the list in comparing the two.

Pioneer is registered as an Eden Home, which follows the philosophy that family, friends, pets, and plants all contribute to create "a human habitat revitalizing relationships, and encouraging residents to be involved with activities that help alleviate loneliness, helplessness, and boredom." Pioneer also provides a respite care program for individuals needing short-term assistance.

And last, the volunteers who were so in evidence during the

evening are a plus. This was a very satisfying evening, another wonderful part of life in Ketchikan.

I've mentioned the "borough" in some of my writing, and will clarify. Residents of Ketchikan formed Ketchikan Gateway Borough in 1963, sixty-three years after incorporation of the City. The borough-council has limited powers: assessing property, collecting taxes, educating children, and animal control. Citizens of Ketchikan who liked the freer lifestyle of the Last Frontier chose the limited form of government with a mayor elected for a three-year term, an elected official who can only vote to decide deadlocks and is overseen by the seven-member borough.

The City of Ketchikan is a home-rule municipality with wide-ranging powers over police, firefighters, utilities, streets, and the library. About forty percent of the community live outside the city. Consolidation attempts have been made but every proposal has been voted down.

"The whales are coming, the whales are coming!" I could hear Nicole shouting all the way upstairs in my apartment. Someone had spotted whales in a cove just around the curve from the inn. Nicole said, "They're something you have to see." But other possibilities took precedence.

Nicole and I were at The Narrows enjoying clam chowder when a friend of hers stopped to chat. Greg Updike is a professional diver. He asked if I'd ridden in a floatplane. My answer was, no. Greg offered to arrange a flight for me; we set a time and were rained out, but set another date. Of course, that's when the whales showed up. I knew from the beginning of this trip I couldn't do everything. The pictures in the paper of the whales were amazing.

At 1:00 p.m., I was at Pacific Air, a floatplane ride-along for delivery of people and cargo to four different small communities on Prince of Wales Island: Craig, Hollis, Klawock, and Thorne Bay. At each stop, people and cargo were waiting to be picked up. It's difficult for me to accurately describe the absolutely breathtaking view of snow on mountains, floating clouds, and—the prettiest I've ever seen—quaint small towns, each expecting Donald Munhoven, my pilot. Donald has been flying the route for ten years. He was most gracious and shared much information with me about the places he serviced.

The plane wasn't big, and I know some of the passengers wished they had my seat, the copilot's spot. There were never more than five passengers at a time, but quite a lot of cargo. The best part to me was that the plane didn't taxi far before takeoff; it just rolled a short distance and we were in the air. Landing—we just plopped down. I would do this again.

On Sunday I returned to the First Baptist Church and met a woman reared in Mobile, Alabama. We knew the same places, but not the same people. She mentioned she and her children had theater practice in the afternoon. I inquired as to when the actual production took place. I couldn't be there, but Nicole talked to someone who gave permission for me to attend a rehearsal.

I loved that all ages were participating in the theater, even an eighty-year-old friend of Nicole's. David is a former mayor of Ketchikan and member of the Borough. He's a mainstay of the theater and performing arts community and was singing and dancing as ably as anyone I saw. In fact, I didn't see anyone out-sing or out-dance David. The production of *Anything Goes* was yet another example of Ketchikan's thriving community of arts, and the promotion of those arts, in all forms.

Leila Kheiry of the *Ketchikan Daily News* was interviewing me today. To make it more convenient, I went to the newspaper's office downtown. I'd planned to be in the area anyway. Staff photographer Tom Miller shot photos, even some outside in the rain. The interview went well, and since I would be leaving before the article was published, they promised to mail copies to me. The day I left Ketchikan, Tom was at the ferry dock to take more pictures of me. There was a guy with a player piano on the back of a truck, playing for everyone, and I was parked next to it on the ferry. You never know what you will see anywhere, at any time.

I spent my last morning in Ketchikan taking care of the odds and ends of departure: delivering the little happies for people who had been so kind to me and enjoying a last lunch at The Point with Nicole, my wonderful landlady and friend. To all the many people I met and the many sights and events you shared with me, Thank you. Ketchikan will always be one of my favorite places.

Boarding the ferry to depart Ketchikan was easier, less anxious for me, than on my arrival. In fact, I felt like a seasoned ferry traveler. My berth was bigger, this time with four bunk beds, which I didn't need, but you take what is available or wait another week. The ferry was a different boat, a little smaller than before. I settled in quickly, had a good dinner in the dining room, read awhile, and slept well.

Eight times walking around the ferry is one mile. I stopped by my car, got rain gear, and made the loop around the ship. Even though it was rainy and quite windy, walking felt good.

An Elderhostel group was watching short movies and everyone on the ship had been invited. I watched several about the Aleutians who were sent into internment camps during WWII; their homes and way of life destroyed. Finally they were given recognition and repatriation. A lecturer with Elderhostel gave a talk about the films. Most interesting.

I dreaded the Port Charlotte crossing, which lasted three hours. It was quite rough. I found a recliner in the lounge and stayed put. After asking one of the attendants about the roughness, he said it was about average—maybe not to alarm me.

From the solarium, I looked back at the "last of Alaska," and the snow on the mountains. It was just getting dark and a hard wind was blowing, but the scene was beautiful. I would be in Bellingham, Washington, at 8:00 a.m., and wouldn't have to wait for anything to begin my journey to Taos, New Mexico.

Surely you're interested in the distance from Bellingham to Taos—2,407 miles. That includes a little detour through Pagosa

Springs, Colorado. The highway scenery rivaled any I'd seen on this trip. Most of the trees were golden or orangey-yellow—all shades from light to dark—contrasting with the greenery of some trees and the snowcapped mountains in the distance. It was difficult to keep my attention on the road and the speed limit. All in all, a good driving day. I reached Baker, Idaho, by 5:30 p.m., ready for a break. One stop did it all, a Best Western with a nice restaurant.

Saturday, October 29th, dawned cool, with snow on the mountains but conditions were sunny. No rain—amazing. I drove miles and miles with nothing but hills and mountains for as far as I could see. Lunch in Burley, Idaho; then I passed through Salt Lake City, Utah, because it was still early, and on to Provo and a Super 8 Motel right at the entrance to Brigham Young University. Tomorrow night I had reservations at Mack and Marie Jones's home and motel in Pagosa Springs, Colorado. I was excited to see my friends again.

I consider friends to be people who, even after a long absence, can pick up right where you left off, as if you never missed a day of seeing one another. That's how I'd always felt about Mack and Marie. Mack P. Jones is former pastor of Chatom Baptist Church, and Marie, his wife, is a musician extraordinaire. Both were missionaries in South America, now retired. Mack taught seminary classes in Uruguay, and each was involved in the ministry. We had a laid-back visit, and after breakfast and devotion, Marie headed to her ham radio responsibilities. Mack and I packed my belongings, said our farewells, and I was "on the road" again.

Chapter Eleven
Taos, New Mexico
November 2011

MY HUSBAND, Fletcher, and I had driven the route to Taos before when visiting Mack and Marie Jones. I appreciated that it was familiar to me. By 1:00 p.m., I was in Taos—a little too early to check into my casita. Lunch sounded good, and so I went to Dragonfly Café at 402 Paseo del Pueblo Norte, the main street in town. It was a perfect day for patio seating, bright sunshine and a cool crisp breeze: the last day of October—no bugs, and a perfect setting.

Dragonfly is an apt name for a café in the state where this particular insect is an important part of legend, both Zuni and Navajo. The Zuni consider the dragonfly to be a shamanistic creature of supernatural powers. The Navajo believe that the dragonfly represents pure water. And it is New Mexico's state insect. I enjoyed my salad lunch, quite good and with a little touch of something different. After lunch I met my landlords at Taos Lodging,

Lovey (I love that name) Jo Supple and her daughter, Christy, and Christy's husband, Ron. The Garcia family built the adobe casitas in 1940. Renovation was done by the present owners, keeping in mind preservation of its history—"a little bit of Taos the way it used to be." Each casita has its own distinctive southwestern personality. Ancient elm trees guard the fenced property, which is in the Taos historical district.

My casita was a great living space with a kiva fireplace. Usually a kiva fireplace is built from the same adobe material as the casita and placed in a corner of the room. Its arched firebox and rounded edges flow upward into a bottle shape that narrows just above the box, and the entire piece protrudes from the wall rather than being built into it. This casita is one bedroom with full bath, a big utility room with washer and dryer and shelves for storage, and a large kitchen. There's a covered front porch, and on the property, an outdoor hot tub, a patio with tables and benches, a barbecue grill, and an unusual birdhouse collection. At night, luminaries light the driveways. Set only half a block off the main street of Taos, the location is ideal for walking, yet secluded.

Taos was established as an art colony in 1898 and incorporated in 1934. The name is from the Taos language and means "place of red willows." Taos is the county seat of Taos County and near the Taos Pueblo, the Native American village and tribe from which its name comes.

Taos sits on the cusp of a variety of climate and terrain zones. From the center of town, you can drive twenty to thirty minutes in different directions and find sagebrush desert, high alpine mountains, the Rio Grande Gorge, or grassy meadows, rolling hills, and hot springs. On average the sun shines 283 days a year in Taos, and it receives about twelve inches of rain annually. The U.S. average rainfall per year is thirty-seven inches. Its semi-arid climate brings extreme variations of temperature. Even the hottest summer day ends with a pleasantly cool night. Elevation is 6,967 feet.

I wanted to see snow, and before I left I got it.

My stay in Taos would be short. I wanted to be home by November 22 and had changed my travel plans to accommodate that. Rather than making a loop down to Santa Fe, Albuquerque, Socorro, and back again to Taos, I'd leave Taos early and spend time in each of those places on the way home.

I always managed to draw attention to myself, but in the wrong way. After my first morning's walk, I returned home to find I'd locked myself out of the house. I had strolled uptown as part of a route that would take me to the Kit Carson Memorial Park, a beautiful area with walking paths, an amphitheater, rest rooms, entrance to the Kit Carson Cemetery and to the Taos Community Auditorium. Uptown, I found an office to buy tickets for the Cashore Marionette Show scheduled for Thursday night.

Finding myself locked out of the casita, I had to call Lovey and wait for her to go to another complex for her tools. She was kind and gracious enough to say it had happened many times before as the storm door latch would sometimes automatically lock when the door closed.

As I sat waiting for Lovey, it began to snow, and continued for an hour. Soon everything was covered: trees, fences, casitas, and my car. What a beautiful sight.

After trying several times to open the door, Lovey resorted to using a kitchen knife to slit the screen, reach inside, and lift the latch. It was a simple solution, but not a good way for her to spend her time.

I'd never seen a performance of any kind quite as fascinating as the Cashore Marionette Show. The word marionette is derived from Mary, and originated in Europe during the Middle Ages when nativity plays were performed using stringed puppets. However, marionettes themselves—puppets controlled by strings—are much older. In Myanmar, once known as Burma, troupes of puppeteers were commissioned and maintained by royalty for entertainment, and sometimes used by the emperor to communicate a reprimand to an errant child or wife. Parables performed by marionettes conveyed unpleasant messages, yet preserved the esteem of the person who had erred. By contrast, the people sometimes convinced puppeteers to pass a message to royalty through the marionettes. It might be a warning, or news of current events. A puppet could say things a human could not get away with. Marionettes replaced actors for some time, as it was a beheading offense to stand with your head above royalty—a difficulty for a performer.

Joseph Cashore created his first marionette from clothespins, wood, string, and a tin can. His goal after making that first puppet was to create the illusion and sensation that the puppet was alive. Cashore soon realized that in order to have the fluid motion he sought in his puppets, he would have to create his own control design. He spent the next nineteen years, while pursuing a career in oil painting, experimenting with the construction of the marionettes and devising totally new control mechanisms.

Cashore graduated from University of Notre Dame with a Bachelor of Fine Arts Degree. He resides in Colmar, Pennsylvania, and has been making marionettes for more than thirty years. Cashore's talent for sculpture and portraiture is evident in his marionettes. The puppets' clothing, all the props, vignettes, and selection of classical music used as background create a magic controlled by the subtle movements of Cashore's hands. A bucking horse, a wrinkly elephant, a young rock star, and an old woman are some of the many characters Cashore has brought to life.

In spite of lifelong shyness, Cashore says he has finally become comfortable with the attention he receives. The audience isn't looking at him, he has realized, but at the creations that come to life under his hands. Strings on the puppets control all the intricate movements, be it playing a guitar, placing flowers on a grave, or rocking a child to sleep. There must have been fifteen or twenty strings on some of the marionettes. Cashore has received the highest honor given a North American puppeteer: the Citation of Excellence from the U.S. Branch of Union Internationale de la Marionette. Citations are "awarded to shows that touch their audiences deeply; that totally engage, enchant, and enthrall." I was totally engaged, enchanted, and enthralled.

When walking into the auditorium for Cashore's show, two ladies spoke to me, admiring the coat I was wearing. Yes, friends and family, it was cold enough to wear a coat. Seeing that I was alone, the women asked me to sit with them. That's how I met Barbara Bartels and Margaret Baucom, two artists, and learned where their paintings were exhibited. After growing up in Texas, marrying and raising her four children in Colorado Springs, Colorado, Barbara Bartels calls Taos home. She is a popular instructor, show judge, and an inspirational speaker on every aspect of art and of being an artist. Her work is shown at Sage Gallery. Barbara says she paints in the Euro-American tradition of *en plein air*, meaning in the open air, and *alla prima*, which is completing a canvas all in one session. Barbara loves being surrounded by the sights and sounds of nature, is passionate about her work, and feels that as an artist she is a historian of sorts, capturing a moment for all time. She is grateful that God has planted her in such a place as Taos and given her the heart and soul of an artist. After a second attempt I was able to view Barbara's paintings at Sage Gallery and buy a small sample of her work.

I asked someone to recommend a nice restaurant and was directed to Antonios of Taos, right off the town square on Dona Luz Street. The old building with an outdoor courtyard is beautiful, with very simple décor inside, and delicious food. I had a first for me: a shrimp, crab, and salmon enchilada with the usual toppings of lettuce, tomatoes, cheese, and sour cream; refried beans and rice; and an amazing flan for dessert.

I think the atmosphere of a restaurant contributes to my eating so much, don't you? Do you wonder that I was even able to walk around after that lunch?

The historic Don Fernando de Taos Plaza, or Plaza Taos as it is often called, was settled by Spanish colonists three hundred years ago. The plaza is in the center of the Taos historic district. It was built for defense, with windows facing into the plaza and limited entrances that could be barricaded. A guidebook suggests standing in the center of the plaza and making a 360 degree scan of the important sights: the first being a statue of Padre Antonio Jose Martinez, whose influence as leader, legislator, priest, and educator had an incredible impact on Taos and New Mexico.

I went into Mariposa Boutique on the plaza, not shopping, just looking. The owner, Katie Iko, invited me to her church Sunday, Taos Valley Baptist.

On my way to Arroyo Seco to see Margaret Baucom's paintings, I visited the famous one-thousand-year-old Taos Pueblo. It's considered to be the oldest continuously inhabited community in the U.S., having endured four hundred years of Spanish and Anglo presence. It is also the largest surviving multi-storied pueblo structure in the United States.

The buildings are made entirely of adobe and have to be replastered annually due to exposure from the four seasons of weather. The Pueblo maintains a restriction of no electricity and no running water within the sacred village. Rio Pueblo, originating high in the mountains of the Pueblo's sacred Blue Lake, is the primary source of drinking water and water for irrigation. Some residents adopted the use of wood stoves for cooking, but many still continue to cook in the fireplace.

Hlaauma/North House and Hlaukkwima/South House are the two main structures of the Pueblo. The entire village is surrounded by an adobe wall, which at one time stood as high as ten feet with five lookout places. The wall served as a boundary for keeping the people safe and undisturbed during ceremonial times. Today this wall is the boundary where traditional cultural beliefs are nurtured and where foreign beliefs do not apply. The native language, Tiwa, is unwritten, unrecorded, and will remain so. Details of traditional values are guarded as sacred, and are not divulged. Past oppressions upon this culture and people require them to keep their cultural details unspoken.

Preservation of the Sacred Village and Blue Lake Wilderness Area are the primary concern of the Taos Pueblo. Their goal is to maintain an area of more than 100,000 acres in its most natural state, protecting trees, water, fish, wildlife, soils, and land from damage. The Taos Wilderness Act provides the tribe with exclusive use of the wilderness area for traditional purposes. It is closed to the general public. Fees are charged to walk around the Pueblo grounds, or to use your camera. Guides are available as well for a fee. Many of the houses are open and residents may offer breads (baked on outside ovens) for sale, or jewelry, and leather goods. This practice sort of contradicts the image they are portraying—in my opinion, but the visit is well worthwhile.

I found Margaret Baucom's paintings on display in Arroyo Seco (which means dry gully), a small village about five miles from Taos. The village is described as a combination of shops in historical adobes and enough other experiences to surprise anyone. I was warned to drive very slowly in "the Jewel of Taos County" because of narrow streets and the many pedestrians on those streets. I had also been told that the shop owners liked to visit with everyone, and I "should not hurry."

Margaret's paintings are displayed in JLI Gallery—Jack Leustig Imaging. JLI had lots of original art, fine art prints, and fine art cards. I bought a print of one of Margaret's paintings.

Strolling through the village, I saw demonstrations in a pottery gallery, browsed Francesca's Clothing Boutique, Antiquarius

Home Furnishings, Sol Food Grocery, Sabroso Restaurant and Bar, Abe's Cantina, and Claire Works. It was at the last location that I saw sculpture by Claire L. Haye and bought an original piece.

My favorite stop of all, the Taos Cow, is an ice cream parlor voted by *Bon Appetit* as one of the top ten in America. A bench outside was painted like a cow. One comment about the shop, "It's pricey, but worth every penny."

Within a block of JLI Gallery is a beautiful old church, locked and cared for by Manuel, a specially designated caretaker called a *major domo*. The privilege and honor of caring for the church has been handed down from generation to generation, from Manuel's father and grandfather before him.

The old church was established in 1834, and built with adobe walls that are five feet thick at the base, and tapering to three feet at the top. I was told there are priceless altar screen paintings inside.

Speaking of churches, I attended Taos Valley Baptist, which required winding down streets into areas I never would have gone otherwise. Katie Iko, from Mariposa Boutique, welcomed me. I felt truly blessed hearing the message from Revelations 3:14-22, concerning lukewarm Christians and churches.

The music was good, and the crowd included lots of children and youth.

A full calendar of activities was listed in a printout, including services available to church members as well as discounts offered by certain businesses related to plumbing, firewood, custom-designed cards, and photography. I had not seen a list like this in other churches.

Long John Dunn is one of the unusual characters who played a part in the history of Taos. According to information inside the old Hotel la Fonda, the hotel site was once Long John Dunn's casino. La Fonda is Spanish for "the inn." Since 1937, the hotel has been noted as one of the places to stay in Taos.

Hotel la Fonda began in 1898 as a mercantile store with a saloon and rooms to rent. When John Dunn acquired the property, he displayed paintings by members of the Taos Society of Artists who had started meeting in the hotel for breakfast and cards. The hotel soon came to be known as an art center.

Reaching Taos in the early twentieth century wasn't easy. Only one road led in and out of town. Dunn took advantage of the situation and built a road, a bridge, and an inn to ease the traveler's way when coming from the north.

A train ran south to Tres Piedras. From there a carriage could be hired for a ride to the Rio Grande River. The length of the trip necessitated an overnight stay at the Bridge Hotel, built by Dunn. For a fee, the traveler was given a ride into Taos. A bridge and a square in Taos are named for the entrepreneur. Remnants of the old inn are still at the site east of the ridge today. Dunn's former home in Taos is now a bookstore, and many quality shops near the store are called John Dunn Shops.

In Taos Plaza facing east, a Union flag flies. During the Civil War, Kit Carson and some of his friends raised the flag to give the message of sympathy with the north, and they stood guard over the flag around the clock. Taos has special government permission to fly this American flag twenty-four hours a day in honor of the event.

During WWII, many members of the New Mexico National Guard fought in the Philippines and were captured by the Japanese. At least half of their number died in the infamous Bataan Death March and in prison camps. To the east of Taos Plaza, a Bronze Cross Memorial is dedicated to those veterans.

On the north side of the Plaza is what used to be the county courthouse. During the Great Depression in the 1930s, the Works Progress Administration, a program designed to put Americans to work, employed artists to paint murals in the Taos courthouse. That area is now blocked from public view. Up the exterior stairs on the backside of the building are paintings by the famed Mexican artist, Diego Rivera, also kept from public view. Stairs go under this structure, which once housed part of the town jail.

Taos Plaza, like the center of most small towns, will continue to change, but the fact remains that history is captured in its memorials, and the space will always be known as The Plaza.

Our Lady of Guadalupe church, first built in 1801, was once a part of the plaza. Rebuilt a second time, due to fire in 1961, the adobe building has curved lines and rounded walls. The interior is rich with stained glass, religious paintings, figurines, and woodcarvings. It was closed when I passed by and I had no way inside. But it looked so interesting. I wish.

The renowned Doc Martin Restaurant on Pasea del Pueblo Norte is yet another Taos historic landmark. I ate lunch there after attending Taos Valley Baptist Church. The restaurant has received *Wine Spectator's* "Best of" Award of Excellence for twenty-five years running.

Doc Martin arrived in Taos in the early 1890s, a typical rural doctor making house calls in a buggy, later a Tin Lizzie, and accepting any kind of payment—chickens, potatoes, and meat, whatever was offered. Over time the doctor and his wife bought several small properties around a small plaza. These are now the location of the lobby and patio of Doc Martin's Taos Inn, built in 1936, and noted by *National Geographic Traveler* as "One of America's Great Inns." The inn has forty-four unique rooms and suites, most with a pueblo-style fireplace. The Adobe Bar is part of the Inn—called by visitors and locals, "the living room of Taos." Adobe Bar offers live music every night—flamenco, bluegrass, jazz, country, Celtic, and folk. Musicians who perform there and audiences who attend say the Adobe Bar is the best performance venue in the territory.

Doc Martin's place is well known for its celebrity clientele. I didn't see any celebrities, but perhaps I was there too early in the day. Ownership of Doc Martin's has changed many times, but it has been the center of social activity in Taos for decades. Just think, the people I saw in the restaurant could have been born there.

Christopher Carson—scout, trapper, Indian agent, rancher, and soldier—better known as Kit Carson, spent forty years traveling throughout the Southwest. He was described as brave, gentle, honest, and wise. Carson spent most of his early childhood in Boone's Lick, Missouri. He was the ninth of fourteen children, and only nine years old when his father died, preventing his education. In 1826, at the age of fourteen, Kit joined a wagon train heading west on the Santa Fe Trail. From Santa Fe, Kit went north to Taos and hired on for a fur-trapping expedition to California.

Between 1828 and 1840, Kit used Taos as a base camp for many fur-trapping expeditions throughout the mountains of the west, from California's Sierra Nevada Mountains to the Rockies. As was the case with many white trappers, Kit integrated into the Indian world, traveling and living extensively among the native people. Because of his associations, Kit became fluent in Spanish and five Indian languages. His first wives were Arapaho and Cheyenne women, one of whom gave him a daughter. The mother died shortly thereafter.

Carson, known for his self-restraint and temperate lifestyle, was described as "clean as a hound's tooth," and "a man whose word was as sure as the sun comin' up."

In 1842, John C. Fremont, an officer and explorer with the United States Topographical Corps, hired Kit Carson as a guide and was accompanied by him on three journeys. Carson found himself caught in the Mexican War, helping Fremont, and when the original mission changed into a military operation, he quelled an uprising by American settlers in the area.

With the outbreak of the Civil War in 1861, Carson joined the First New Mexico Volunteer Infantry Regiment. He served as a colonel and fought in support of the Union cause. Carson also led campaigns against some Native American tribes in the region. Part of his work was to relocate Navajos to Bosque Redondo, a reservation located at Fort Sumner in New Mexico. The Navajo were starving and exhausted and finally surrendered. Nearly eight thousand men, women, and children were forced to march about four hundred and fifty miles to the reservation. The journey, known as the Long Walk, was brutal, and it cost hundreds of Navajos their lives.

Carson was promoted to brigadier general in 1865. After the war he moved to Colorado. He became commander of Fort Garland, and negotiated a peace treaty with the Ute Indians in the area. Carson died in 1868. His remains were moved the following year to a small cemetery near his old home in Taos.

In 1909, action was taken to begin a long struggle to raise funds necessary to first purchase, then restore, and finally, to maintain Carson's historically important house in Taos. The house served mainly as a place of residence, or business, before becoming a museum. Today there are guided living-history interpretive tours, a summer lecture series, and a large gift and bookstore. New exhibits, storyboards, and videos keep the Carson legend a favorite subject of tourists, historians, and biographers.

I visited the museum late in the afternoon and nothing was open, but I walked around and looked at the buildings and read the storyboards. Before this I didn't know anything about Kit Carson. A long list of places have been named after Carson, including forests, army posts, mountains, campsites, schools, roads, and parks. Now I'm a little more informed about his importance.

Each morning when walking, I pass Fechin House, once the home of the Russian artist Nicolai Fechin, who moved with his family to Taos in 1927. I found a schedule of open times and made plans to visit the museum. My husband and I had been in Taos before but the museum was never open. I was excited to go inside, although I learned there wouldn't be any furnishings—only an exhibition of Fechin's work.

The house features three architectural styles: Russian, Spanish, and Pueblo. Fechin had made brief sketches of his ideas for the house, and a cardboard model was in his studio. The final building is reminiscent of the composition in Fechin's paintings. Fechin's extraordinary use of wood in his Taos home showed the influence of his years of living in the forest heartland of Kazan, capital of the Tatarstan Republic in Russia. It was in his father's craft shop that Fechin learned about construction, carpentry, carving, and gilding.

The elder Fechin was a gilder and carver of *iconostases*—the Eastern Orthodox Church's high screens decorated with icons. Nicolai Fechin recreated a Russian atmosphere in his home, carving furniture and sculpting decorative motifs in the woodwork. He blended design elements such as triptych windows and intricately carved doors, with traditional Southwestern adobe construction. Metal work (light fixtures, door hardware) in the house was designed by Fechin and forged by a local blacksmith. The artist finished downstairs adobe walls with a pearly-gray clay and straw mixture, sealing them with sweet milk. He enhanced wood surfaces with ashes or a gasoline torch. A paste wax added finish and protection to the walls. The two-story house could have been dark and dreary. Instead, its many windows and beautiful woodwork, carved doors, and arches lighted the house.

Fechin's marriage ended in 1933. He and his daughter, Eya, left Taos for New York City. Fechin's wife, Alexandra, lived in the Taos house until about 1976. Eya opened Taos Art Museum at Fechin House in 1981. One write-up stated, Fechin's "exuberant use of line and color to define form creates an immediate impression of energy and purpose." Fechin is considered one of the greatest portrait artists of our time.

Walking one morning I met the nicest lady. It didn't take long for me to share with her the story of my trip. She suggested I call the newspaper for an interview. Since I had done this in other places, I wasn't hesitant at all at following up on her suggestion.

Newspapers and television stations seem to send their most charming people to interviews. Teresa Dovalpage, Ph.D., Spanish instructor at the University of New Mexico, Taos, fits the description. She put me at ease, even while I questioned her about her background because I saw that she was an interesting person. Teresa is a native of Cuba, but has been in the states for many years. The interview went well, and the picture taking. Not knowing a publication date, Teresa said she would send me copies of the article for *Taos News*.

My time in Taos was limited, and I had only scratched the surface of things to do and see. I took another walking tour. Los Comadres Women's Cooperative Gallery, 288 Paseo del Pueblo Norte, at the south end of the John Dunn Shops, has existed for fifteen years. Los Comadres means "the women friends." The gallery handles the usual array of pastels, oil paintings, and watercolors, but it also has works in tin, glass, photography, pottery, sculpture, painted gourds, and wearable art. Geraldine Liermann, one of the artists, was manning the shop that day. I bought one of her painted Christmas gourds, a small one. It was a little expensive, but I'm happy to have a sample of her work.

The Geoffrey Lasko Gallery is next door to Los Comadres and features Lasko's paintings as well as mezzotint prints. Mezzotint is a process invented in 1625 by Ludwig Von Siegen. Geoffrey prepares the surface of copper plates in the same way Von Siegen did. Another process employed by Lasko is called aquatint, which means "like a watercolor." Aquatint is an intaglio technique developed in England in the 1770s. I mentioned before how willing everyone has been to chat with me. Geoffrey was so interesting, talented, and easy to talk with, and loved the idea of my trip.

My next stop was the Hulse/Warman Gallery operated by painter and sculptor Clint Hulse and Jerry Warman, whose background is in science, design, and architecture, according to the gallery's website. The gallery specializes in contemporary fine art and sculpture and purports that "works exhibited must be critically examined based upon artistic merit, irrespective of medium."

Brodsky's Bookshop is in Long John Dunn's former home. Rick Smith from Baton Rouge, Louisiana, and Jay Moore own the independent bookstore. Rick and I chatted about my writing, family, and about Alabama-Louisiana State University football.

After lunch I took a driving tour to Red Willow Farmer's Market, which is closed at this time of year, but is reported to be quite an endeavor during the spring and summer. The Taos Town Hall and Library caught my attention too. Both new buildings are built in the local adobe style. My next stop was Tony Reyna's Indian Shop, which is next door to his home in Taos Pueblo. Ninety-five-year-old Tony was twice governor of Taos Pueblo. He served in WWII and is a survivor of the Bataan Death March. In 1950, Tony opened his shop selling Indian-made art from his hand-built adobe. Phillip Reyna, his son, and an artist with many creations of stone and steel, runs the store now.

San Francisco de Asis Mission Church, four miles southwest of Taos in Ranchos de Taos, is the most photographed of all Spanish

Colonial churches, and the subject of four paintings by Georgia O'Keeffe. The eighteenth-century adobe historic landmark is an active church and stands as a living testament to the strong faith of generations of Catholics. The church was built between 1772 and 1816 when Spanish colonists began permanent settlement in the area. To defend themselves against Comanche raiders, adobe homes and other buildings were built close together around a common plaza. The church sits on that plaza. The uniqueness of the mission church is found in its twin bell towers, and the arched portal entrance that overlooks an enclosed courtyard. Architectural features inside the church include two large, carved and painted *reredos* (altar screens) with painted panels, hand-hewn *vigas* (ceiling beams) that rest on hand-carved *corbels* (support timbers), and a wooden choir loft.

The church was sponsoring its 1st Annual Arts and Crafts Fair November 19 to November 20 to benefit the school gymnasium. I would have loved to be there to see the quality handcrafted gifts and enjoy the good food.

I was headed to see the Rio Grande River Bridge, locally known as Gorge Bridge. It's another "most photographed" site. The bridge has a six-hundred-foot span with a steel deck arch flying 565 feet above the Rio Grande. Gorge Bridge is the seventh highest span in the U.S. The wind almost blew me away, but I had to get out, look at the site, and peep in some of the booths where Native Americans were selling jewelry, coins, leather goods, and blankets.

Riding a little further, I was looking for the remains of the John Dunn house. I did a double take when I saw what looked as if I'd drifted into a futuristic era. The world headquarters of

Earthship Biotecture—an earthship-looking building—looms in the middle of nowhere. I shot some pictures to prove what I had seen. The structure is built from recycled materials, and claims to be the most versatile, economical, sustainable green building design in the world. According to the website for Earthship Biotecture, "No part of sustainable living has been ignored in this ingenious building." Water harvesting, contained sewage treatment, solar/thermal heating and cooling, solar and wind electric power, and food production are all disciplines used at the facility. Tours were available, but I got out and walked around instead. I felt guilty for not paying the five dollars for a tour.

Before arriving in Taos, New Mexico, in 1919, Mabel Dodge was already a prominent figure in the arts and society of New York City and Europe. Born into wealth and privilege in 1879, Mabel Ganson was the daughter of a banker in Buffalo, New York. Her first husband, Karl Evans, was the son of a wealthy steamship owner. Evans died in a hunting accident just two-and-one-half years after they married.

With her third husband, Maurice Sterne, a painter and sculptor, Mabel's salons in New York City drew well-known artists, activists, writers, and thinkers of the day to dine and discuss the new ideas of the century. Salon participants often formed lasting relationships and fomented ideas that had far-reaching influences. Among Mabel's friends were Emma Goldman, Alfred Stieglitz, Margaret Sanger, John Reed, and others of the political and artistic avant-garde.

Mabel sent Sterne west to scout places. They settled in Taos in 1919, and Mabel immediately fell in love with Tony Luhan, a full-blooded Taos Pueblo man. The whole world was watching. *New*

Yorker cartoons quipped about Mabel. Shakespearean production sets were based on adobe architecture. But many notables such as Georgia O'Keeffe, Willa Cather, Ansel Adams, and other artists found their inspiration while visiting Tony and Mabel's home that would shape their life's work. Carl Jung's visits to the Taos pueblo came to influence mainstream conception of the "native mind." Political wheels set in motion by Mabel's friend, John Collier, would affect legislation benefitting Native American communities for generations to come. These and other events can be traced at some point to Mabel and Tony's commitment to one another and to the life they built in Taos.

The property Mabel and Tony Luhan purchased contained a typical four-room adobe house: thick-walled, low, squatty, and dark. The couple added an addition that is high and full of light. Mabel and her second husband, Edwin Dodge, had remodeled a villa while living in Italy. That Mediterranean influence can be seen in Mabel's Taos home and courtyard. A solarium with glass all around graces the top floor. The second floor has a sleeping porch and bathroom with glass on three sides. The living room features a beamed ceiling, the beams having cost eight dollars each at the time of construction. Above the *vigas* are aspen *latillas* (crosspieces placed between the beams), topped with sage, then mud. The rainbow room, built for reading, has long low windows, easier to see out of if you're sitting on the sofa with a book.

The dining room was patterned after an Italian villa with a chandelier, silver wall sconces, and red and black floor tiles. The ceiling is painted with earth pigments, resembling a Navajo rug. Mabel's kitchen remains much like it was in her day. Mabel served her female guests breakfast in bed, while the men ate at the large table in the dining room. The Mabel Dodge Luhan House is now an inn and conference center. There are nine bedrooms, not open for touring. I took in the public rooms at a leisurely pace. One writer said, "Many who came to the Luhan house were at a critical point in their lives: physically, psychologically, or vocationally. The house functioned as a kind of life crisis center, breaking down and healing and making and sometimes unmaking love affairs and marriages."

Throughout its history the Mabel Dodge Luhan House has served as a retreat and a center for personal growth. Those who have enjoyed its ambience, and those who are yet to be introduced to the experience of the Luhan house, can look forward to many more years in celebration of creativity with workshops in the arts and humanities and support of local cultural activities. I would love to go back and rent the solarium for some length of time.

I had long been curious about a particular restaurant in Taos—Lambert's. Since my maiden name is Lambert, I decided to check it out. In Foley, Alabama, is a very popular restaurant called Lambert's Throwed Rolls, where the waiters toss rolls from a basket to their customers with great accuracy. I wanted to see if this Lambert's was in any way like the Lambert's in Alabama.

It was not at all the same I learned, in such a nice way. The building is old but has been beautifully renovated, and is quite elegant with just the right lighting, white tablecloths, and silver, crystal, and china. Service was excellent too. I was early, the only customer when I first arrived, giving me an opportunity to meet the staff, tell my story, and enjoy a wonderful meal.

I splurged with the filet mignon—cooked perfectly—potatoes thinly sliced into a sauce, and served like a slice of pie. Add to that: asparagus, salad, yummy bread, and, as a treat to me, my rich dessert of chocolate mousse was offered compliments of the manager. I think I tipped too much, but everyone in the restaurant heard about my trip and I was feeling good. What a nice evening.

And now, I was leaving a special place again. This time was quite different because it would be my last time to pack the car and tell folks good-bye; I was a little sad just thinking about it, but I needed to go home. I wanted to go home. Yet I really didn't want the trip to end.

I slept a little late. It took longer to pack the car, and so I didn't get to tell Lovey, my landlord, thanks or good-bye, but her daughter, Christy, and Christy's husband, Ron, were there and I wished them both farewell.

I was not really on a schedule, but I had several places still to visit—places mentioned in Kuralt's book—on my way to Austin, Texas, where I would spend the night with my sister, Janie, before heading home.

Artist Georgia O'Keeffe purchased a house called the Ghost Ranch a few miles northwest of Abiquiu, New Mexico, and lived there part of each year in the 1930s and early 1940s. Ghost Ranch is approximately sixty miles from Santa Fe, surrounded by the stunning landscapes that inspired O'Keeffe's art for more than five decades.

Also to be found in the tiny community of Abiquiu is a home and studio that O'Keeffe restored, making it her permanent residence after the death of her husband, Alfred Stieglitz, in 1946.

O'Keeffe's husband was an American photographer and modern art promoter, instrumental in making photography an accepted art form. Stieglitz had met O'Keeffe in New York and, through his gallery, helped to promote her abstract paintings: large-scale depictions of flowers, leaves, rocks, shells, bones, and other natural forms. She also painted New York cityscapes and paintings of the unusual shapes and colors of the architecture and landscape of northern New Mexico.

Georgia was a member of an avant-garde group headed by Alfred Stieglitz. O'Keeffe and Stieglitz married in 1924, having been associated for more than six years. The photographer made hundreds of photos of his wife in an effort to capture her in a portrait.

One of the most significant artists of the twentieth century, Georgia was devoted to creating imagery that expressed what she called, "the wideness and wonder of the world as I live in it." Her body of work equaled in importance that produced in Europe. O'Keeffe played a major role in disabusing the art community and the general public of the notion that gender was in any way a determinant of artistic competence or creativity. She established a new and significant space for female artists in a realm that was, and continues to be, dominated by men.

In 1997 philanthropists Anne and John Marion opened the Georgia O'Keeffe Museum in Santa Fe, New Mexico. The museum is dedicated to perpetuating the artistic legacy of O'Keeffe and to the study and interpretation of American Modernism. More than three thousand artworks, photographs, and archives dating from 1901 to 1984, as well as O'Keeffe's homes in Abiquiu and Ghost Ranch are owned and managed by the O'Keeffe Museum. The museum offers diverse learning opportunities on site and across the state throughout the year. Lectures, art workshops, reading clubs, and creative writing classes are available. Concerts, walking programs, and exhibition-related special events are also offered. Many of the programs are free.

I walked the grounds and looked in O'Keeffe's home, just to acquire a feel for how she lived and to view the landscapes she loved to paint.

I was off to the little village of Chimayo and wished I had hours to explore everything there, but it was already late afternoon. Chimayo is about thirty minutes north of Santa Fe, New Mexico, in the foothills of the Sangre de Cristo Mountains. Spanish settlers near the end of the seventeenth century founded Chimayo. The Santa Cruz River nourishes the fertile valley, which is protected by the surrounding foothills. The settlers became experts in farming, raising stock, and weaving wool. To protect themselves from threats inherent in their frontier life, they built the fortified Plaza of San Buenaventura (now Plaza del Cerro). The plaza is the last of its kind surviving in the United States.

Legend has it that Chimayo is the site of miraculous healings, which occurred two hundred years ago. A friar was performing penance when he saw a strange light coming from the ground. Upon investigation, he unearthed a wooden crucifix. Three times the crucifix was taken to the neighboring village and three times it disappeared, only to be found again in its hole in the hillside. In 1816 a chapel was built on the site of the discovery. The chapel, El Santuario de Chimayo, draws thousands of pilgrims and travelers each year who come for various reasons. Some hope to be healed. Some are only curious, and some hope to be restored by the tranquility and hospitality of the surroundings. At Chimayo, a chapel in honor of Santo Nino de Atocha was built in 1856. The pious legend of the wonder-working little Santo Nino is set in a community in Spain.

In Atocha, a suburb of Madrid, many men were imprisoned because of their faith. The *caliph* (head of state) issued an order that their jailers would not feed prisoners, and no one from the prisoners' family could deliver food except children twelve years old or younger. Those men with young children managed to stay alive, but others suffered. The women of the town appealed to Our Lady, begging for help to find a way to feed their husbands, sons, and brothers.

Soon the children came home from the prison with a strange story. Prisoners who had no young children were being visited and fed by a young boy. No one knew who he was, but the little gourd he carried was never empty of water, and his basket was always filled with enough bread to feed the needy prisoners. The *nino* came at night, slipping past sleeping guards, or smiling politely at those who were alert.

The women who had asked the Virgin of Atocha for a miracle began to suspect the identity of the little boy. As if in confirmation, they discovered the shoes on a statue of the child Jesus were worn down. When those shoes were replaced with new ones, those too soon wore out.

In the early 1850s, Don Severiano Medina, of an influential family in Chimayo, became seriously ill and learned of the Santo Nino de Atocha. Medina traveled to a shrine in Plateros, Mexico. Upon his recovery, he received permission to build a private chapel in Chimayo, in which he placed the papier-mâché doll he'd brought from Plateros—a manifestation of the Christ Child. The chapel Medina built eventually fell into ruin but has since been renovated into a children's chapel.

During WWII, some of the first American troops to see action were from the New Mexico National Guard. They fought bravely on Corregidor, with its underground tunnels and defenses. Many of the soldiers made a vow that if they survived the war, they would make the pilgrimage from Santa Fe to Chimayo on Thanksgiving. At the end of the war, two thousand pilgrims—veterans of Corregidor, Bataan, and Japanese prison camps—along with their families, began the tradition of walking to El Santuario de Chimayo in honor of Santo Nino de Atocha, and in memory of the Bataan Death March.

The descendants of Chimayo's early settlers are still expert in the traditional skills for which the community became famous: weaving, growing red chiles, horse and sheep reining, and keeping fruit orchards. Hispanic and Tewa Indian arts such as woodcarving, the paintings of saints on *retables* (flat wood slabs) and creating *bultos* (sculptures) are still practiced. Other ancient crafts kept alive are tin working, the making of *colcha* (bedspreads, quilts, and blankets), and creating pottery.

It was late afternoon, time to leave, and the landscape was breathtaking—sunset against mountains covered with snow, all colors but more reds in the sky, and leaves of every reddish hue, with the narrow, hilly roads winding ahead. I should have left an hour earlier, but wanted to soak up the atmosphere while I could.

The next day I was a little late getting started, but I was enjoying this unhurried time for breakfast, and I just one suitcase to put in the car. The ride to Albuquerque wasn't long. One could spend much time in Santa Fe and the little surrounding towns, too. I passed several that I had intended to at least ride through. One of those was Madrid.

Madrid is nestled in a narrow canyon in the Ortiz Mountains, between Santa Fe and Albuquerque on the Scenic Turquoise Trail (State Highway 14). The town has evolved into a bustling mountain community of some three hundred people. Once a historic coal-mining town it still has remnants of its past: the Mineshaft Tavern and Coal Mine Museum. Madrid is now a thriving artists' community with more than forty shops and galleries lining the Turquoise Trail. Several miles north of Madrid is the quaint village of Cerrillos, encompassing Cerrillos State Park with its five miles of hiking trails, the Broken Saddle Stable, and the Cerrillo Mining Museum.

My main goal in Albuquerque was to find the Man's Hat Shop on Central Avenue N.W. The hat shop is a famed cowboy hat store, but has thousands of hats from caps to fedoras to western straw hats. If you can't find the hat you want, they'll design one for you. I was met by Bill Fisk and then introduced to a Mr. Brown and another fellow named Steve. The Man's Hat Shop has been in business since 1946. I explained my reasons for being there. One of the men remembered Charles Kuralt being in the shop, but didn't recall his buying a hat. According to Kuralt's book, he did not.

C. Stuart Dunlap, president of the company, wasn't in the store that day but I was given his card and told to call. It was fun talking to the men, wandering the store, and trying on a hat. I had my picture made in it. The shop's logo reads: "Excellence in

Men's Headwear Since 1946," featuring cleaning, blocking, custom fitting, and accessories—all a cowboy could want.

On my way back to the car, I passed a shoe store, then walked in and was greeted by a young man whose grandparents live in Samson, Alabama. That meeting necessitated a nice long talk about Alabama.

Albuquerque is easy to drive around in, and I circled some areas several times. The streets are wide and open; everything is clean. I loved the buildings. A stunning Venetian Gothic Revival style, built in 1917, is home to Occidental Life.

The First National Bank on Central Avenue (Albuquerque's main thoroughfare once known as Railroad Street) was the city's first skyscraper. The nine-story building was erected in 1922. Albuquerque is an exceptional town, a wonderful mix of old and new.

Old Town is the city's historic district, dating to its founding by Spanish settlers in 1706. Ten blocks of historic adobe buildings surround a central plaza, typical of Spanish colonial towns. Many of the adobes are houses that have been converted to restaurants or small art and souvenir shops.

San Felipe de Neri Church, built in 1793, is one of the oldest surviving buildings in the city. In 1867, Jesuit priests from Naples, Italy, gave the church and adjacent structures a major and impressive facelift. At one time the church was the most elaborate building in the area and served as the social center for the entire community. Administration of the church and adjoining buildings was returned to the clergy of the Archdiocese of Santa Fe in late 1965. After ninety-eight years of service, the Jesuits left Old Town.

Prominently mentioned in Charles Kuralt's book is Jaramillo's Barbershop in Belen, New Mexico. Belen is an old railroad town. I stopped and asked people about the barbershop, but they didn't even recognize the name. So I moved on to Socorro, disappointed, but not wasting time. I knew from the beginning I wouldn't find every place or person Kuralt wrote about, yet it has always been worth a try. And I have succeeded more often than not.

Bosque del Apache National Wildlife Refuge is nine miles south of Socorro and home of the Festival of the Cranes. If you're a birder, photographer, or a nature lover, then you'd want to visit the Refuge in mid-November and attend the annual festival.

Nine miles of the Rio Grande River wind through the Bosque del Apache Refuge. The river is banked with cottonwood and willow trees. The refuge is situated between the foothills of the Chupadera and San Pascual mountains. Adjacent farmlands, through cooperative agreements with local farmers, are used to plant cornfields and crops that benefit the wintering birds—an estimated twenty thousand snow geese join the gray sandhill cranes. Tens of thousands of migrating birds take advantage of the federally managed wetlands and impoundments, the rich cornfields, and the nearly thirty thousand acres of designated wilderness. It is wild country that draws many birds in winter.

The regal sandhill crane is tall with a red forehead, white cheeks, and a long dark pointed bill. His call is a loud trumpeting sound. In cultures of the Far East, cranes are thought to be a symbol of longevity. Greek mythology associates cranes with Apollo the Sun god, symbolizing light and life.

The sandhill crane winters at Bosque del Apache, to the delight of local, national, and international crane and geese watchers who gather for the annual Festival of the Cranes. Enthusiasts delight in the predawn liftoff of thousands of cranes and snow geese, and in their return at sunset to roost in the ponds and wetlands of the refuge. Despite the bite of brisk cold air, the faltering light as winter dawns, or the moody sunsets, the watchers persist, knowing that they're seeing nature's beauty in a unique, unforgettable manner—this "wonder of wings."

Touring the refuge is made easy by a twelve-mile loop auto tour. Additional roads create shorter loops winding through the well-protected refuge. Closer approaches to feeding or nesting birds are possible, and there are viewing trails and viewing platforms along the way. A sampling of what is available to be seen or done during the festival: workshops and outings on sandhill crane behavior, snow goose ecology, songbirds of the Rio Grande Valley, raptor ID, duck ecology, and birds of Bosque.

At Bosque del Apache, nature follows her own magical schedule at sunrise and sunset. People gather at key sites known to provide excellent photographic opportunities, and visibility, at those particular times. I had planned to be a part of this wonderful festival, but when I got to Socorro, I didn't feel great. I made food to eat in my room, planning to get an early start the next morning. But I didn't feel well the next morning either. I decided to begin my trip home, and forego time in Socorro.

Although I had no one to complain to, having spent ten-and-one-half months on the road, I wouldn't have dared complain about not feeling up to par either. How could I? I had eaten in hundreds of restaurants, and remained well and active doing what I wanted to do. I would not think of complaining.

Once on the road again, I felt quite nauseous and had to pull over on the side of the road at least half-a-dozen times, but I kept driving until I'd made it to Brownsfield, Texas, for the night.

After a not-too-early start the next day, I drove to Janie's in Austin, Texas, arriving late in the afternoon. She introduced me to some of her friends at her apartment complex and in the evening, her son, David, and his family: wife, Ann, and sons, Jacob, age seven, and Josh, five, came by. The boys were adorable, blue-eyed towheads, so nice and polite; we all had a nice visit. It was good to see them. Janie seemed to be better, but still couldn't maneuver the best in the world. She was in less pain, but the problem hadn't been resolved—a work in progress.

We were in bed early, and I awoke early. Rather than making breakfast, I decided to stop for a bite on the way. Janie and I planned to start work on the book the first of January. I was scheduled to arrive home at noon the 22 of November, eight days shy of the eleven months I had intended. I was in no hurry. I wanted time to unwind after the roller coaster I'd been riding. It would take a while to learn how not to be scheduled to see new places and people every day.

Janie and I never mentioned the disagreements we had on the trip. They weren't important now. If we were together again for any length of time, it would be the same. We aren't ever going to like, or care, or agree about the same things all the time. We're just different, in our circumstances, lifestyles, and outlook on life—just about everything concerning us is different. But we love and care about one another nonetheless.

My solo journey home gave me opportunity to think about re-entering "life after trip." How do you end an adventure such as mine? Well, you really don't, and you don't want to. Each time I think about a particular place, certain people, the things we did, and I did, the past becomes present. I don't want those memories to fade away. I want everything to remain very clear, to be remembered in detail.

I'm a seventy-eight-year-old lady, sheltered in certain respects as to where I live and what I've done travel-wise and in life. To think I could be so bold as to leave for almost a year and revisit the places Charles Kuralt visited in his book *America*—how did I even begin to think I could do such a thing? I really prayed about venturing out and doing something totally not me. And the more I prayed and seriously thought about taking such a trip and began to plan, the more it seemed right. The right time, the right thing to do. I was not worried about coming home. I knew I'd seem a little out of sorts for a while. I was not concerned about how my family, friends, or my community would react to my return. There was no reason for anything to be different. And it wasn't.

The same family members and friends and neighbors who had sent me off on my trip were lining my driveway, waiting in the drizzling rain to welcome me home just as they had stood when I left. "Welcome home, Miss Lou, we missed you neighbor," read the library sign across the street.

With the help of everyone, especially the grandsons, my car was soon unloaded, and I was getting reacquainted with everyone, walking around my house, looking at all I had left behind.

Two wonderful friends and neighbors, Maudene Thompson and Glenda Donald, had cleaned my house to perfection in anticipation of my return; the lawn was manicured and the shrubbery trimmed. Just perfect.

I could only think, "I don't deserve this." My homecoming would always be a very special part of the trip.

The End

Lou's Epilogue

It didn't take long for me to settle into the routine of being home. I gave up many of the responsibilities I had had before leaving. I planned to devote much of my time to writing the book about the trip. Everyone seemed to accept my decision.

Still I felt that I didn't have the words, the intellect, the capability or the "whatever" it takes to make the book come alive for you as vividly as the experience has been for me. My words are inadequate to really capture the magnificent beauty of our country or completely describe the wonderfully inspiring people we met. But this book is my attempt to share with you, forever grateful for the opportunity, amazed that my health allowed me to do all that I did, and eternally grateful for the wonderful love and support of family and friends, and the watchcare of Jesus Christ, who never ceases to inspire and awe me with his presence.

I hope you read, and enjoy, and that you are inspired to do whatever you've always dreamed of doing, however simple, however grand. Don't wait until it's too late.

Thanks so much for being a part of this adventure.

Lou Schell

Janie's Epilogue

Now that some time has passed since I returned from the trip, I seem to have only happy memories and have forgotten frustrations, arguments, or any problems along the way. It was a once-in-a-lifetime experience, and I am grateful to have been a part of it.

Having to come home early because of my medical problems still makes me sad. I knew Lou would continue the trip without me—so that did not factor in my decision. The pain from what would be diagnosed as three herniated discs was excruciating and constant. It never lessened. I couldn't continue to travel.

It was both pleasure and pain to hear from Lou as she continued the trip. So many things I had wanted to do. Our niece, Jo Anne Sims, was to have met us in Montana, and I had wanted to visit with her. I really wanted to see Alaska. However, I realize I was lucky to be able to make as much of the journey as I did.

Every day, I think about the trip. Anything can trigger a memory. I recall a place, sometimes because it reminded me of home, sometimes because it was so different. I remember people we met and the fascinating things I learned from them. It was a wonderful experience. I learned a lot. But mostly I just had fun.

Thank you, Lou

Janie Gass

Acknowledgments

"It takes a village to raise a child."

It took the prayers, support, and encouragement of my family and community to make my trip possible. I'm so thankful for each expression of your love and support.

I would also like to thank: Jeff Eason of *The Blowing Rocket*, Blowing Rock, North Carolina; Audrey Richardson of *The Vermont Standard*, Woodstock, Vermont; Lisa Kristoff of the *Boothbay Register*, Boothbay Harbor, Maine; Terry Jackson of *The Ely Echo*, Ely, Minnesota; Leila Kheiry of *The Ketchikan Daily News*, Ketchikan, Alaska; Teresa Dovalpage of *The Taos News*, Taos, New Mexico; Ellen Williams of *The South Alabamian*, Jackson, Alabama; Jo Anne McKnight of *The Mobile Press Register*, Mobile, Alabama; and The Breeze, Dauphin Island Woman's Club, Dauphin Island, Alabama.

And writer Tory Minus and manager Stan Wilson of *Alabama Living*, Clarke-Washington Electric Corporation; editor Janice Fink, *Alabama Alumni Magazine*, Tuscaloosa, Alabama; *The Washington County News*, Chatom, Alabama; editor Marlin Scott of *FishMonster Magazine*, Key West, Florida; and Susie Steimie, WCAX-TV, Rutland, Vermont.

And for help with our accommodations: Cottage Connections, VRBO, Brooklyn Hospitality, Home Away, and Resort Quest.

Appreciation also goes to the Washington County Public Library, Chatom, Alabama, and M.W. Smith Library, Jackson, Alabama.

And, last but not least, many thanks to Robert Mitchell for the beautiful cover photographs, Judith Richards for her editing help, Cissy Hartley and Susan Simpson for cover design and publishing efforts, Lee Carpenter for help editing my photographs, and Jeanne Devlin for her tireless work in whipping my manuscript into shape.